THE GOSPELS COME ALIVE

Study These Words…

Share Your Words

Robert G. "Bob" Newman, PhD

ISBN 978-1-0980-7961-1 (paperback)
ISBN 978-1-0980-7962-8 (digital)

Christian Faith Publishing, Inc.
832 Park Avenue
Meadville, PA 16335
www.christianfaithpublishing.com

Printed in the United States of America

This volume is dedicated with everlasting love
to the sacred memory of
Patricia Lynn Keenan Richardson Newman.
First of all, Patricia Lynn was my student in undergraduate studies,
then she became a colleague in study and
practice of ministry and faith.
Finally, we were united in holy matrimony,
a sacred relationship we shared
for fifteen years, until she was called to an untimely departure
from this life at age seventy-four.

Patricia Lynn, my dearest darling,
thank you with all my heart and soul for the precious love you
brought to our household, for the devotion and wisdom
with which you cultivated our lifestyle with beauty,
harmony, and creative domesticity only you
could achieve.
During these years I live alone, my desire
for you and your precious love
drives my need for reunion with you, which shall only be
realized with our anticipated reunion in the eternal loving arms of
Almighty God, our Heavenly Father.

Until then, I remain, lonely yours,
Robert G. "Bob" Newman, PhD

CONTENTS

FOREWORD

Preachers and teachers are always looking for new resources. No matter what the profession, finding new resource material to help in your profession is something to discover, explore, and celebrate.

As a student of the Bible and religion, Bob Newman dedicated his life to learning and teaching. As a young child, he was taught the importance of the love of Jesus and the importance of discovering the love of Jesus in the Gospels. Over the years, Bob has grown in that sense of discovery and has shared his learning through his many years of being a professor of religion, including years in Alaska and West Virginia. His students have grown in the sharing of his lifelong learning not just in factual knowledge but in the passion for learning.

In his retirement, he has not stopped learning or teaching. In West Virginia, he voluntarily took on the years of freely issuing weekly reflections on the Gospel lessons from the Revised Common Lectionary. As many who teach, one learns much in the process of learning in preparing to teach. Bob is no exception. As he continues to learn and continues to teach, Bob brings his years of study, perspective, and personality, including occasional humor, bringing his own life history within his writing. As he brings his own stories, he paints a picture in which one feels you are there with him.

Given the immense task of sifting through a mountain of material, in thinking about the three-year cycle of the Revised Common Lectionary, Bob has condensed the three years into one year of Gospel lessons, following the seasons of the church year. Each of the five church year seasons' Gospel lessons are included in this one volume work for you, starting with Advent and continuing on through the season of Pentecost.

Why the church year? It is a framework to help us on a journey that is lifelong. Each year, it helps us to remember, giving us new insights to guide, comfort, and challenge us. It is a part of God's way in opening our hearts to the Holy Spirit's presence in our lives. Who is this man Jesus? Who sent him? Why? To whom was he sent?

Chapter 1. During Advent, a time of preparation, we explore Jesus's ancestry, the history of his people, and the world of his time. As we explore, we find issues, attitudes, emotions, situations similar to those around us in today's world. We also recognize the shortcomings, the need for help, the need for a Messiah in our own lives and the world around us.

Chapter 2. During Christmastide, Epiphany, and the Transfiguration, we encounter amazing, bewildering, often confusing confrontations of the nativity, the epiphany, Jesus's childhood, his baptism, his transfiguration, and the responses and feelings of those around him. We are moved, enchanted, mystified, and challenged by them at the same time.

Chapter 3. During Lent, we follow Jesus's life through his travels, teachings, healings, and miracles. They touch our hearts and our consciousness, but the demands may often seem troubling and unreasonable. We walk with Jesus and the disciples through the confusing and horrific events of Holy Week, only to find ourselves completely spent and alone on Holy Saturday.

Chapter 4. During Eastertide, we stand as an Easter people with joyful hearts but bewildered by what this all means. What next? With the disciples, we wait, reflect, and ponder for fifty days.

Chapter 5. During Pentecost, we are filled with the Holy Spirit, and we feel called. We have a sense of purpose. Taking baby steps forward, we often stumble as we return again and again to the story for the grace, guidance, inspiration, hope, faith, and love that moves us forward.

A writer is always conscious about the audience for whom a resource is being written. The audience for this new resource are preachers, teachers, and those serious about exploring the Bible. This work gives you the years of learning and teaching of Bob Newman. You do not have to be a biblical scholar to appreciate Bob's writing.

He avoids the technical and biblical scholar terminology to encourage the learner. He believes in lifelong learning, and he has continued to learn through his study and writing. He invites you to join with him in the learning process and to join with him in the reflecting and discussing of the Gospels and making the Gospels come alive.

The Gospels Come Alive provides the reader new material to read, ponder, question, reflect, with an eye toward application. How will this new material help you as you grow in knowledge and faith? How will it call you to know more about the love of God in Jesus Christ? What difference will it make in your teaching and preaching? What difference will it make in your life?

There are many Bible study resources that have been produced over the centuries, each one developed for the audience of that time. This work is written for the audience of this time. If you have ever visited the home or office library of one who takes Bible study seriously, you are likely to see book after book written by many authors over the centuries. For the beginning learner, just seeing so many books can be overwhelming. Bob invites you into the learning process with him.

These are not sermons. He believes everyone should think for themselves. He invites curiosity and questioning, which means we need to have an open mind. With an open mind, you take on the responsibility for your own learning and how these writing may apply to you.

Bob takes joy in helping to make connections for people. "Every word I write is an encouragement for people to think for themselves. Then when you leave this, you use your own words and experience."

You are invited! You are invited to take a step at a time and to read a lesson at a time, to bring your curiosity with you, to question, to think, to learn, to help make the Gospels come alive for you!

Forrest and Barb Palmer

Dunbar, West Virginia

ACKNOWLEDGMENTS

This publishing project would be impossible without the contributions of many contributors whose hard work and creative vision make this product much stronger and viable than would otherwise be true. While I cannot mention them all, I list the following with deep appreciation and thanksgiving for their unique contributions without which this project could not have developed as it has. I present and describe each person or process as an example, hence an *exemplar*, or necessary, invaluable ingredient whose hard work is indispensable to the historical development that culminates in this opportunity for learning more about the human participation in both knowledge and faith.

Example One

I begin with my birth family, my dear father, Corley Graves Newman, and my precious mother, Margaret Henrietta Hirschi Newman, who brought me into this world. I was their first child, Robert Glen Newman, and they soon gave me a sister, Alice Elizabeth, and two brothers, Roderick James and Stephen Frank. My parents made sure I was baptized in the Presbyterian Church, nurtured in this faith, and they proceeded to make sure my siblings and I became organic elements, student components of the public education system of the state of Florida. We were blessed with teachers, both men and women, whose competence and vision for our learning literally exerted lifelong influence upon us. Many examples of these role models come to mind, and I shall mention one whose dedication and competence represents them all. This was Mrs. Myrtle Taylor Blair, whose Christian faith and service, expressed especially in music, was balanced by her labors that demanded academic excellence in equal proportion in every other academic discipline. We, my siblings and I, graduated right on schedule as expected and as facilitated and were promoted forward to find our necessary, rightful posture in the public system of higher education.

Example Two

In my case, it was the University of Florida in Gainesville. There I was immersed in the arts and sciences, especially the humanities. Nearby I was adopted by the Westminster Fellowship and especially claimed by the campus pastor, the Reverend Dr. Neely Dixon McCarter, who lathered me with biblical and theological studies and convinced me how academic achievement and spiritual depth were two sides of the same human mind, heart, and soul. Under his elaborate tutelage and my need for paternal and fraternal fellowship, his skillful guidance made it clear that I should pursue graduate studies in the Theological Seminary. Dr. McCarter soon became a national leader and figure in graduate theological education and eventually became president of the Pacific School of Religion, in San Francisco, California. His influence continues forever!

Example Three

For me, the nearest Presbyterian seminary was Columbia Theological Seminary in Decatur, Georgia. There I found myself absorbed in a student body of divergent academic orientations, to my advantage, balanced with superpious devotion to evangelical principles. I was blessed with inclusion in the honors program, where my academic adviser was Professor Shirley C. Guthrie Jr., recently a student of the Swiss scholar Dr. Karl Barth. Courses of study in Hebrew language and Greek language occupied much of my time, but I was blessed to become an assistant who helped support the work of Dr. Guthrie as he wrestled with his first edition of his now classical publication *Christian Doctrine, Revised Edition*, which, as one reviewer puts it, has introduced thousands of laity, students, and theologians to the tenets of the Christian faith.

Example Four

Upon graduation with honors and the MDiv degree, I was ordained to the Christian Ministry of Word and Sacrament by the Presbytery of Florida (1961), and although pastoral duties beckoned, I was motivated to pursue advanced graduate studies at Drew University, Madison, New Jersey. The internationally renowned faculty and cosmopolitan student body kept me occupied with one seminar after the other, but I was honored to be invited to teach New Testament Greek when the occasion arose. I shall mention only two of that faculty for acclaim, Dr. Howard Clark Kee and Dr. Robert W. Funk, both of whom became original contributors to the growing world of biblical scholarship.

Example Five

Having completed my doctoral dissertation, "Tradition and Interpretation in Mark," and awarded the PhD degree, I found myself teaching at Lees-McRae College in rural North Carolina when one day a call came from Dr. Marshall Buckalew, who invited me to consider his invitation to join the faculty of Morris Harvey College in Charleston, West Virginia, where he served as president. When he invited me to visit this college campus, he also introduced me to the First Presbyterian Church of Charleston, which he, serving as a ruling elder, explained was a living example of the family of God. In other words, college and church were two communities, side by side, that together compose the living family of Almighty God. This intimate human family—Marshall and Mary and their children Ronald, James, and Marsha—was a living example of the family of God, whose love shares both faith and learning. College and church, mind and faith, working together, I became convinced, witnessed to the spiritual and academic opportunities here in Charleston when we cultivate the blessings of both heart and mind. Such has been true over all these years because the Buckalew family, among many others, including especially the First Presby family, showed the way to learning with both heart and mind.

Example Six

This reach for wholeness—heart, faith, and mind—has continued to characterize First Presby ever since my adoption by the Buckalew family, and I shall call attention to a special pastoral family, or couple, who gave inspired leadership to this direction of behavior. This was the Reverend Dr. Dean K. and Rebecca Thompson, who served First Presby for nine years (1995–2004) and who reached out to embrace elements of the community not yet included. They cultivated shared ministry with the African American congregations, with the Jewish community, and with the Muslims and the Indian community, just for starters. They encouraged shared learning, for heart and mind, with the academic community, the University of Charleston now having succeeded Morris Harvey College. Rebecca Thompson, for example, was a professional musician who cultivated choristers among the youngsters of First Presby and who reached out to share her vision and expertise with the Appalachian Children's Chorus. When Pastor Thompson left to become professor of ministry and president of Louisville Presbyterian Theological Seminary, he was motivated to encourage continuation of his vision and explorations. He achieved this goal when he became coeditor of a brand-new work of scholarship, *Mentoring: Biblical, Theological, and Practical Perspectives* (Wm. B. Eerdmans Publishing Co., 2018), a multiauthored volume whose contributors all together provide the contemporary vision and skills we need to merge human faith and knowledge together into the new creation our Creator promises for us all.

Example Seven

It is appropriate to include one final example of leadership that makes a difference in our serious education, which cultivates the unity of the human heart and soul with the human mind, and thus calls for the shared ministries of church and academe. I call attention to the leadership among us of Dr. Edwin H. Welch, now president emeritus of the University of Charleston. Dr. Welch and his dear wife, Janet, have continued to recognize and encourage the necessary coordination between church and campus as advantageous to both communities. One summer, for example, they dedicated one week of their vacation to participation in an international colloquium on the work of British theologian C. S. Lewis, held in Oxford, England. Upon return home, Ed and Janet hosted several seminars and lectures both on and off campus to share their learning with as many constituencies as possible.

Dr. Welch has adopted the theme of *innovation* to describe the new graduate programs of study, the new School of Pharmacy, etc. and to reach out to include the Muslim and Indian communities, again, just for starters. Surely, *innovation* is an appropriate vision for the creative movements, changes, and encouragements called for and necessary for well-rounded education, especially when we seek to include both faith and reason. Thanks to Dr. Edwin H. and Janet Welch for their years of dedicated witness and service to both campus and church.

Summary

These seven examples to which I call attention are only a few, although exceptional, persons who have deliberately become involved in the leadership and direction that we all need to encourage and support. You probably know several, if not many, others who should be included in this list. Make sure they receive appropriate and proper identification, recognition, acknowledgment, and thanksgiving just as well.

Soli Deo gloria!

TO YOU, THE READER PATHWAYS TO ADVENTUROUS LEARNING

Hello, and welcome to this adventure in learning. I have been working on this project on and off all my life, and I am very happy if you will join me in my studies of the Holy Scriptures in order to grow stronger in your faith and practice as citizens/members of the kingdom of God.

For me, it all began in a Southern Baptist Sunday school class for three-year-olds when I learned to sing, "Jesus loves me. This I know, for the Bible tells me so. Little ones to him belong. They are weak, but he is strong. Yes, Jesus loves me. Yes, Jesus loves me. Yes, Jesus loves me. The Bible tells me so!"

Here are two points I learned that still stick with me today: (1) Jesus loves me and (2) the Bible teaches me how and why this is true. Early on, I was blessed with family, friends, teachers, and pastors who made sure I learned several different lively versions of these two foundations for my Christian faith. For example, my paternal grandfather was an ordained Southern Baptist minister and my grandmother was a vigorous Christian scientist, a lifelong member of the Mother Church in Boston, Massachusetts. My mother, however, a native of St. Louis, Missouri, was a direct descendant of German Lutherans and Swiss Reformed immigrants. Family reunions were occasions for rigorous exchange on just who Jesus was/is and why/how the Bible is still so important today.

If we still accept Jesus as our primary teacher, as well as Lord and savior, Jesus assures us the love of God is much more important than the laws of God. Let's listen to Jesus's argument in Mark 12:28–

34. Long before laws appear on the scene, God gives us his love, always and forever. And what does God expect, need, deserve, desire in return for his love? Actually, God always loves us, each and every one of us, whether we do or do not love in response. But you can be sure God yearns to receive some love in return from us, because God thrives on companionship, sharing, partners hugging and kissing. And so God creates us with special lovemaking resources deep down inside ourselves. Jesus points to our heart, soul, and strength, and then he adds a fourth resource, the human mind. This means put your intellect to work and add the knowledge you learn to what your heart, soul, and strength already provide.

When you do this, you become the well-rounded, fully equipped human being God loves and needs to share his creation. And notice, this love for yourself and for God does not stop here but is also aimed outward, in order to bless and to benefit your neighbor, whomever he or she may be.

This whole scenario is our Creator God's incredible gift of who we already are, created in the very image and likeness of God himself. But there is so much more when our God promises who we shall become when we trust, accept, and plunge ourselves into the loving work God promises to equip us to share with him as his very special colleagues in Christian ministry.

Check out the promises Jesus makes to his disciples in John 14:1–32. Understandably, Jesus's disciples—normal, run-of-the-mill *Homo sapiens*—trust this rabbi they are used to, but lately, he keeps warning them he is leaving them, going away. And this makes them nervous, if not scared to death. How will they possibly survive without him? They know all too well how ignorant, weak-kneed, and ill-equipped they are to face their world without him.

They fear his absence when, ironically, Jesus has the best possible news for them. Only because he is going away can he assure them he shall return, more ready, able, and useful to and for them than ever before. How so? Because he shall return as the Holy Spirit of the Almighty God he truly is, to move into and live within each one of them and empower/enable them to fulfill the mission of the arrival of the kingdom of God.

As Jesus himself puts this good news, "This means anyone who welcomes me, who trusts me, will do the same works I have been doing, and what is more, can or will do even greater works than these, because I am going to the Father" (John 14:12). Are they ready, able to hear, understand, trust, assimilate, implement, put to work this new leadership Jesus promises they shall do?

You and I, everyone who hears, welcomes, responds, seeks to obey, and serves this very same Lord and Savior, Jesus of Nazareth, will receive these same promises Jesus makes over and over in John 13–17, often entitled the Farewell Discourses. And as Jesus explains in Mark 12:28–34, this same Holy Spirit promises to live deeply within us, each one of us, including all the potentials and resources arising out of and nourished by our heart, soul, strength, and mind. And to be sure, the most valuable element living and working deeply within each one of us is the Holy Spirit himself, whose love and spiritual presence makes all the difference.

And just why do we suppose Jesus himself adds the human "mind" to the short list of resources we human beings enjoy at our disposal—heart, soul, strength, and our neighbor (Mark 12:28–34)? The answer is, our/your mind is where we begin our adventure in learning. Here are the first three basic steps each of us can/should take to launch our adventure into learning why/how Jesus loves us and how/why the Bible assures us this is true:

- *Curiosity.* Begin with your natural experience of *curiosity*, a most valuable gift of God, who inspires us to desire to know more about how and why Jesus loves us as he does and how the Bible teaches us this is true.
- *Open mind.* Growing out of your *curiosity*, you need to be sure you have an *open mind*, ready and eager to work hard to learn for yourself more knowledge of these two questions. And with your open mind, you need to study serious, disciplined exercise of your God-given/inspired intellect, which Jesus promises to generate and perfect, living deeply within you as the presence of God's Holy Spirit.

- *Independent thinking.* And make sure you learn how and when to think for yourself, not dependent upon anyone else but trusting yourself as your response to and enthusiastic participation in relationship with the Holy Spirit within you.

I have prepared this volume, *The Gospels Come Alive*, following the five seasons of the church's annual worship/study calendar and providing a lesson for most weeks growing out of the Revised Common Lectionary. Each lesson offers you an opportunity to explore, to pursue your *adventure in learning*. You may do this alone or with partners in Bible study.

As you tackle your adventure in learning, my hope and prayer is that you will grow step-by-step in your understanding and knowledge of why/how Jesus loves you as he does and how the Bible teaches us this most profound truths of all.

May your labors, your adventures in learning be rewarded by the eternal blessings that Jesus promises you and all of God's creatures shall receive. In your adventures in learning, you will find an elaborate apocalyptic description of these blessings in the final volume of the New Testament canon, the book of Revelation. I shall quote this brief but positive promise: "Then the one seated on the throne said, 'Look, and behold! I am making all things new'" (Revelation 21:5).

CHAPTER ONE

The Season of Advent—the New Church Calendar Begins

Lesson One: Read Mark 1:1–8

As we begin to study this lesson, we should remember that Christmas (Advent season) is not the most important festival we celebrate during the church year. The anchor, the foundation, the pivotal turning point of the church calendar is Easter, the resurrection of the Lord. All the other liturgical festivals reflect and grow out of the resurrection of Christ Jesus from the dead. Without this cornerstone for the new covenant, there would be no truth to the claims of Christian witnesses. With this solid rock of reality and truth, Jesus's disciples are commissioned and empowered to witness through the celebration of this and all the other elements that make up the story of Jesus's life and work. (Check out 1 Corinthians 15:3–28 and Acts 1:6–11.)

However, as the immanent Franciscan theologian Dr. Ilia Delio reminds us, we love cuddly, innocent, cooing infants, whereas we shy away from gruesome executions and cemeteries, which are somber and sad and may promise new life beyond death, but new life that calls for faith in a world still lacking and waiting for redemption. And so truth to tell, no Easter, no manger in Bethlehem. But with Easter, we share a faith that is hopeful, waiting, and trusting in God's promises to make all things new (Revelation 21:1–5).

Nevertheless, contemporary culture so saturates us all with traditional symbols and contexts of the Christmas season, beginning as early as Thanksgiving and not slowing down until Epiphany at the earliest, we are overwhelmed with Bethlehem, shepherds, magi, angelic choruses, and St. Nicholas and his reindeer. We are certain the arrival, or advent, of Jesus into this world is adequately remembered and described in the two longest Gospels, those of Matthew and Luke. We are not prepared for the shortest and first Gospel to be written, that of Mark, which knows nothing of the journey to Bethlehem or of the charming lure of an infant born to a virgin mother and laid in a manger, because there was no room anywhere for his family to stay in an inn.

Indeed, here in Mark, the good news of the career of Jesus Christ, the Son of God, does not focus directly upon Jesus at all, it appears, but upon Old Testament prophets and a strange, new prophet called John the Baptist. Not calculated to promote record holiday sales at the local mall. Why does this Gospel writer ignore the beautiful nativity story and look backward to the Old Testament?

The answer is, Mark is convinced the good news of Jesus Christ does not begin in Bethlehem but long, long before in the wilderness, in times when God's people suffered exile from their homeland, partly due to their human weaknesses and failings and partly due to the turmoil—social, political, and military—tearing the world apart, the world in which their God calls them to live and work.

And so you check out what their God tells them to hear and believe when they were tempted to give in to despair and lose all hope in themselves and the future their God had promised for them. How could they trust God's promises in their predicament?

Mark has the answer. God spoke then and God speaks now, Mark is confident, "As it is written in the prophet Isaiah [who draws upon words from another prophet, Malachi]." What do these ancient prophets have to say? "Look, and behold! I am sending my messenger to you so you can see him and hear how he prepares the way of salvation for you" (paraphrased). "Listen for the voice of this messenger, for he will be crying out to you in the wilderness, saying to you, 'Get ready, prepare the way for the Lord, make his pathways clear, straight, and not crooked so he can bring my salvation to you who need and want deliverance from all sin and evil'" (paraphrased).

The history of Christianity has always and consistently explored and experimented with the arts as an effective language for cultivating human response to and involvement in the spirituality the four Gospels express, originally in the Greek language. Let's examine one example of an artist who takes his inspiration from this very passage we are studying. George Frideric Handel (1695–1759) was born a German Lutheran but lived most of his life in England, where the King James English Bible provided the text for his best-known work, the oratorio *Messiah*.

Handel and his librettist, following Mark, chose Isaiah 40:11–3 to present the words of God in the first vocal number in this oratorio, featuring the tenor voice, which reminds one of the trumpet: "Comfort ye, comfort ye my people; comfort ye, comfort ye my people, saith your God, saith your God. Speak ye comfortably to Jerusalem. Speak ye comfortably to Jerusalem, and cry unto her, that her warfare, that her warfare, is accomplished, that her iniquity is pardoned, that her iniquity is pardoned. The voice of him that crieth in the wilderness, prepare ye the way of the Lord, make straight in the desert, a highway for our God."

In these words and in this composition, which the artist coops from the Old Testament prophets, Handel calls our attention to Mark's announcement of "the beginning of the good news of Jesus Christ, the Son of God." And how shall this good news now arrive in person in the rural Judaean countryside? Behold, John the Baptist, the new prophet of God the Father, "appears in the wilderness, proclaiming a baptism of repentance for the forgiveness of sins." As the first tenor aria in *Messiah* makes clear, this is a voice crying in the wilderness, "Comfort ye, comfort ye, my people."

In the second vocal number, the same tenor voice continues to quote from Isaiah 40:4, "Every valley, every valley shall be exalted, shall be exalted, shall be exalted, shall be exalted, and every mountain and hill made low; the crooked straight, and the rough places plain, the crooked straight, the crooked straight, and rough places plain, and the rough places plain."

And how shall "every valley be exalted, every mountain and hill be made low, and the crooked become straight and the rough places plain"? The answer is, John, this new prophet, brings baptism, calling for repentance and forgiveness of sins.

The same tenor voice continues, "Every valley, every valley shall be exalted, every valley, every valley shall be exalted, and every mountain and hill made low; the crooked straight, the crooked straight, the crooked straight and the rough places plain, and the rough places plain, and the rough places plain. the cooked straight, and the rough places plain."

The third vocal number is for chorus, which quotes from Isaiah 40:5, "And the glory of the Lord shall be revealed, and all flesh shall see it together, for the mouth of the Lord hath spoken it." Handel obviously found the King James text appropriate to express the excitement and grandeur of the Baroque style of composition and performance. *Messiah* was first performed in Dublin, Ireland, in 1742.

And how does Mark show the source for Handel's celebration of the glory of the Lord being revealed so that all flesh sees this together? Mark describes how the people of God respond to this new prophet, John the Baptist, among them, "And people from the whole Judaean countryside and all the people of Jerusalem were going out to him and were baptized by him in the river Jordan, confessing their sins." This momentous event reveals the beginning of the good news, the imminent arrival of Jesus Christ, the Son of God. John's announcement and call for response elicits overwhelming, shall we say, universal response of God's people, who participate in welcoming, receiving the comfort promised long ago and now realized in their confessing of their needs, their sins, and their trust in this impending arrival of the glory of the Lord in all its grandeur.

It is important to recognize the dominance of the theme of the wilderness in this passage. The great Old Testament prophets (e.g., Isaiah, Malachi, and Elijah) all lived and worked in the wilderness. Indeed, God's people knew themselves all the while to be people identified by their experience defined by their wilderness worldview. Not only was their natural environment, usually harsh desert, an example of unfriendly wilderness but they also defined themselves, as God's people, by their struggle to survive physically and to thrive spiritually, as deprived people who are called, adopted, and equipped to respond to their creator and redeemer by confession of sins and commitment to and trust in the promises of the Lord.

Notice John the Baptist here is clearly a servant identified and certified by his wilderness profile. He not only is sent to do his job in the wilderness, at the Jordan River, but his new clients must also leave their urban neighborhoods—in the cities such as Samaria, Antioch, and Jerusalem—and make a pilgrimage out to the wild riverside hills and valleys where their only consolation from a hostile environment is their response to this new prophet who calls for their confession of sin as their necessary preparation for the promised imminent arrival of the Son of God. And John fits the looks appropriate for his role. "Now John was clothed with camel's hair, with a leather belt around his waist, and he ate locusts and wild honey." His rustic lifestyle, in other words, dispensed with any and all luxuries, and he sacrificed himself, symbolically speaking, on the altar of extreme devotion and commitment to the one God for whom he behaves and speaks as he does. It is appropriate to recognize that Mark presents this new prophet, John the Baptist, as the long promised and expected return of the ancient Old Testament prophet hero Elijah the Tishbite.

Jewish tradition, of course, as presented canonically in the Old Testament, reports that the first Elijah did not die but ascended into heaven in a chariot of fire, propelled by a whirlwind (2 Kings 2:11). Jewish tradition insists Elijah not only did not die but also continued to wander the earth, until the appropriate time when he will return to usher in the *Messiah* and the final redemption of humankind.

Every year when the Passover Seder is observed in faithful Jewish homes around the world, an extra cup of wine is poured for Elijah, and some families draw up an empty chair at the table for him. During the service, the door is flung upon to let him in, and one of the favorite songs of the Passover evening is "Elijah the Prophet, Elijah the Tishbite, Elijah the Gileadite, may he come quickly to us with the *Messiah*." And these same Jewish families, living in exile, in the Diaspora, are fond of repeating this profound expression of hope, "Next year, in Jerusalem!"

Mark's prologue to his completely written Gospel presents John the Baptist as the return of Elijah, whose anointed task is to announce the imminent arrival of the *Messiah*: "The one who is more powerful than me is coming after me. I am not worthy to stoop down and untie the thongs of his sandals. I have baptized you with water, but he will baptize you with the Holy Spirit."

No sooner said than done! Suddenly, in the long line of participants, there appears, arrives a man whose name is Jesus, from Nazareth, and is baptized by John in the Jordan River. Coming up out of the water, Jesus sees the heavens splitting open and the Spirit, like a dove, coming down upon him and hears a voice from heaven, "You are my Son, whom I dearly love. In you I find happiness!"

This Spirit immediately propels this baptized Jesus to his appointed work. Where is this blessed work? Into the wilderness, of course!

If we listen closely and carefully, we can already hear the soaring voices and instruments of those musicians and artists who present the inspiring and eloquent climactic chorus of Handel's oratorio *Messiah*, whose title is the single-word "Hallelujah"!

Lesson Two: Read Matthew 1:18–25

This is probably the first description or report of the birth narrative of Jesus, the second one emerging prominently, with much more elaborate development, in the Gospel of Luke (1:26–2:40). The earliest documents in the New Testament canon, notably the letters of the apostle Paul, do not refer to this as a specific historical event, although they consistently describe or reflect a so-called high Christology understanding of the origin and purpose of the career of Jesus of Nazareth. If we assume that the Gospel of Mark was written first and serves as a source for Jesus's itinerary for both Matthew and Luke, then we may ask why and how Matthew and Luke begin their narratives not with Jesus's adulthood, as Mark does, but with genealogies and birth narratives and then only thirdly with Jesus's adult baptism by John the Baptist. The short answer is, both Matthew and Luke found Mark too abbreviated and they had access to other sources of narrative information, which begged to be included in order to flesh out, so to speak, the meaning and significance of Jesus's career, first to strengthen the foundation of Jesus's career within Judaism (Matthew) and second to expand this same career to include the larger Hellenistic world (Luke).

This lesson in Matthew follows in sequence the elaborate genealogy of Jesus, thus resting upon the solid foundation of three epochs of fourteen generations each (Matthew 1:1–17), beginning with no less than the patriarch Abraham and reaching climax in the continuing presence of the house of David, now occupied by a man named Joseph, who presumably lives in the city of David, Bethlehem. (According to Matthew 3:19–23, Joseph later took his newly expanded family and settled in Nazareth of Galilee, thus fulfilling a scriptural prophecy.)

In the normal scope of events, Matthew wants to show that this Joseph seeks and finds a suitable spouse, since ancient tradition foresaw a long line of descendants issuing from King David of old. Joseph's courtship of the young maiden Mary advances to their relationship known as engagement with intent to be married, usually arranged or promoted by their parents or larger families.

Engagement was a time of serious, formal betrothal or covenantal commitment, which bound the two individuals together in promise and expectation. But this commitment prohibited them from living together until the ritual celebration of formal union after which the groom would take his new bride home to live with him in the warm hospitality of his parents or family of origin. Now, as has been observed often, "In closely knit neighborhoods, there are few secrets and no unanimous benevolent congruencies." Or as Matthew puts this development, "Mary was found to be with child of the Holy Spirit." Matthew, the narrator, of course, is the only one who knows and can reveal the source of this pregnancy. No one else knows this just yet. But Joseph hears this rumor and no doubt is immediately stressed to his limits to know what to do.

First of all, Joseph is a righteous man, Matthew tells us, seeking justice according to the law of Moses. To grasp the harsh and even cruel but nevertheless legal requirements for dealing with elicit sexual behavior, read Deuteronomy 22:22–30. No doubt the severity of these laws was mitigated through rabbinical processes of leadership over the centuries. But even so, they weighted heavily upon the minds and hearts of all citizens who, like Joseph, trembled at the very idea of stoning someone to death, or at the penalty for not stoning someone to death, as required by the law.

Because Joseph seeks to express righteousness or justice, this first option is not open to him, who, Matthew implies, seeks to be faithful to the spirit of the ancient Mosaic law and not merely to the letter of the same law. And thankfully, there is a second option available. Conformity to the first option would mean public scandal and disgrace for all the families involved. Matthew explains that because Joseph is a righteous man and thus, above all, unwilling to put Mary to shame, he also has the option to divorce her quietly, without shame, to preserve her dignity and her peace of mind.

But before Joseph can ponder the negotiations necessary to proceed with this second option, divorce, a third option arrives in the form of a dream Joseph has in the middle of the night. Matthew describes this annunciating event this way, "Now while Joseph was strategizing on how to engineer his anticipated divorce proceeding, guess what? An angel [messenger] of the Lord appeared to him in a dream, saying, 'Joseph, son of David, do not be afraid to take Mary to become your wife, because the child which is conceived in her is being sent to her from the Holy Spirit. Issuing from this conception, Mary will give birth to a son, a boy child, and you yourself shall give him an appropriate name. You shall call him Jesus. Why this name? Because this is the Greek form of the Hebrew name Joshua, which means he will save his people from their sins'" (paraphrased).

Now Matthew wants to put this narrative sequence into ancient, prophetic context. He says, "Now all this happened to fulfill, to bring to pass exactly what the Lord promised through the words of the prophet Isaiah [7:14], who said this: 'Behold, the virgin shall conceive/become pregnant and give birth to a son. And everyone will address him by his proper name, Emmanuel, which when correctly interpreted means "God is right here with us"'" (paraphrased).

When Joseph woke up from his sleep, he was shaken up and overwhelmed by this dream, but he immediately did what the angel of the lord commanded him to do; he took his wife, Mary, under his oversight and protection but knew her not (intimately) until she had borne her son. And then as the angel had instructed him, he named him Jesus. Luke's version of this narrative adds this description: "After eight days had passed, it was time to circumcise the child, and he was called Jesus, the name given by the angel before he was conceived in the womb" (Luke 2:21).

In order to clarify just what the angel, messenger of God, intended to communicate to Joseph during his dream, we may profitably recognize that this announcement from God has understandably produced confusion, consternation, and exaggeration, to say the least, among interpreters down through history.

First, let's begin with the quotation from the prophet Isaiah. The word translated *virgin* in English is *almah* in the Hebrew text and means "young woman" rather than "virgin" explicitly. "Young woman" may imply virgin, but the word itself is ambivalent and open to further definition after exploration of facts. The Greek text uses the word *he parthenos* (*Parthenos* in English). The difference comes about because Matthew quotes from the Septuagint or Greek translation of the Old Testament, which uses the word *parthenos.* This same word appears in the name for the monument in Athens, Greece, called the Parthenon, to honor the virgin goddess Athena, goddess of wisdom and patroness of the Athenian city-state. The original use of the word *almah* in Isaiah refers to a sign being born to show King Ahaz of Judah that the Lord is still with his chosen people and will bring for them deliverance from their enemies. While an important event, this sign apparently points to military leadership and thus does not appear to equate 100 percent with the redemptive, sacrificial role that Jesus appears to be sent from God to fulfill if he is indeed to save his people from their sins. Thus, while Matthew's anchor for the conception of Jesus is perhaps understandable, it was not likely to be convincing to most Orthodox or faithful Jews who preferred a more convincing or authentic understanding of the word *almah* in its original context.

A second attempt at interpretation of Matthew's use of "virgin" to anchor Jesus's conception and birth emerges in later centuries among Christian theologians. This is the claim that because Jesus was not conceived through normal conjugal relations, he miraculously avoids the inheritance of "original sin," which was traditionally associated with or transmitted by human sexuality, the primary source and conduit for universal human sin and evil behavior. The weakness in this argument is the sharp connection of original sin with human sexuality above all else. This direction of thinking is shallow and limited when it comes to a full and more faithful interpretation of Jewish theology, especially as presented in the Old Testament canon.

A third example of this perennial exploration and struggle to interpret the significance of Matthew's anchor of Jesus's conception and birth in the reality of virginity emerges in the Western world in the modern era. This is the insistence on the dualism between the natural world and supernaturalism. This outlook is especially popular since the arrival of modern science, which thrives on empiricism and scientific method that prefers truth based only upon experimental methods that render proven facts. The concept of a virginal conception, which defies naturalism and thrives on the supposedly opposite world of spiritualism, is very attractive to many thinkers or practitioners who also find no problem with the heresy known as Docetism. This is the outlook that Jesus was always, in every way, 100 percent spiritual and only appeared to be in any way a normal human being with physical or material components to his personality. As such, he could not truly suffer and die and thus has no need to rise from the dead. Again, this outlook says Jesus only appears to be a real integral component of and participant in the natural world, which, by the way, the Creator thought was in no way inferior but pretty darn good (Genesis 1:31).

The above three theological references point us to the need for much more investigation and wrestling with the meaning and significance of Matthew's use of this world "virgin" in his version of the nativity. For our present purposes, let us listen to the theologian Charles M. Wood who concludes, "It is best construed as a pointer to a more central and truly indispensable affirmation, namely, that in

Jesus, God has assumed our humanity." That is the gracious mystery conveyed in our text and in the event for which the Advent season has us so expectantly waiting.

Lesson Three: Read Luke 1:26–38

This is the time of the year when we are inundated with artistic, aesthetic, or stimulating media of all types, which urge us to respond to the entertaining, inspirational, or captivating images that appeal both to our five senses and to our deeply emotional, esoteric, and transcendental dimensions of reality. Having participated in the annual worship service entitled Nine (or Seven) Lessons and Carols, modeled on the traditional service pioneered by King's College in Cambridge, England, we are likely to be riding high, saturated with bells, drums, candles, angelic children's voices, and brass ensembles during this Advent season, which propel us forward to our celebrations on Christmas Eve, Christmas Day, and indeed the raucous "twelve days of Christmas" itself.

Perhaps we should recall how the presence and power of art is a central, perennial feature of the biblical narrative, both Old and New Testaments. From the creation stories of Genesis 1–4 all the way to the fantastical but moving images of the book of Revelation, the Holy Scriptures consist primarily of memories, stories, plots, and counterplots that recall, recount, and repeat for consumption, assimilation, and repetition vivid images in order to grasp us, include us in their spiritual shenanigans, and promise us divine blessings, redemption, and salvation from all sin and evil. Consider that the book of Psalms, to take one strong example, is a comprehensive collection of 150 poems, some simple, many more complicated, which weave scenarios of complex, positive, and negative images that invite us and move us to encompass within and among ourselves all the heights and depths of spiritual experience available to members of the human race.

Of course, there is great risk at every turn in this artistic worldview. Consider one example of where the narrators of the Bible are acutely aware of the limitations involved in serious participation in the attractive features of human artistic endeavor. Let's refer to Exodus 20:1–7, the first reading of the Ten Commandments, where God reminds his people of his rescue of them from Egyptian slavery and of their appropriate response to this act of mercy, which calls for worship of him alone and exclusion or rejection of any and all competing gods that are condemned as idols or false gods. This warning especially excludes from use graven images, such as those dominating the Egyptian culture they are leaving behind.

This commandment carries serious consequences, including negative and positive outcomes as specified in verses 4–6, and includes "wrongful use of the name of the Lord your God" (verse 7) and thus includes storytellers and orators as well as painters and sculptors. But it is important to notice that this discussion neither rejects nor condemns art *per se* but only wrongful use of art, for example, as it soon took place, as described in Exodus 32:1–35.

Indeed, this cautionary warning about the power of art to produce worship of false gods is superseded most extravagantly in Exodus 15:1–21, where Moses and the Israelites sing and dance their hearts out, seeking appropriate artistic expression to advertise their thanksgiving for the salvation their Lord has worked in saving them from the Egyptians (Exodus 14:13–30), using such expressions as "Who is like you, O God, among the gods? The Lord will reign forever and ever." And who should miss this vivid description of artistic choreography hard at work: "Then the prophet Miriam, Arran's sister, took a tambourine in her hand, and all the women went out after her with tambourines and with dancing. And Miriam sang to them, 'Sing to the Lord, for he has triumphed gloriously; horse and rider he has thrown into the sea.'"

This overview of the prevalence and importance of creative or artistic sensitivities hard at work through the biblical writings brings us to the lesson for today, Luke 1:26–38. The writer Luke has assured his patron Theophilus that he will produce his own orderly account after carefully investigating all the materials he has inherited, and his goal as he takes pen to papyrus is "so that you may know the truth concerning the things about which you have been instructed" (Luke 1:1–4). Scholars are in agreement that the writer Luke was a learned, cultivated, dedicated Christian servant, knowledgeable of Judaism, steeped in Hellenistic culture and traditions (perhaps a physician), and committed to evangelize the Gentiles, especially the weak and underprivileged. He displays admirable skill in control and manipulation of the Greek language, sensitive to style and artistic dimensions of syntax, appealing to aesthetic opportunities and limitations as he composes his prose, sequence by sequence.

For example, today's lesson, Luke 1:26–38, flows smoothly out of the previous one (1:5–25), "in the sixth month," following the conception of John the Baptist in the womb of Elizabeth, relative of the young maiden Mary, upon whom the angel Gabriel now calls. Luke, the Gospel writer, calls attention to this young woman's commendable condition before he mentions her name or the name of her betrothed. She is a virgin, more important than the name of Joseph and his status as a leader of the house of David. And it is this virgin who now also has a name, Mary.

Luke, the artist, now uses the Greek word *parthenos* (virgin) twice in rapid succession. Connoisseur of Hellenistic culture, he calls attention to how the same word, as every Greek-speaking citizen knows, becomes the name of the most prestigious work of art in the Roman Empire, the temple/monument known as the Parthenon, situated prominently on the Acropolis in Athens, named for the virgin (*Parthenos*) Athena, goddess of beauty, integrity, and knowledge; esteemed patroness of the city-state of Athens; and highly symbolic of the entire positive cultural heritage of classical Greece.

Luke tells us this virgin's name is Mary, perhaps because this was a Hebrew name for one who is obstinate. The angel Gabriel begins to deliver his announcement, and thus, this event becomes known as the Annunciation. Gabriel addresses this maiden, "Greetings and salutations, for you have been chosen above all others to receive a special assignment" (paraphrased). Such words greatly disturb Mary and prompt her to wonder just what in the world is going on. But before she can modify her shocked facial expression, Gabriel continues, "Do not be afraid, Mary, for our God has come to admire your strong commitment and dedication to fulfilling all your responsibilities, even when confronted by serious obstacles. And because of your dependability, our God has chosen you, from among all other women, to perform a very important role." Mary is speechless to hear these words but is eager to hear more and curious above all. Gabriel continues, "Soon you will conceive in your womb and bear a son, and you will name him Jesus [Savior]. He will become great and will be called the Son of the Most High God, and God his Father will give to him the throne of his ancestor David. He will reign over the house of Jacob forever, and there will be no end to his kingdom."

Astonished beyond all measure, Mary recognizes the significance of this scenario Gabriel has proposed and envisioned for her consumption, nothing less than the present, future, and everlasting reality of the long-promised kingdom of God, working to save all creation from sin and evil. But her way of taking seriously her role in this vision, as Gabriel has explained it to her, is to be honest with herself and express her practical problem-solving nature. She asks, "How can this possibly happen as you promise since I do not know a man?" (Mary is cautiously careful not to use the word *virgin* for herself because she is reluctant to associate herself too closely with the popular goddess Athena.)

The angel, messenger from God, is quick to explain the plain and simple answer to Mary's very practical concern. "You don't need a man, because the Holy Spirit will come upon you, and the power of the Most High will overshadow you. And this means this child to be born will be holy, created, called, and set aside for a very unique role and destiny, and he shall bear the title Son of God." Mary is dumbfounded, weak at the knees, and must sit down in order to allow all this incredible vision to sink into her consciousness!

Gabriel continues, "You are not alone in being singled out and called for a very important task as a participant in the eternal work of our great Lord God. For already, your relative Elizabeth, even in her old age, has also conceived a son. And this is the sixth month of her pregnancy, she who has always been looked down upon with disgrace for being barren. And these events taking place, with you and with her, make it clear that nothing is impossible or beyond the reach of our God's fulfillment of his promises to his people."

The smile on Mary's face as she rises to speak directly to her visitor is indicative of her experience of being overwhelmed by the presence of the Holy Spirit now operating within her heart, soul, mind, and body. She speaks strongly with but a slight tremor in her voice, "I give myself to you, blessed messenger from God, for I am ready, able, and willing to do what you call me to do. I shall be our Lord God's servant, just as your words call me to become." Gabriel, his journey to Nazareth now fulfilled, nods, smiles, and takes his leave.

As we pause, ponder, and survey this impressive scenario composed and presented in the Koine Greek language by the writer Luke, we may identify three notable characteristics that this writer incorporates in his finished product.

First, we observe that the writer Luke seeks to be an artist as he works with his medium, not chisel and marble or brush and pigments but words that flow from his pen onto papyrus or parchment with creative finesse that gains our attention and involves us closely in the dynamics of the exchange between two figures, Gabriel and Mary. But these two figures encapsulate in their encounter the reality, the will and purpose of Almighty God, recaching from creation to eschaton.

That is to say, the artist Luke communicates to us his profound insights by creatively blending raw, natural material elements in human nature and social environment with transcendent, spiritual, invisible, and eternal realities whose origins and functions reach far beyond our temporal, physical limitations to encompass the divine blessings only the creator and redeemer can and will, or promises, to fulfill. This delicate and profound synergy, raw matter blended and intermeshed with aesthetic inspiration, succeeds in connecting our fleshly sensitivities with our need for participation in spiritual realities, which both reflect and feed our heart, soul, mind, and body.

Second, this artistic balance permits Luke to show how, through the angel Gabriel's words, the great Lord God of Israel is determined to continue to work his process of salvation in and through basic elements of his good creation, most notably through his own chosen people. And although this promised event does connect with the earlier promises to the house of David, it is now in and through this birth event and its outcomes that God makes special promises that Mary's offspring shall enable this work of the house of David to extend into eternity. In other words, Mary represents all of God's people when she is given the choice of servanthood or not and, despite her humble, inadequate circumstances, agrees to accept her role in sequence with all those who have preceded her and all those who shall succeed her.

Third, Luke, the artist, makes clear—first in the example of Zechariah and Elizabeth, too elderly to conceive and bear a son (Luke 1:5–25), and then in the example of Mary, who has never known a man and thus a virgin—that nothing shall be out of the question or impossible for God to make work when he sets his mind to get it done! And Luke makes clear, in both of these cases (Zechariah and Elizabeth and Mary, the adolescent maiden), that God chooses to work not through the high and mighty but through the lowly and humble, those who present themselves when called, they who live simple, unpretentious, but dedicated lives, making themselves responsive and pleased to become instruments for their master's divinely ordained service.

And now some homework! Locate a comprehensive edition of *History of Fine Art*. If you do not own a copy, your public or church library should provide one. Or you may google "Da Vinci; Annunciation: Uffizi." Locate information on Leonardo da Vinci (1452–1519). This foremost artist, sculptor, engineer, architect, scientist, mathematician, and inventor is known as a genius among Renaissance geniuses. His most well-known paintings are *The Last Supper* and the *Mona Lisa*. For our purposes, locate a reproduction of *Annunciation* (1472–1475, Uffizi Gallery, Florence). This dramatic portrayal exhibits for our study how the artist Leonardo da Vinci seeks to capture the visual, physical details of the encounter of Gabriel with the maiden Mary, as presented in the work of the earlier artist Luke. But the rich visual details that so sensitively portray the angel and the maiden, each in his/her own integrity, more strongly draw us deeper and deeper into the exchange going on between them and through them, leading us beyond them to the spiritual and metaphysical heights and depths encompassed in the temporal/

eternal worldview of which they are one part yet so poignantly captured in this timeless interpretation provided for posterity by the artist Leonardo da Vinci.

Thanks be to the artist Luke, who, seeking faithfully to serve his patron Theophilus, captures in Greek language this encounter, this dialogue that rivals and surely supersedes the traditions associated with the popular figure enshrined in the Parthenon of Athens. But thanks as well to those storytellers, those architects, those sculptors whose creativity inspired and motivated Luke to build upon their labors and be alert to this opportunity that comes his way to capture in the Greek language the devotion of this later virgin, Mary of Nazareth, as a necessary and inspired encounter early in the narrative, which he develops into his complete version of the career of Jesus of Nazareth, the Son of God.

And thanks be to all those later writers who draw out of Luke's work their own inspiration to carry forward the impetus Luke here provides. The apostle Paul is most likely one example of the messenger who does this, according to what we read in his letters and according to what Luke describes in his second written volume, the Acts of the Apostles.

And thanks be to all the theologians, preachers, artists, musicians, and teachers, among whom we list both Leonardo da Vinci and George Frideric Handel, knowing that the list of their colleagues and successors keeps on growing year by year, hopefully wherever and whenever each one of us does her or his part to take seriously, with critical discernment, all the pioneering artists, such as Luke, who have gone before us.

Lesson Four: Read John 1:1–18

It is important to take notice that this the fourth Gospel joins the Gospel of Mark by ignoring, bypassing, or overlooking the sequence of nativity events, which are so central to both Matthew (1:1–2:23) and Luke (1:1–52). However, this Gospel of John does agree with the first Gospel to be written (Mark) that John the Baptist plays a primary role in the arrival of Jesus on the historical scene, because John is the human witness who points to and interprets the meaning of the divine *Logos*, who becomes flesh and dwells here with and alongside other members of the human race.

But we must first identify and seek to comprehend the worldview of the Gospel writer John, which is both consistent with that of Judaism and startlingly inclusive of Gentile worldviews that permeate Hellenistic cultures. John 1:1 affirms Jewish monotheism and thus the origin of the universe, or all created reality, deriving from one common source and thus, by definition, exhibiting characteristics that presumably express unity or a consistent whole. However, this view of creation or origins lacks the prominent horizontal linear calendar of chronology or progressive time (past, present, future), so characteristic of the three Synoptic Gospels.

John achieves this contrast between his worldview and Genesis 1 by introducing the persona of the *Logos* ("speech, word, reason, or truth"; *logic* in English), which gets first mention, whereas Genesis 1 knows only the one God who stands before and outside of all creation and history. Here, the Logos takes center stage, coworker with God and coequal with God and, indeed, identical with God himself.

Now John's sources are steeped in Jewish tradition, where the one God from time to time gains alternative personas, such as Spirit, High God of Israel, etc. or such as the feminine noun *Sophia*, or "wisdom," in the Writings (Proverbs). Outside the canon, this same concept, Logos, was adopted by Philo of Alexandria (30 BCE–45 CE), a Jewish scholar who reflected strong Stoic and Neoplatonic influences, where Logos was a favorite concept for discovering truth and unity across different realms of human need.

This means the Gospel writer John does not abandon the Jewish worldview, but he does seek to include this Hellenistic concept of Logos as an organic, essential component of the reality of the Jewish God. He does this in order to reach out to include Gentiles, whose cultural milieu already includes this concept of truth, familiar and fully operative for those who study natural law, as pioneered by the philosopher Aristotle, for example, and as operative for ordinary citizens who rely on the familiar and pervasive philosophies of Stoicism and Epicureanism to sustain them in solving the problems of everyday life.

Back to John 1:1–2, notice the verbs for *being* in Greek are third-person singular, imperfect tense, active voice, denoting timeless, unwavering unity, equality, and identity of Logos with God and God with Logos. And yet at the same time, the preposition *pros* is introduced twice, which describes *God* and *Logos* standing over against each other as two complimentary but different entities. But suddenly in John 1:3, it is the Logos who gives birth to everything or through whom all that exists comes into being. The Greek verbs here are in the aorist tense, which means singular activity happening one time only. To paraphrase, not one singular thing of what came into being did so without this Logos being its source. This is an affirmation of universal monotheism and a categorical denial of polytheism in any form whatsoever!

The good news of this new reality is trumpeted in the next verse, John 1:4, "In him, Logos, was life, or became life, and this life was the lifeblood of humanity." And as if to make the total picture of reality here completely true, however confusingly, suddenly darkness enters the picture, "And this light shines in the darkness, and this darkness does not take control over it." The Greek verb here, *katalambano*, is notably difficult to translate. Where does this darkness come from, and why does it mess up the picture? It certainly appears as if a dualism now exists in this creation, implying a competition between the light and the darkness, with the light destined to prevail over the darkness. And this dualism between light and darkness, of course, comes as an integral, necessary part of this new creation, absolutely all of which comes from the same source, the Logos.

This contextual review brings us to today's lesson, John 1:6–8. Suddenly, a human being enters this overview of this new creation for the first time. This man's name is John, and he is explicitly sent by God. Why does God send this person? To point to or to bear witness to the light, the life of all humanity. This need for witness to point to the light suggests that the darkness, while subservient to the light, nevertheless, may produce trouble in its struggle with light, and thus the light may need this support or added strength, lest the darkness should begin to prevail. God's motivation in sending this person, John, therefore is to promote the goal for all of humanity to trust in the light instead of the darkness.

And the narrator finds it important to make clear that this new person should not be confused with the light since the two work closely together, but this person has arrived to point to or to witness to the light.

Quick review of John 1:9–18: Here, the Gospel writer ventures an overview of the story of this light, which his Gospel narrative will develop in great detail (John 1:29–21:25). To wit, this light needs the witness of John the Baptist because even though all things are made by this light (Logos) and even though all humans are enlightened by this light, nevertheless, this world does not acknowledge him and even his own people (the Jews) do not recognize him. But as many as shall recognize him, he will give to them the energy to become children of God. "Children of God" are, by definition, human beings who shall have been born not through natural processes involving blood, flesh, and insemination by a husband but newly born or reborn from above, by the will of God. Notice this theme of rebirth from above is a favorite theme throughout this Gospel (cf. John 3:1–10). No wonder the witness of this first human being on the scene, John the Baptist, is so important!

Continued quick review: Suddenly, "The Logos became flesh and tabernacled among us" (John 1:14). The words in Greek here—*sarx* (flesh), *egeneto* (became), *eskenosen* (pitched his tent)—are very important. Apparently, the Logos, Jesus, arrives on the scene as a fully grown adult. The verb for *became* is third person, singular, aorist tense, a historical singular, unrepeatable event. The word for *flesh* is a radical change for the Logos, who suddenly joins the human race, flesh and blood, just as vulnerable, subject to natural laws as everyone else; and the verb for *tabernacle*, pitched his tent among us leaves no room for a manger in a stable. Only an adult can pitch his own tent and, by doing so, join his neighbors, adopt their lifestyles, language, temptations, and citizenship, which means pay taxes to the Roman government like everyone else! John, the Gospel writer, speaks for his generation: "Because of this radical new event, we have gazed upon his glory, glory as of one whom the Father has sent to us, full of grace and truth!"

In John 1:15–16, this sudden and radical change of the Logos from being a prehistorical component of the one God himself to moving in next door to Judaean peasants means John the Baptist has his work cut out for him all the more! John scrambles and cries out, "Listen up now because this one whom we now see is the one who I promised was coming after me. Because this one, the Logos, comes to us from Almighty God, we are already now receiving grace upon grace!"

In John 1:17–18, John continues with his witness to this new event, "I say this and point to this Logos among us, because while the law, the *Torah*, was given to us by Moses, grace and truth have now been given to us through Jesus Christ." And what is the ultimate outcome of this new event, the arrival of the Logos among us in the flesh? Here is the simple truth: "No human being has ever seen God the Almighty Father, but now it is the only begotten Son of God, the one who dwells in the bosom of the Father, this one has made him known to us." Here, the Greek verb is *exegeomai*, third person, singular, aorist tense, middle voice, a concept from the Hellenistic world, which means the actor, God himself, is in serious process of explaining who he is, leading outward from his deepest guts, revealing the whole, full, explicit truth about himself for the whole world to behold. This revelation is possible and takes place only because of the initiative of God who sends out the Logos, part of himself, to live in historical time and circumstances in human flesh.

In John 1:19–28, John the Baptist's witness, his testimony to the incarnation of the Logos, stirs up enough tension to prompt the Jewish officials in Jerusalem to investigate just what is going on with this rabble-rouser out in the wilderness along the Jordan River. Priests and Levites descend upon him, asking, "Who are you?" Apparently, rumors were flying.

"I am not the Messiah," he assures them.

Not likely, they think, but more likely, they ask, "Are you Elijah or some other prophet?"

Again, his answer is, "No."

"Then tell us who you are, on your own terms," they insist, not wanting to return to Jerusalem empty-handed. They set him up, give him the stage for the honest truth, which John is eager and quick to provide.

Like the earlier Gospel of Mark, here, the Gospel writer John makes sure that John the Baptist anchors the arrival of Jesus on this scene in the words of the ancient prophet Isaiah: "I am the voice of one crying out in the wilderness, 'Make straight the way of the Lord'" (Isaiah 40:3).

Having been sent from the Pharisees, these priests and Levites press John to defend his behavior. How can he be baptizing like this without authority to do so? The Jewish authorities, the establishment, assume they must enforce the written, enshrined authority of the Torah and the Prophets, and this maverick troublemaker does not appear to fill the bill. Indeed, John does not fulfill their expectations, but he seizes this opportunity to renew and continue his witness to the very recent arrival of the Logos in the flesh. He explains, "I am baptizing with water, but even now, already there stands one among us all, one whom you do not know, the one who is coming after me. I am not worthy to stoop down to untie the thong of his sandals."

CHAPTER TWO

The Season of Christmastide

Lesson Five: Nativity of the Lord; Read Luke 2:1–20 and John 1:1–14

The prominence of the Roman emperor Augustus and the governor of Syria Quirinius repeat and emphasize the Gospel writer Luke's aim to situate the entire Christian story squarely in the middle of secular, comprehensive/inclusive world history. Actually, Luke does this more elaborately and completely in 3:1–6, and now this later announcement focuses upon John the Baptist, who launches Jesus when he becomes an adult, ready for his baptism, being about thirty years old.

Here (Luke 2:1–20), however, the nativity is foremost in Luke's strategy. God's only begotten Son arrives in this world history to an ordinary, modest couple, members of a backwater tribal culture, Judaism, subservient to the Roman emperor who monopolizes and moves his subjects around at will like players on a chess board. The ninth month of pregnancy is not the time to journey from Nazareth to Bethlehem. And although they have relatives in their extended Davidic family of ancestry who will welcome them into their living quarters, this child who arrives inopportunely must be nestled for warmth and safety among the lowly household of cattle and sheep.

Although Luke seeks the truth in all these events (1:1–4), his language here is plain and simply pure poetry. The Roman Empire projects its version of truth based upon brutal enforcement of strict order, power, and control. The creator and ruler of the entire universe expresses himself in the faithful, humble lifestyle of a homeless couple, begging for food and water, desperate to provide for this newborn infant, the weakest, most helpless, most vulnerable of all living creatures, totally dependent upon his parents or whomever or whatever will humble themselves to assist and promote his survival.

When the angel (messenger of God) arrives to announce, to reveal, to share the reality, the truth, the significance of this humble birth, he/she does not seek out the Roman power structure to receive this incredible news. No gladiators, senators, proconsuls (such as Pontius Pilate or the Herodians), generals, legionnaires, or vestal virgins are chosen and addressed with this special news. Likewise, no religious officials from within Judaism receive this visitation from heaven.

Instead, the angel of God chooses to seek out and visit the lowest of the low, socially and economically, shepherds out in the fields, plodding with rhythmic repetition to perform their daily duties. Long past is the legendary role of the least of the sons of Jesse, the shepherd boy David, chosen and anointed to become the second monarch of ancient Israel (1 Samuel 16:1–13). Long past is the popular image of the Shepherd as the Lord himself, faithfully caring for his weak and often lost sheep (Psalm 23). These days, shepherds were looked down upon and despised and all too often weak, untrustworthy, undependable, shifty, and of negligible value to society.

But to these peripheral citizens of Judaea, the angel of God appears replete with heavenly glory. Response from the shepherds? Terrified, of course. Opposites meeting. What is the angel's first word? "Do not fear!" Why no fear? "Because I bring you good news that calls for great rejoicing, the opposite of fear." What could this good news be all about? "Today is born in the city of David a savior who is the Messiah, the Lord. This great, good news is for everyone, for all the people. But to you, here and now, I bring this news. You are the first to hear what is true for everyone."

Now we should remember that the Jews always seek signs to point them to abstract truth before they take such a message seriously. "This will be a sign for you. If you look, you will find a child wrapped in bands of cloth and lying in a manger." Suddenly, the mountainside is ablaze with heavenly choristers who praise God, reaching from horizon to horizon, "Glory to God in the highest, and on earth peace among those whom he favors."

These shepherds are certainly those whom God favors, because they are the very first across the world to hear this incredibly good news. But the angel has made it clear that this good news is for all the people. This great, good news comes first to the simple, poor, deprived, and neglected, weak in spirit, whom God has called and promises never to forget. But Luke envisions this same great, good news now arrives in order to be shared, sent out, projected across the whole world, even "to the ends of the earth" (Acts 1:8).

These shepherds are persuaded. They make haste to check up on the angel's announcement and find for themselves the small family in Bethlehem as instructed. They connect the angel's message with their experience at the manger and begin to spread this news to everyone. Mary remembers her earlier experience when she was visited by the angel Gabriel, "He has brought down the powerful from their thrones and lifted up the lowly; he has filled the hungry with good things and sent the rich away empty" (Luke 1:52–53).

Luke's powerfully poetic and aesthetic narratives here pose for his readers the clear and persuasive stimulus they need to trust their God who promises to save the whole world, to make all things new (Revelation 21:5), beginning with the lowest and most humble and moving through them outward to transform the whole creation.

Read John 1:1–14.

Each of the four Gospel writers brings his/her own hermeneutical (manner, system, or habits of interpretation) orientation to bear on just how to go about this task of putting together a truthful and convincing portrayal of the career of Jesus. The first three to be written—Mark, Matthew, and Luke—stick to Mark's narrative and itinerary for Jesus's life and work. Mark, of course, begins with Jesus already an adult and works forward from his baptism. Both Matthew and Luke find Mark too skimpy and thus must elaborate, and so each in his own way proceeds to fill in the birth and infancy narratives, including genealogies.

The fourth Gospel, John, is the most independent of the four. John begins his labor with creation or, more correctly, long before creation, with eternity, when there is no beginning or end. To paraphrase, "Always has been the word [in Greek, *ho logos*] and this word was with God and indeed this word was God. This word has always existed with God. All things that exist come into being because of the work of this word. Indeed, absolutely nothing at all that exists has ever come into being apart from his work.

"He, this word, is the source of all life and this same life gives light to all human beings. There is also darkness, and this light shines in the darkness and dominates the darkness. As the human race grows, there comes a man sent from God whose name is John. This man, John, comes to call attention to this great light that shines in the darkness in order that everyone may believe and trust in this light and not be distracted or sidetracked or consumed by the darkness. Now to be very clear, John himself is not this light but comes to point everyone to this light.

"This light we are talking about is the true light, who enlightens every human being, and this light is coming into the world. Indeed, when he comes into the world, this is the very same world he creates, and yet this world does not recognize him. He comes to his own, whom he has created, and his own do not receive him. But as many as do receive him, to them he opens the way for them to become children of God, to the ones believing and trusting in his name. These are the ones who are born not of blood or of the will of the flesh or of the will of a husband but out of the will of God.

"And the word [*ho logos*] became flesh [in Greek, *sarx egeneto*] and tabernacled among us [in Greek, *eskenosen*]. Literally, he pitched his tent among us." To paraphrase, "He moved in right next door to us, in our encampment, joining us and accepting normal citizenship roles alongside all the rest of us."

In other words, the fourth Gospel writer, John, adopts the Greek concept of *ho logos* ("word, reason, truth, or knowledge") in order to move the nascent Christian Gospel message from its previous homeland, the Jewish worldview, outward to embrace the Hellenistic worldview. The prominence of John the Baptist shows, however, that

John does not intend to abandon Judaism completely. Indeed, John holds on to the context of Judaism and moves it forward, intensifies it, and indeed radicalizes it with his central affirmation in 1:14 that "the word became flesh and pitched his tent among us." This means that the eternal reality of *Ho Logos*, who is both with God and an integral component of or part of God and who creates all historical reality, becomes a physical and material part of this same reality, and thus, eternity is present then and there, here and now, and always.

This event, which is to use Greek concepts, both *kairos* (timeless, eternal occasion) and *chronos* (historical, calendar time), brings the eternal reality and purposes of God to happen, take place, occur, become historical reality in Bethlehem and thus leads to the theological conclusion that this Gospel writer champions the concept of "realized eschatology." This means that the incarnation, the process of becoming flesh of the eternal *Logos*, makes the reality of God's eternal purpose already present and operating in Judaea on behalf of the whole creation.

Lesson Six: First Sunday after Christmas Day; Read Luke 2:41–52

This is a Lukan episode not found in Mark or Matthew and thus derives from the hypothetical source known among scholars as the L source. Annual observance of the Passover Festival in Jerusalem shows extraordinary piety on the part of this family. Normally, women and children did not make this pilgrimage, but this scenario makes it look like a community/family affair. One may ask, where are Jesus's brothers and sisters? Presumably, they are not precocious as is Jesus and cause no anxiety for their parents.

One can identify with the frightened parents when their son is missing. Could he be kidnapped by the Romans and forced into military slavery? Ironically, this incident both suggests Jesus's strong sense of calling and destiny, which presumably his parents are also committed to fulfilling, and his precocious independence, willing to outpace his parents in vision and behavior.

There is such glaring inconsistency here in his parents' expectations and demands upon him and their previous knowledge of who Jesus is and what roles he is destined to fulfill (cf. Luke 1:26–56 and 2:1–40). There is a positive, happy tension here between the Jesus who necessarily enjoys a two- to three-day seminar with the professional Jewish elders and officers in the temple complex and his need to behave in a respectful, dignified, decent, "nice young Jesus boy" role as one who causes no anxiety for his parents and who always makes them proud of his conformity.

Luke's two summary overviews (2:40 and 2:52) make it clear that Jesus fits the perfect image demanded across the Hellenistic world for human development from childhood to adulthood. Jesus's maverick self-indulgence for dialogue on questions and issues of eternal significance (2:46–50) makes it equally clear he is committed to his divine origin, calling, and destiny.

His mother to the rescue, Mary, reliving her spiritual meditations in her earlier *Magnificat* adventure (Luke 1:46–55), weaves all these bits and pieces together and "treasures them in her heart" as she produces a tapestry of divine and human energies intertwined and destined to mold her son Jesus into the grown man whom John the Baptist will introduce to the world (Luke 3:21–22).

Lesson Seven: Epiphany of the Lord; Read Matthew 1–12

The English word *epiphany* is derived from the Greek verb *epiphaino*, which means to facilitate, produce, or provide a manifestation, an appearance, a revelation, a showing forth or clarification, where before there was only darkness, ignorance, or obscurity. This concept carries the assumption that some hidden treasure of immense value begs to be released from negative darkness into the positive, bright light of freedom, released from prison to serve and save a waiting constituency in dire need of this new blessing.

Originally of Eastern origin, this one festival marked the nativity of Christ, the baptism of Christ, and the manifestation of his glory in the Cana wedding feast (John 2:11). When the Western church settled on December 25 as the best date on which to celebrate the nativity of Christ, epiphany began to be associated with the manifestation of Christ to the Gentiles (Matthew 2:1–11). Today in the West, epiphany occupies the twelve days devoted to the celebration of the nativity. Note how our popular culture celebrates "the twelve days of Christmas," with a parody focusing upon the many, many gifts "my true love brings to me," concluding with the "partridge in a pear tree." The Eastern Orthodox churches still tend to associate epiphany with the baptism of Christ.

Our Old Testament lesson for this Sunday reminds us of how this promise of blessing we call epiphany has an ancient origin. Read Isaiah 60:1–3, "Arise, shine, for your light has come… Nations shall come to your light and kings to the brightness of your dawn." How do our Gospel writers draw upon this classical prophet and each one contributes his version of epiphany, or the bright light of the arrival of Jesus the Christ as the good news Isaiah promises?

Notice each Gospel writer is an independent individual, drawing upon the same divine spiritual source but inspired and eager to compose a narrative that reveals his particular insights and visions aimed to influence his readers to respond with new knowledge, insight, and inspiration. In other words, they, the Gospel writers, seek to unveil and thus reveal convincingly the great, good news the prophet Isaiah foretells, but each one must do this relying upon his personal creative strengths as well as weaknesses.

As far as we know, each Gospel writer thinks and writes in the Koine Greek language in order to reach and effectively communicate with as many readers as possible, near and far, across the Hellenistic world. Each one may know Hebrew and/or Latin or various dialects floating around, but Koine Greek is their necessary literary tool. Jesus himself spoke Aramaic, a dialect of Hebrew. We may assume he was literate, conversant with the Hebrew Scriptures, but not a dedicated writer, if he wrote at all. All evidence shows Jesus prefers one-on-one, face-to-face oral communication.

The Gospel writer we know as Mark wrote first, with Matthew and Luke using his narratives as their basis for the itinerary Jesus follows in his adult ministry. Mark anchors his narrative in the vision of the ancient prophet Isaiah, apparently dependent upon

Isaiah 40:1–5 as the strong promise of an epiphany event Mark describes in 1:1–11. Once baptized, Jesus is off and running, full steam ahead!

Along come both Matthew and Luke, who find Mark too short and simple, so much rich material missing. No infancy narratives. Was Mark ignorant, bashful, tongue-tied, or what? Both Matthew and Luke have rich knowledge and beautiful, delicate, elaborate stories, too valuable to leave out, sure to move readers to tears. But let us not miss their differences as well, which point to the variations each writer wishes to put forward as his best, most faithful contribution to this his calling to publish this great, good news.

A couple of examples to move this comparison forward. When we listen to Luke's promise to his patron Theophilus (Luke 12:1–4), Luke's ambition reflects a highly sophisticated scholar, equipped with rich and complex resources upon which to draw. He meticulously composes an artistically inspired and motivated composition as he intertwines the two birth narratives, that of John the Baptist and Jesus of Nazareth (Luke 1:5–80). For example, the poetry that emerges from the brain/mouth of the virgin Mary (Luke 1:46–55), to become known in modern musical circles as *the Magnificat*, reflects Luke's desire to elevate this maiden into friendly competition with another virgin (*parthenos*), the goddess Athena, patroness of the city-state of Athens, goddess of beauty, justice, wisdom, and integrity.

Matthew's version of the birth narrative shrinks by comparison, neatly confined to Bethlehem, although no less serious in motivation and content (Matthew 1:18–25). But missing is Luke's drama in the imposed travel from Nazareth to Bethlehem and the suspense when the couple and infant must survive in primitive living arrangements among the lowly animals (Luke 2:1–7). Both Matthew and Luke present genealogies of Jesus, but compare their strikingly different, unique contents. Matthew traces the descent of Jesus through a carefully calculated list of ancestors beginning with Abraham. In other words, this birth and blossoming career continues and fulfills the promises of the Creator God to bless his covenant people descended from the original patriarch, Abraham himself (Matthew 1:1–17).

Luke, by way of contrast, traces Jesus's genealogy from age thirty, meticulously cataloging ancestors not to the patriarch Abraham but all the way back to Adam, the very first human being brought into existence as the father of the entire human race, not only the chosen Jewish segment but the multifaceted Gentiles as well (Luke 3:23–38).

Now both Luke and Matthew are eager to express "epiphany," revelation, clarification of the good news to which each of these genealogies and this nativity point and which lead to open, public presentation. How does each Gospel writer go about this task, this opportunity?

In Luke's version of epiphany (Luke 2:8–20), an angel, messenger from God, suddenly appears alone, unannounced, to shepherds, the lowest of all socioeconomic strata, nearby, close to Bethlehem. This mouthpiece "spills the beans" to this vagrant group. They, most humble of all Jewish servants, are the first to receive the incredible news that shall bring joy to all people, which is delivered first on the mountainside. "To you is born this day nearby, in the city of David, a savior who is the Messiah, the Lord. This will be the sign for you: you will find a child wrapped in bands of cloth and lying in a manger." One angel quickly becomes a multitude of the heavenly hosts, and the mountainside is ablaze with heavenly voices who sing, "Glory to God in the highest heaven." And what is to be the outcome of all this commotion? "Peace on earth among those whom our Lord favors!"

The message is delivered. This birth is explained, made clear, and promised to all people but comes first to these shepherds and, from them, soon to share this news down in Bethlehem so that all the world shall know, be blessed, and benefit. Luke is preparing his Gospel narrative to show how important the Messiah is as the Savior who is now born in Bethlehem; he comes to be revealed not to the high and mighty but first and foremost to the humble, the ordinary, the lowly servants. Just as Jesus's most significant ancestry includes but is not focused upon Abraham but rather upon Adam, the father of the human race, so this epiphany has good news that shall eventually reach out to embrace all the Gentiles. Or to put this blessing in another word, this is a project of blessing "which shall reach to the ends of the earth" (Acts 1:8).

We should remember that Luke and Matthew both accept Mark as their model for Jesus's itinerary, but they do not know each other's work, as far as we know, and so each Gospel writer reports epiphany as he envisions it, perhaps drawing upon other documents or sources such as the hypothetical Q or M or L sources. Let's examine how Matthew goes about dealing with this subject.

Matthew begins his narrative (Matthew 2:1–12) at the other end of the socioeconomic scale, with royalty, or pseudoroyalty, since King Herod was not a Jewish monarch but a Roman subject. But Herod receives reports of *epiphany* when an entourage of privileged travelers arrives for a high-level consultation. Who are these pilgrims? We have learned to call them kings, magi, and wise men, from the East. They were not kings but probably astrologers, members of a learned fraternity who devoted themselves to scholarly examination of the heavenly bodies, calculating and measuring cosmic phenomena and the relationship of such objects to earthly developments, both natural and human.

These astrologers were aware of the history of Judaism and probably operated out of an academic stronghold such as Babylon, crossroads of many prophetic resources, academic fraternities, and visionaries who interacted with one another. We have been indoctrinated to sing the hymn "We Three Kings," but all we know is, they brought three gifts. Their number may have been much larger. Whatever their number, they were corporately turned on by astronomical movements of some powerful sort. One scholarly opinion suggests they may have been confronted by an unusual mixture of two or more stars coming together to produce an effect that was a rare merger that triggered their research into documents, which offered prophetic visions of the relationship between the heavens and the complicated careers of Jewish dynasties interacting with one another over many centuries.

Where better to seek wisdom, fascinated as they are by the alluring Jewish traditions the scribes have collected and cataloged, than to ask the current monarchy in charge down in Jerusalem.

Confident that the child destined to be king of the Jews has already been born, trusting the astronomical display they have experienced, they come seeking simple information. The current occupant of the throne, Herod the Great, faces a crisis. Is he not already king of the Jews? Ostensibly, but he knows how tenuous his rule actually is. The experts search the scriptures. The prophet (Micah 5:2–5) points to Bethlehem as the key location being sought.

Still following the same heavenly constellation, the travelers find the house in Bethlehem, where, overwhelmed with joy, they pay homage to the child and his mother, presenting gifts of three valuable items, signifying their understanding of the scene before them (epiphany). The three gifts are gold, fit for a king; frankincense, suitable for the work of a priest; and myrrh, indicative of suffering and necessary for dignified burial of the dead.

King Herod tries to piggyback on the successful location of the newborn child, but the visitors from the East, warned in a dream, are quick to avoid any further collaboration with the current Jewish power structure and, sufficient within their own Gentile resources, complete their pilgrimage on their own steam, thus basking in their own experience of epiphany, returning to Babylon by a safer route.

Contrary to Luke's strategy, wherein the epiphany launched with the shepherds will eventually spread to include the Gentiles, Matthew describes this epiphany as already arising from the Gentiles themselves, stimulated by their academic study of the heavenly bodies, continuing with their shrewd encounter with King Herod, and their spiritual strategy, which enables them to serve as messengers who will share their exposure to this newborn child with their Gentile coconspirators back in the East to which they return.

In both narratives, that of Luke and that of Matthew, it is the encounter with this newborn child that is the catalyst that opens up—hence *epiphany*—new knowledge, spiritual dimensions of worship and communion, and new opportunities for service to humankind that promise blessings for all those who find favor with the great Lord God who sends this child as the gift who will save his people from all sin and evil.

Lesson Eight: Baptism of the Lord / First Sunday after Epiphany—Exploring this Baptism Event in All Four Gospels; Read Mark 1:4–11, Matthew 3:13–17, Luke 3:15–17 and 21–22, and John 1:1–51

Scholar's consensus: The narrative event of Jesus's baptism by John surely happened because it caused serious embarrassment for his disciples and had to be explained. For example, did Jesus confess his sins like everyone else? Did John exercise superior rank and authority over all those whom he baptized? Before the first written Gospel (Mark), the bulk of narrative communication was transmitted by word of mouth, which is designated as the "oral tradition." The first written documents included in the New Testament, of course, are the letters of the apostle Paul, which contain little narrative and mostly confessional, kerygmatic/instructional, therapeutic/ethical, and doctrinal/Christological concerns.

The first written Gospel, Mark, appears roughly 65–70 CE, probably written in Rome to Gentile readers who need to have the oral tradition redacted (edited) and interpreted in order to be meaningful to their Gentile ears/minds and who also need to hear it anchored in its original Palestinian/Jewish context. The only human recognition and confession in this Gospel of Jesus to be God's Son comes from the lips of the Roman centurion who witnesses Jesus's last breath in Mark 15:39. Finally, at last, a Gentile gets the point and hears the truth Mark has been wrestling to show his readers and Jesus's disciples from day 1.

Mark's readers, of course, get the word and know who Jesus is right from the start (Mark 1:1 and 1:11), and Mark does this by linking John the Baptist directly to the Old Testament prophecy of Isaiah whose words provide the solid anchor for the work of John, who attracts his fellow countrymen to respond to his call for repentance of sins in preparation for the imminent arrival of one greater than John, this one being Jesus, who arrives from Nazareth to Galilee to join the crowds who are responding/listening to John's announcement.

Jesus joins the long line and takes his turn to be baptized by John, and suddenly, he looks upward and sees the heavens fractured/

split wide open and the Spirit of God descending like a dove upon him. A voice from heaven cries out, "You are my Son, the Beloved. With you I am well pleased." Mark, the narrator, does not make it clear if anyone else, the crowd, for example, sees this spectacle or if, as it appears, Jesus alone sees and hears this voice. But Mark's readers surely get the point that this is the one whom John has been speaking when he says, "The one who is stronger than me is soon coming. I have baptized you with water, but he will baptize you in the Holy Spirit."

Baptism as a liturgical ritual was never a standard initiation practice in Judaism, as circumcision was. But baptism was an increasingly innovative, somewhat controversial and sectarian (Essenes) ritual, no doubt influenced by widespread practice among Gentile cultic traditions. Both John and his cousin Jesus show cultic influences from the Essene sectarian cult arising from within Judaism. Mark wants to show how the arrival of Jesus on the scene ties directly both to his Jewish heritage and reflects the Gentile practice of ritual ablutions as practiced across the Roman Empire and reaching into Judaism (the Essenes).

But there is danger his Gentile readers will identify Jesus's arrival with the popular Roman expectation that their new emperor, when he arrives, will be zapped into divinity and adopted as the new god everyone must automatically worship, honor, serve, and adore. When the heavens split open and Jesus sees the Spirit descend like a dove upon him and hears the voice identity him, "You are my Son, the Beloved. With you I am well pleased," this event reaffirms the link already established with the Old Testament prophet Isaiah. Gentiles in Rome, Mark hopes, should hear this recognition and celebration of Jesus not as a repeat of their Caesar's present-day adoption ritual but as reaffirmation of the eternal Jewish God's fulfillment of the long-standing promises quoted unmistakably from the exemplary Old Testament prophet Isaiah.

This scenario clarifies how John the Baptist's promise that the one soon coming "will baptize you not with water, the usual everyday element, but with the Holy Spirit" links Jesus firmly with the long-familiar concept of God's Spirit at work in history and contradicts the Gentile notion that the spirit of naturalism or humanism stands ready to divinize whomever the gods choose as the next royal emperor waiting in line for his elevation to popular, heroic, divine stature. Baptism, now, here, receives a new definition both for Jews and for Gentiles, but baptism was always waiting in both cultural contexts (Judaism and the Hellenistic Diaspora) for this new interpretation.

The writers of the next two Gospels are both disappointed and impatient with Mark's choice of adoption as a scenario for Jesus's arrival on the world scene. Matthew thus provides genealogy and birth narratives to flesh out what is lacking in Mark (cf. Matthew 1–2) so that when Jesus arrives for baptism, his identity is already well established and cemented in stone by the divine promises fulfilled in Bethlehem and witnessed to by the journey of the magi from the East (cf. Matthew 3:1–17).

Now the issue is not Jesus's identity but the question of why Jesus would submit to a baptism deemed necessary for forgiveness of sins. John's role now is to clarify this discrepancy and thus magnify the task Jesus has been prepared to fulfill step-by-step from the time of the patriarch Abraham. When John tries to prevent his baptism of Jesus, Jesus insists this act is necessary: "Let it be so now, for it is proper for us in this way to fulfill all righteousness." This event does not announce who Jesus is, but this event "fulfills" or brings to climax the long, slow process that began in Abraham so very long ago. And this event "fulfills all righteousness," not some, a few, or partial righteousness but "all righteousness." This means it is necessary and imperative that Jesus identify with sinners, with all sinners, whose guilt he must now take upon himself, in order for grace, mercy, salvation, and peace to arrive and be freely distributed, shared with all of God's people, not with the few deserving ones alone but with the entire human race, not to mention, all of creation.

Jesus gladly submits himself to John's baptism, and when he emerges from the water and sees the heavens open and the Spirit descending, the voice this time does not speak directly to Jesus alone, with a private personal message, using the singular pronoun *you*. This time, the heavenly voice speaks to everyone, making a public announcement, for those gathered nearby and for the whole world to hear, including Matthew's readers, saying, "This is my son, the beloved, with whom I am well pleased." We may be sure that this writer, Matthew, is happy he has corrected and magnified Mark's rather skimpy and error-prone introduction to the Gospel.

The third Gospel writer, Luke, as far as we know, does not know Matthew's work, but he does know Mark's version, and he is equally disappointed and impatient with the first Gospel's comparatively weak and inadequate portrayal of Jesus at the hands of John the Baptist. Luke, one of the fathers of classical Greek literary style and aesthetic extravagance, writes to provide his patron Theophilus with the truth about "the matters of which you have been instructed" (Luke 1:1–4). Drawing upon his own reservoir of resources, consisting of both oral and written traditions, Luke proceeds to elaborate upon Jesus's family and cultural origins, especially his family tree or genealogy, that includes John, son of Zechariah and Elizabeth (Luke 1:57–80). This resourceful writer provides the announcement delivered by the angel Gabriel to the maiden Mary in Nazareth known as the Annunciation (Luke 1:26–38) and the beautiful hymn of response delivered by the Virgin Mary to her cousin Elizabeth known as the Magnificat (Luke 1:46–56).

Luke portrays the birth and significance of John as equally revelatory of the long-awaited fulfillment of the ancient covenant now coming to fruition (Luke 1:57–80), whereas Matthew recalls the journey of the magi from the East first to Jerusalem and then to Bethlehem, thus connecting Jesus's birth with the national and international power systems and structures (Matthew 2:11–12). Luke is careful to stress the humble circumstances of this birth with divine revelation brought by the angelic choirs to the lowly shepherds hard at work out in the fields and yet prime candidates for the event known as the epiphany of the Lord (Luke 2:8–20). And Luke has John the Baptist develop the relevance of baptismal confession of sin to include social ethics from across a broad public spectrum (Luke 3:7–14).

Moving from the Synoptic Gospels to the fourth Gospel, John, we do not know if this writer had access to the three Synoptics or not. It is more likely, some scholars observe, that John knew some or all the writings of Paul the Apostle. At any rate, while there is no baptism with water, as far as we can tell, John gives the strongest and most fully developed portrayal of John the Baptist and his announcement of the arrival of the Son of God within human history (John 1:1–51). John, this Gospel writer, does this of course by acknowledging both Jewish and Gentile contexts for both John the Baptist and the Jewish covenant and, above all, by anchoring his narrative not primarily in Judaism or in Gentile cultures but by tracing Jesus all the way back beyond and before creation, before all natural and human history, to precreation.

And most importantly, he does this by identifying Jesus who becomes flesh with the Word of God (in Greek, *Ho Logos Tou Theou*), who, as equal to and part of God himself, does the work of creation and continues this work when he becomes flesh and "moves in and pitches his tent right next door" deliberately to be present with and to work among humans and all creation as the Light, the Word, the Truth, etc. Thus, this fourth Gospel writer magnifies the identity of Jesus far beyond the synoptic writers by introducing up front this Greek concept of *Ho Logos*, reason, truth, or natural law coeternal and coequal with all creation and indeed all reality however defined. English language cognate for this Greek concept *Logos* is the word *logic*.

The event of the baptism of Jesus, first recorded in Mark, thus continues to grow, expand, and remain a constant element of the Gospel message, as each of these four Gospel writers seeks to show how the concept of adoption needs extensive development within the resources of human language and intelligence.

Lesson Nine: Second Sunday after Epiphany; Read John 2:1–11

This lesson presents the first of the seven (or eight) signs Jesus works in the fourth Gospel, and it may be helpful to review the organization the writer John gives to his document. We may take all of chapter 1 (John 1:1–51) as the prologue to this Gospel. In the eternal

Word of God (*Ho Logos Tou Theou*), God himself becomes flesh and moves in and adopts the Jewish cultures of Judaea and Galilee as his own residency, him being full of grace and truth.

This means that although the law was previously given to Israel through Moses, now grace and truth arrive, and this comes about finally, fully, and completely only through the incarnation of Jesus Christ. No human being has ever seen God, but the only begotten Son of God, who is in the bosom of the Father, this one now reveals God the Father to his creation (paraphrased, 1:17–18).

But how can this be true if Jesus Christ moves into and becomes the product of a trivial village such as Nazareth? Surely, the incarnation of Almighty God would choose to begin his reign in the capital city of Jerusalem, or at least in a prosperous Greek-speaking city like Sepphoris or Tiberias. When one of Jesus's first disciples hears their master hails from such a down-and-out hamlet, he, Nathaniel, exclaims, "Can anything good come out of Nazareth?" (1:46).

As Nathaniel gets to know Jesus better, he recognizes the irony of his own consternation and also exclaims, "Rabbi, you are the Son of God! You are the king of Israel!" Jesus counsels Nathaniel this way, "Do you believe because of what I have said to you? Truly, truly I tell you, you will see heaven opened and the angels of God ascending and descending upon the Son of Man" (1:51). Does Jesus here point forward to the signs he will be presenting to his audiences/constituencies as this Gospel progresses?

In other words, the all too ordinary village of Nazareth becomes the first metaphor for the career of Jesus. John, the Gospel writer, is prepared and begins to show when, where, and how Jesus of Nazareth does indeed bring the grace and truth of salvation to Israel and beyond this nation to the whole world.

What does this concept "metaphor" mean? This concept combines two Greek words, *meta* ("beyond, across, over") and *foreo* ("bear, carry, transport"). A metaphor is a linguistic symbol that functions to carry across or transport meaning, truth, or ideas from the known to the unknown. You begin with the known and move from what you do understand, the familiar, across the chasm separating you from what you do not yet understand, the unfamiliar, in order by this process to gain new knowledge.

Nazareth here serves as Jesus's new home, his new environment, his milieu, where he moves in and sets up residency in order to bring the love of God his Father to share grace and truth with the human race, indeed with the whole world (3:16).

Jesus (*Ho Logos Tou Theou*, the Word of God) now moves from the eternal, divine milieu to his temporal, all-too-human milieu in order that he may facilitate, become a divine catalyst to move human minds from little or poor knowledge, indeed probably gross ignorance, across the great divide to arrive at saving knowledge of God his Father and their creator (3:16–21). The signs up ahead will be Jesus's instruments for his task of showing forth the eternal God hidden until now but now seeking through this his only begotten Son to share his eternal covenant with the whole world, concentrating especially upon fallen humanity.

In order to flesh out (pun intended) this metaphor of this man from Nazareth, John arranges his source material into two major sections or books. The first is the book of signs (chapters 2–12), and the second is the book of glory (chapters 12–20), with a final epilogue (chapter 21).

Scholars have identified seven signs in the book of signs and one final sign in the epilogue: 2:1–11, water into wine; 4:46–54, healing of the royal official's son; 5:1–18, healing of a lame man; 6:1–14, feeding of the five thousand; 6:16–21, Jesus walking on water; 9:1–4, healing of a blind man; 11:1–44, the raising of Lazarus; and 21:1–14, the miraculous catch of fish.

Our lesson (John 2:1–11) narrates the first such activity (sign) of Jesus, whereby this man from Nazareth, full of grace and truth, reveals his unknown Father God to Jewish citizens who appear to be ready and eager to receive this special blessing but who lack, need, and receive Jesus's presence.

To paraphrase, it was the third day of a wedding feast taking place in Cana, a village nearby to Nazareth, in Galilee. (Customarily, a wedding was an all-inclusive, extended family and neighborhood celebration that lasted for seven days.) The mother of Jesus was a part of this extended celebration, and on this third day, Jesus and his disciples are also invited to join the festivities. (The mother of Jesus is never mentioned by name in this Gospel, only by her relationship to Jesus.) On this day, the celebration was not even halfway to conclusion and the supply of wine was running out. Jesus's mother grows concerned and calls him aside, saying, "They are almost out of wine!" Jesus replies, "Why should we be concerned, woman? It is not time yet for me to be leading this celebration!" His mother winks her eye at him and steps over to speak to the servants who are huddled with worried looks on their faces. She whispers, "Now when he calls you to work on the water jars, be sure to do exactly what he tells you to do." (How's that for a dedicated "Jewish mother" taking good care of her extended family!) She waves her hands over the water jars and smiles at Jesus.

As a matter of fact, there are six huge stone water jugs nearby, ready to be used for the Jewish purification rites. Jesus addresses the servants, "Fill these jugs with water." They get busy, pleased someone is taking control. Pretty soon, they have all six jugs filled to the brim.

Jesus thanks them for filling the water jars as he requested and continues, "Take some from these jugs to the master of the feast." (This person is the chief butler, or Mr. Carson, for all of you *Downton Abbey* fans.) He has to sample and approve all refreshments before they can be served to the guests. As he rolls this liquid around his palate, a big, wide grin takes over his face. He does not know the source or circumstances that have produced this new wine, although the servants know very well. He seeks out the bridegroom, the host in whose home all these festivities are taking place. "Hey, Chief, look how crafty you are. Normally, everyone serves the good wine first and waits until your guests are all tipsy, and then you put out the weak stuff, when nobody knows the difference. But you, you saved the good wine until now. Great strategy, boss!"

This is what happens when Jesus of Nazareth presents the first of his signs, this one in Cana of Galilee, and he shows forth his glory to everyone, including his own disciples, who find their trust in him and his promises growing stronger.

Many, if not most, commentators refer to this event as a miracle and define *miracle* as "an act of power or performance that exceeds or defies the normal, natural laws, which science and/or common sense expect and demand." The problem with this reading is that it reflects a version of modern science that sees the physical/natural world as operating on its own according to a closed system of natural laws not subject to interference from any other outside source.

It is understandable that this modern worldview has come to dominate Western civilization since the time of the Enlightenment. This closed mathematically and experientially predictable natural universe has no room for the presence and involvement of spiritual dimensions such as the biblical God. This development leads modern philosophers and theologians to the worldview known as deism. According to deism, God was perhaps active in the original creation but did such a good job he can now move away and take a rest, uninvolved in the natural world that operates according to the perfect and predictable laws God has established once and for all time.

There is a Greek word for the phenomena that do not conform to the natural laws but appear to be empowered or controlled by divine or spiritual forces. This word is *he dunamis*, usually translated as "power, wonder, miracle." (Notice the English collateral word *dynamite*.) But in this Gospel, John uses another Greek word to refer to Jesus's activity, *to semeon*, translated as "sign, symbol, signal, explanation," an event that enables and promotes communication, understanding, or knowledge and thus covenant communion. In other words, the issue is not one or power, as in the term *miracle*, but of sharing ideas, news, reality, truth that being shared promotes and builds covenant relationships.

The biblical worldview has no concept of God the creator being separated from or uninvolved in his creation, contrary to modern deism. Instead, God the creator is always closely involved in all his creation. There is no place, no time, no one where God is not present and seeking the welfare of all his creation. Psalm 19:1–4, for example, expresses this omnipresence, omniscience, and omnipotence of God the creator and sustainer of all reality.

At the very same time, however, there is a huge problem of communication between God and one very special element of his creation, and this is the human race. Genesis 1–2 affirms that human beings alone of all living species are created in the very same image and likeness of God, which means granted freedom to accept, cultivate, and seek covenant relationship with their creator or choose to exploit their freedom and go in a different direction. All creation is very good, according to this narrative, and all creation is loved absolutely and unconditionally by the Creator (John 3:15). But there exists lack of communication, or weak versions of communication, and this reality is the challenge Jesus faces when he becomes flesh and launches his ministry from Nazareth. How to reach out to this fallen creation? How to share, express, communicate the grace and truth that he brings, sent, motivated, and empowered as he is to reveal God his Father to these human creatures who have never seen God?

At Cana in Galilee, God in Jesus presents this sign when water becomes the best wine available. He lives and will work within and out of his Jewish heritage, where wine is a powerful symbol for the reality of celebration, celebration of divine love and deliverance from slavery, as in the Passover Festival. In this episode, Jesus finds himself as a guest, involved in a traditional cultural occasion, the celebration of the covenant of human marriage. The sharing of wine is a necessary, expected element of this celebration, just as it is in the Passover Festival. When the supply of wine runs low, Jesus, with his mother working as his catalyst, seizes this opportunity and takes advantage of this threat to the festivities to bring about a living metaphor, in order to heal the stress and promote the covenant bonding relationships this festival offers.

It is worth repeating that Jesus has a strong colleague in his mother, she who initiates this opportunity to present his first sign in the fourth Gospel. But it's the two of them working together, with available props such as the huge stone jars, with willing servants, and with the master of the festival who aptly praises arrival of the new wine, even in his braggadocio. And the climax of the whole event belongs to Jesus's disciples. They are just beginning their pilgrimage journey with this Jesus of Nazareth, watching this little drama as they do from the sidelines. If the communication from God in heaven facilitated in this extravagant arrival of the best wine stimulates them to strengthen their trust in their new master, surely, John is thinking to describe this marriage feast as dramatically as possible and to look ahead to such future signs and to the time of Jesus's glory (trials, rejection, suffering, death, resurrection, and ascension) and to the arrival of the kingdom of God on earth, which Jesus's career in human form inaugurates, promises, and promotes.

Lesson Ten: Third Sunday after Epiphany; Read Luke 4:14–21

It will be helpful to study the context in which the Gospel writer Luke places this episode. Both Matthew and Luke follow their primary source, Mark 1:1–11, in stressing the importance of the preparation of John the Baptist and his baptism of Jesus in the Jordan River. For Mark, this is the occasion when the Holy Spirit appears on the scene and anoints the adult Jesus as the Son of God. We should remember that in Mark's context, writing in Rome for Gentiles around 65–70 CE, this may be interpreted to mean adoption to divine status, as was assumed to happen to prominent Romans, such as the emperor.

At any rate, in Mark's original version, this means the Spirit is now ready to begin the necessary work in and through this newly anointed Son of God. What does the Spirit do? The Spirit "drives" Jesus out into the wilderness. The Greek verb here, *ekballo*, has a cognate in English, *ballistics*, referring to firearms. Perhaps a better translation is, "The Spirit propels Jesus outward toward the wilderness or desert." This verb suggests Jesus may be reluctant to go there and has to be prodded or forced to do so. A better reading is that Jesus is empowered by the Spirit, equipped and made ready to go in this direction.

We should recall that both Matthew and Luke bring their own interpretations of what Jesus's baptism means. Matthew (3:13–17) is motivated to explain just why Jesus participates in John's baptism for repentance from sin. Not because Jesus is guilty of sin but because he identifies with those who are guilty of sin, and this means "it is proper for [them] to fulfill all righteousness." In other words, he is taking the sin of the whole world upon himself.

Luke (3:21–22) has Jesus join the queue of the multitudes whom John is baptizing and take his turn. Luke's Jesus wants to identify with the multitudes, the *hoi polloi* (in Greek), the ordinary, working stiffs, the poor of the world with whom and for whom Jesus is empowered here with the Holy Spirit in order to minister to their most serious needs (looking ahead to Luke 4:16–19).

Now this baptized Jesus is ready for the next step. Neither Matthew nor Luke chooses to use Mark's verb, *ekballo* ("drive out"), as if Jesus may be reluctant to go forward. Instead, Matthew (4:1) uses *anexthe*, aorist tense, passive voice, from *anago*, "to lead, guide, or facilitate." In translation, "Then Jesus was led into the wilderness by the Spirit to be tempted by the devil." In other words, Jesus is ready, willing, and able to begin his ministry and welcomes the leadership and direction of the Holy Spirit in order to get this done. Jesus is not reluctant, as Mark may intimate, but ready and willing.

Luke (4:1) chooses the same verb in Greek as Matthew does, *ago*, in the form *egeto*, imperfect tense, passive voice. In translation, "Now Jesus, full of the Holy Spirit, returned from the Jordan River and was being led continuously by the Spirit in the desert throughout forty days, being tempted by the devil."

Whatever words they choose, all three Synoptic Gospel writers agree that this exit from the Jordan River and the next forty days in the wilderness or desert launches Jesus's ministry, his mission on behalf of God his Father, empowered as he is by the Holy Spirit, anointed to bring good news and salvation from sin and evil to God's chosen covenant people and, through them, beyond them, to the whole world.

Mark, the minimalist writer, paints a helicopter overview of this cosmic spectacle, reflecting the players and dimensions characteristic of the Jewish apocalyptic worldview. At issue is the eschatological battle or contest or showdown between cosmic good and evil. "Forty days" is the proverbial occasion and time allotted for this struggle to take place. And notice, it does have to take place! God cannot or will not push a button or pull a switch from far away at a distance. After all, this arena of encounter is God's creation, and this creation is very good, meaning God's appointed choice of environment is suitable, appropriate, and necessary for this historical encounter (Genesis 1:1–31a). These forty days of dramatic confrontation reflect God's commitment to his creation, his precious, divine milieu he loves so very much (John 3:16).

Without in any way meaning to trivialize or lessen the eternal significance of this encounter of good with evil, Mark says it all when he summarizes this inauguration of Jesus's career with the symbols of "forty days of temptation by Satan, with the wild beasts, and the angels ministering to him." Enough said!

Not enough, say both Matthew and Luke. Mark is much too skimpy for them. Here, in the hypothetical Q source, they receive three obviously Spirit-inspired versions of what transpired during these unforgettable forty days. What is the most basic of all human needs? Food.

To survive, you have to eat. Jesus's own forty-day fast is weakening, humiliating, and exhausting, putting him at the extreme limit of human deprivation just minutes before physical death from starvation. With one foot already in the grave, Jesus is a ripe, prime candidate for Satan's tempting offer. Satan has the solution to this crisis, "Turn this stone into bread if indeed you are the Son of God." Jesus replies, "It is written that human beings shall not live by bread alone"—and Matthew supplies the needed completion to this basic truth—"but by every word that the mouth of God speaks." Thus refuted, we may call this the first temptation by Satan "the economics temptation."

Satan does not give up or weaken his resolve. Satan ushers Jesus up to a satellite view of the planet Earth. This cosmic guide offers to turn over rule of all the kingdoms on Earth to this Son of God, if only he will fall down and worship his host. Jesus is certainly human, but not stupid. He knows this claim by Satan to be an honest entrepreneur is a falsehood. But the offer is tempting, nonetheless. How could a little worship of Satan now and then hurt? Jesus knows he already has more claim to ownership and rule of this planet than Satan has or could ever have. It doesn't take a jury deliberation to reach this verdict, "You shall worship the Lord your God, and him only shall you serve." Let's call this "the political temptation."

Satan has one more ace up his sleeve, according to Luke's recall. Quick journey to Jerusalem and, poised on the highest pinnacle of the temple, Satan urges, "Here's your big chance to show your true power. Jump off, and surely, angels will rescue you in midair. You'll make headlines with your huge splash on Broadway. Surely, a ticker tape parade will soon follow!" Notice Satan can quote scripture too. Let's call this "the glamour temptation." By this time, the devil must have exhausted his resources for effective temptation, but as he slinks away with disappointment, Luke is quick to conclude this is only a temporary setback for this tempter supreme. The devil will reconnoiter himself and bide his time, waiting patiently until better opportunity opens up.

Interestingly, Matthew and Luke both have the second and third temptation events reversed in sequence. Luke probably reports these events in a sequence that will build anticipation for what is coming up in 4:14–21 (22–30). The three Synoptic Gospels agree that after his baptism and temptations and after the departure of John the Baptist due to his arrest, Jesus begins his ministry in Galilee, moving among towns and villages, probably having settled in Capernaum as his virtual headquarters. One can only speculate why his hometown of Nazareth was not his headquarters. His absence there most likely has to do with his need to serve outside of and away from his established relationships among family, extended family, and close neighbors. He must distance himself in order to develop his new post-baptismal identity and mission. And the reports are that he meets with welcoming crowds and warm receptions, including accolades of praise (Luke 4:14–15).

But sooner or later, Jesus most surely came home, even though the Spirit now calls him out and away from his past and forward across Galilee and even beyond, eventually to reach the ends of the earth, as Luke emphasizes in his second volume, the Acts of the Apostles. Luke makes his homecoming to Nazareth a big deal, as if it may serve as a formal coming-out or inauguration of his now official mission. Note the similarities and differences between Mark's version of this event (Mark 6:1–6) and Luke's more formal, stylized, almost ritualistic portrayal of Jesus's homecoming (Luke 4:14–30).

Luke first emphasizes Jesus's long-established connection, indeed his integral belonging to Nazareth and its synagogue. He is now where he has always been and slips naturally and smoothly into the grooves that await him, as normalization takes over. Back where he belongs, he repeats the roles he has always performed and fulfilled. When he stands up to read, is this his choice or has he been appointed for this role on this Sabbath? Does he choose to read from the scroll of Isaiah the prophet, or is this scroll chosen for him?

And why does he turn to the passage that Luke quotes from the lips of Jesus: "The Spirit of the Lord is upon me, because he has anointed me [1] to preach good news to the poor. He has sent me [2] to proclaim release to the prisoners and [3] recovery of sight to the boing, [4] to send forth all those oppressed into freedom, and [5] to proclaim the year of the Lord's special favor."

Now some scholars are confident that the writer of the book of Isaiah intends to speak in the Spirit of the Jubilee year, long established as a traditional observance. After seven sequences of seven years, thus forty-nine years, on the fiftieth year, the Lord proclaims grace, forgiveness, and freedom for everyone. Ancient property rights were honored and restored, debts were forgiven, prisoners were released, and slaves were granted freedom.

Jesus rolls up the scroll, hands it back to the attendant, and sits down. He has moved from reader to teacher, according to formal ritual, and dutifully all eyes and ears are focused upon him as the prepared, appointed, honored teacher for this Sabbath day. When he begins to speak, it is Jesus's words and teaching that Luke wants his readers to hear, absorb, and take seriously as the good news his Gospel document has to present: "Today this prophecy has now been fulfilled in your hearing!"

What? Does he refer to himself? They all recognize the prophet's description of the Jubilee year and are pleased to hear this good news, which will benefit them all in some or many ways. They smile and welcome this pleasant vision of gracious promise all too much needed among all their people. But they are also somewhat surprised, puzzled, and even amazed that such words reach them from one of their very own neighbors. This question buzzes through their ranks, "Is this the son of Joseph?"

Jesus is both pleased and prepared for their ambiguous response. "No doubt you wish to speak this advice to me, 'Physician, heal yourself first' and 'Everything you did in Capernaum now do here for us too.'" Jesus affirms, "I know very well that no prophet is going to be welcome in his own hometown. But I must remind you of this truth: In the days of Elijah, many widows suffered from a drought and famine, which lasted for three years, but Elijah sent help to no one but a poor widow woman in Sidon [a foreign land]. And there were many lepers in Israel during the time of Elisha the Prophet, and none of them were cleansed but only Naaman, the Syrian [again a foreigner]."

This reminder from history shows that the God of Israel loves and cares for foreigners and aliens and sometimes, it appears, before or instead of his own chosen people, which prompts a growing rage of strong disappointment, anger, and hostility among all in the synagogue. Luke describes the scene this way: "Rising up, they drive Jesus out of their synagogue, out of their city, and their newly energized mob propels him toward a cliff where some would like to throw him to his death. But Jesus slips through their midst and continues, walking away, to be about the business his anointment with the Spirit propels him to perform."

And so the hometown boy, son of Joseph (as was supposed) and Mary, has gone off, associated with John the Baptist, got himself anointed and filled with the Holy Spirit of God, endured abrasive temptations in the desert, and now flexes his spiritual muscles to teach and heal in Capernaum, all across Galilee, and here finally in his own hometown where he grew up.

What a delight for his neighbors to hear the ringing promises to come in the Jubilee year of the great Lord God. So what if he brags that today these promises are already being fulfilled, right now in himself and his leadership, but then he jumps ship and veers far off course when he compliments the prophets Elijah and Elisha for extending the healing mercies of God beyond and away from Israel to foreigners, outsiders, aliens, Gentiles, who reap the benefits of the Jubilee year, which are denied to God's chosen people? The prophet Isaiah speaks of the poor, captives, blind, oppressed, and the Lord's special favor, but surely, these blessings belong to the chosen people and not to the pagans and heathens.

And so Luke prepares his readers for more of Jesus's proclamation and presentation of the Spirit at work in Jesus and his disciples, concentrated initially in Jesus's native neighborhood of Galilee but ultimately intended to bless the Gentiles and indeed the entire human race. "Beginning in Jerusalem, in all of Judaea and Samaria, and even beyond Sidon and Syria, to the ends of the earth" (Acts 1:8).

Lesson Eleven: Transfiguration of the Lord; Read Luke 9:28–43

The Gospel writer Luke is dependent upon his source Mark for the content of the transfiguration event (Mark 8:27–9:1). For Mark, Jesus's arrival with his disciples at Caesarea Philippi denotes a transition from the ministry in Galilee, toward movement now into and through Gentile territory, and attention to the identity of Jesus both anchored in his Jewish origins, his approaching journey to Jerusalem, and his ministry there in Jerusalem.

For Luke, the geographical context is not as significant as the involvement of Jesus alone in prayer (9:18). Recall Jesus's baptism, an experience of Jesus in prayer and clarification of his identity (Luke 3:21–22). Jesus in prayer leads Luke to follow Mark's questions, including Simon Peter as spokesperson for the disciples. He diminishes Simon Peter's role positively and negatively, however. Luke's Jesus agrees with Mark's Jesus who predicts the approaching suffering, rejection, crucifixion, and resurrection, and very importantly, that one who trusts and follows this Jesus must expect to share these same responsibilities as his own identification and service of discipleship (Luke 9:19–26).

Thus, for both Mark and Luke, the big questions here are (1) how to explain and make real and true who Jesus is and just how his roles will be expressed in his ministry in Jerusalem and (2) how his disciples can understand and accept this truth including their own roles and identities committed to him. Two sides of the same overall dilemma/opportunity, as Luke sees it, through Mark's eyes.

Both Matthew and Luke follow Mark's Jesus when he counsels his disciples to keep all this tough talk quiet, acknowledging the difficulty they and most people have understanding it. But all three Synoptic Gospel writers accept these words from Jesus: "Truly, I say to you, there are some standing here who will not taste death before they see the kingdom of God come with power" (Mark 9:1). Luke and Matthew follow Mark's transition now to address these two questions—who Jesus is and just how his disciples' own identity and mission grow out of and should express their solidarity/unity with what they discover about their master.

About a week later (six or eight days), Jesus takes his three inner-circle disciples—Peter, John, and James—aside, in order to address these two questions: his identity and their identity/roles. This episode, known as the transfiguration event, takes place because Jesus leads them apart, up a high mountain, symbolic of profound spiritual experience. Note, for Luke, the mountain is not as important as Jesus's motivation to pray. While in the process of praying, "his facial appearance becomes different and his clothes become dazzling white." And suddenly, the disciples see two men, Moses and Elijah, conversing with Jesus. Note, Mark and Matthew immediately report Peter's address to Jesus: "Lord, this is great. We are there. So let us make three booths, one for you, one for Moses, and one for Elijah." And Mark adds, "He did not know what to say because they were overwhelmed with fear."

Luke gives us a different take on Peter's response to Jesus's transfiguration and his talk with Moses and Elijah. Luke says, "And behold, two men were conversing with him, Moses and Elijah, who, having appeared in glory, were speaking of his exodus [departure], which he was soon to fulfill in Jerusalem" (Luke 9:30–31). Luke adds that these three disciples are weighed down with sleep but are wide awake, despite their tired bodies and minds, having witnessed Jesus's change in appearance and his conference with Moses and Elijah. Only at this point, as Moses and Elijah leave, does Luke quote Peter, "Master, it is good we are here. Now let us make three tents, one for you, one for Moses, and one for Elijah," not knowing what he was saying.

Noting the emphasis in Jesus's conversation with Moses and Elijah on his exodus (departure) soon to be fulfilled in Jerusalem, some scholars detect here reference to the Feast of Sukkoth or Tabernacles, which Peter perhaps anticipates soon to observe in Jerusalem. This Feast of Sukkoth remembers and celebrates the divine protection given to the people of Israel during their wandering through the wilderness, both literally and symbolically, on repeated occasions over the centuries.

Perhaps in Peter's mind, when Jesus, Moses, and Elijah converse, they are relating divine deliverance in history to the approaching events through which Jesus in Jerusalem will once again fulfill his role as Son of God who delivers God's people from their oppression. Thus, Peter's offer to set up three booths or tents is not a plea to prolong this divine conversation for the wrong reasons but rather the intention of himself, John, and James to join together to share Jesus's approaching experience of exodus (departure) once again. In other words, perhaps Peter discovers through this transfiguration event both the truth about who Jesus is and affirms his own commitment to and participation in the destiny of Jesus as Son of God.

Suitable transition from this powerful moment of epiphany occurs in their sudden engulfment in the cloud, moving from the mountaintop experience of transfiguration back down the mountain to everyday reality once again. Surely, this is a fearful moment of transition. And now this voice from heaven points to the significance of all that has transpired: "This is my Son, the one having been chosen. Listen to him." Be sure to hear the repetition here of the event of Jesus's baptism, according to Luke's version (Luke 3:21–22).

And now the cloud dissipates, and Jesus stands alone. Jesus belongs for all time in the same company as Moses and Elijah, representing the Law and the Prophets, but when all is said and done, Jesus remains after Moses and Elijah have appeared, conversed, shared their respective leadership roles, and departed. Now only Jesus alone remains. Moses and Elijah have spoken, but now only of Jesus does the voice command, "Listen to him." In other words, Jesus is who he is, and Jesus does and will fulfill his baptismal calling and anointment only in teamwork with Moses and Elijah, but Jesus's new exodus, his delivery of God's people from slavery to sin and evil, is both present and soon to be fulfilled in his departure—all this is his alone to perform. But at the very same time, as his identity grows clearer, can and will his disciples recognize, accept, and also perform their respective/necessary roles as members of his team? Perhaps Simon Peter finds his own mind and heart to be in the right place.

Perhaps Luke wraps up this transfiguration event with the arrival of the cloud that engulfs Jesus and his three disciples as they descend from this epiphany experience in order to remind his readers of the ambiguity that still characterizes the complex dimensions of human involvement with this divinely anointed Son of God. Terrified as these three disciples are when they enter this cloud, and no doubt mesmerized by the voice that points directly to Jesus as their source of authority, nevertheless, as the cloud disappears, Luke describes their conclusive response to this experience in these words: "And they kept silent and in those days told no one any of the things they had seen" (Luke 9:36).

In the very next pericope (Luke 9:37–43), Luke describes Jesus's apparent frustration, even exasperation, when his disciples cannot, or do not, participate in the exorcism and healing that Jesus then performs. Continuing this theme, when Jesus seeks to teach his disciples what lies ahead, Luke reports, "They could not understand his teaching because this meaning was concealed from them, and they were afraid to ask" (Luke 9:44–45). Likewise, when his disciples argue among themselves as to which one of them is the greatest, Jesus assures them, "The least among you is the greatest" (Luke 9:46–46).

Perhaps Luke organizes these teaching quotations from the lips of Jesus to suggest that the symbolism of the cloud that engulfs Peter, John, and James as they descend from the mountaintop is just as indicative of the human dilemma as is the transfiguration experience up on top of the mountain. Continue to read/study Luke 9:49–62 to follow how Jesus has still more opportunities to teach his disciples and, by implication, of course, Luke's readers their need to grapple with their opportunities to understand and participate in Jesus's exodus/departure, soon coming up in Jerusalem. What's good for Luke's readers then, of course, is probably good for Luke's readers today. Let's welcome the cloud, our clouds, and put them in proper perspective.

CHAPTER THREE

The Season of Lent

Lesson Twelve: Ash Wednesday; Read Matthew 6:1–6, 16–21

This lesson draws its context from two sources. First, from within the work of Matthew. Following Mark, all is prepared for Jesus to begin his ministry in Galilee, which he does with strong responses (Matt. 4:12–25). If, as many scholars are sure, Matthew seeks to present Jesus primarily as the new Moses, then these verses show Jesus leading God's people out of slavery or oppression and toward liberation, freedom, and new experience of salvation.

Just as Moses did, therefore, Jesus seeks to launch his ministry with an inaugural presentation of the new version of the law of God, or *Torah*. Like Moses, Jesus goes up into the mountain. Today, you can visit the Mount of Beatitudes, a traditional site of Jesus's sermon, not far from Capernaum, overlooking the Sea of Galilee. The spacious slope of the mountainside suggests multitudes gathered and united to hear this unforgettable Sermon on the Mount. My memory of popular religious art always shows Jesus preaching to the crowds stretching out before him, covering the picturesque slope below.

But Matthew's text is ambiguous. Matthew 5:12 says when Jesus sees the crowds, he goes up the mountain. But is this move to accommodate the crowds or to escape from them? When he sits down, assuming teaching posture, his disciples come to him. Do his disciples find him in a spot or niche apart from, separated from the crowds, or all together with the crowds? Does Jesus open his mouth to teach thousands or to teach only his disciples as a special, chosen, cultivated cadre of devotees?

On the one hand, the inclusive message of the Sermon on the Mount addresses all humanity and thus is relevant for both individuals and crowds whomever, wherever, or however involved. For example, the Greek word translated *blessed* is *makarioi*, which covers a broad sweep of human conditions from sacred context which seems to dominate these nine pronouncements, reaching out to include Aristotelian concepts of natural attainment and fulfillment, such as the Greek concept of *eudaimonion*, which means happiness or well-balanced and rounded-out harmony of all human physical and mental processes, social as well as individual, spiritual, or private.

On the other hand, the English word *blessed* does not appear to translate the Greek *makarioi* at all but rather the Latin word *beati* derived not from Greek but from the Latin Vulgate translation of the New Testament. In this context, the word *blessed* refers not so much to human social environments but rather to the direct action or initiative of God the Father Himself as opposed to normal, regular human responsibilities and behaviors.

When Jesus clarifies his long-range goals and objectives in Matthew 5:17–20 and identifies his negative role models (scribes and Pharisees), he no doubt means to encompass the human race. The most explicit indicator, however, is Jesus's use of the plural English pronoun *you* in chapter 5, verses 13 and 14. The Greek word *humeis* is in the plural nominative case, or "you all" in Southern American English, and matches the Greek verb *este* in the plural number. Looks like Jesus intends to address and include the crowds, the cross section, inclusive of everyone taking positive notice of his beginning days of ministry.

Jesus now plunges into analysis of the six examples of how the law needs serious wrestling and stretched, tossed-and-tumbled, turned-inside-out, and not-simply-crystalized-into-static dead legalism, such as exhibited by the scribes and Pharisees (Matt. 5:21–47).

Jesus tops out this portion of his sermon using the Greek concept *teleios*—that reality which, in the process of movement or growth, will inevitably reach maturity, completeness, or fulfillment

(Matt. 5:48). (Try the concept of teleology in English.) The word *perfect* in some English translations (e.g., Be perfect, therefore, as your heavenly Father is perfect.) smacks of Plato and Neoplatonism and detracts from Jewish/Hebrew interest in natural, living organisms/history rather than static, spotless, timeless mythic purity.

Having examined the context for this lesson in Matthew's document, look briefly now at two contexts for our use of this lesson today. Our word, *Lent*, is Middle English from the Old English word *lencten* (to lengthen), referring to the days getting longer or the anticipated, approaching arrival of spring. Presumably, longer days meant more daylight and thus less hunkering down to survive winter darkness. Instead, more time to venture out and prepare for or participate in the disciplines of repentance and devotion leading to Holy Week and the celebration of Easter / resurrection of the Lord.

Probably from medieval times, *Lent* came to mean identification with Jesus in his forty days of testing/temptation by Satan in the wilderness and allowing his trials and testing to strengthen us as we learn from him. The season of Lent includes the forty days between Ash Wednesday and Good Friday, excluding Sundays. Sundays, being the Sabbath, are never days of fasting and repentance but always days of joyful celebration. No long faces on Sunday, please!

Ash Wednesday became the day for the imposition of ashes—all the more reason to enjoy reveling on Shrove Tuesday (*Mardi Gras* or Fat Tuesday). The liturgy for Ash Wednesday stresses prayer for illumination, invitation to the observance of the Lenten discipline, the Litany of Penitence, and the imposition of ashes by the celebrant upon the forehead of the penitent with the words "Remember that you are dust, and to dust you shall return."

We come now to Matthew 6:1–6 and 16–21. These verses in the Sermon on the Mount, probably emphasized to strengthen Jesus's case against the scribes and Pharisees as poster child hypocrites, remind me of my own boyhood school days in the deep rural American South. Every public school day opened with a reading from the Holy Bible, the recitation of the Lord's Prayer, and the pledge of allegiance to the flag of the United States of America, which, if I remember right, did not yet include the words "one nation under God." These ritual activities were mandated by state laws.

We faithfully conformed our behavior to the letter of the civil law, which means we were publicly and politically correct; but how did we, do we, take seriously Jesus's call to be more concerned about expressing our faith, our piety, our spiritual dimensions of human behavior in secret or privately? As Jesus puts this tension, we certainly received our reward outwardly, but did we, do we, receive that reward or result or response God desires so that God can reward us inwardly in secret?

When I settled here in the state of West Virginia, I arrived in time to participate in the Great Kanawha County School Textbook Controversy. Some evangelical Christians mounted a protest against allegedly corrupt, perverse, if not, down-right evil textbooks that were assigned reading in the public schools of Kanawha County. The fireworks erupted, and sparks flew back and forth for some months. As I remember the stalemated outcome, there was much more concern for public victory, one way or the other, than discussion of integrity focused on the issues Jesus raised in his Sermon on the Mount.

About the same time, newspaper columnist and pundit L. T. Anderson responded to vociferous insistence by some "evangelical Christians" that every public sports event, and certainly every Friday night high school football game, had, of necessity, to be opened with public prayer, invoking divine blessing upon the competition about to commence. This writer, L. T. Anderson, made the calm suggestion that instead of imposing Christian prayer upon a pluralistic gathering, it made better sense to save the prayer until the game was over, and whoever wanted to remain for the blessing could do so or leave as preferred. As I remember, this somber advice prompted many "letters to the editor."

Now, here in his Sermon on the Mount, Jesus reminds his listeners three times to express their faith and piety in secret, not in public, and to expect their recognition and blessing in secret, not in public. Above all, this is the pathway to storing up your treasure in heaven and not on earth. "For where your treasure is, there your heart will be also." Sounds like a good investment policy or strategy, but does it guarantee to beat the Wall Street odds?

Jesus knows the odds, of course, and he seeks to counsel not only the scribes and Pharisees but all the crowds and his disciples included. And his primary goal in this sermon is to draw attention to the imperative to fulfill the Spirit of the law rather than the letter of the law. Perhaps the poetic imagery of "treasure in heaven" rather than treasure on earth offers to his listeners both the mystery and the reality of human participation in his mission, which will take him, and hopefully his disciples, from Galilee to Jerusalem, and then, in Matthew's version of his resurrection appearances (Matt. 28:16–20), back to Galilee again.

Lesson Thirteen: The First Sunday in Lent; Read Luke 4:1–13

With these two more recent modern contexts (Lent and Ash Wednesday) in mind, we are perhaps better prepared to welcome this lectionary study/lesson for the first Sunday in the season of Lent. The immediate context for this lesson, however, is Jesus's baptism by John the Baptist (Luke 3:21–22), when Jesus identifies with his fellow human beings in the queue and, while praying, receives the Holy Spirit and his heavenly Father's explicit blessing.

It's no accident Luke places Jesus's genealogy next, true to the pattern of historical work pioneered by Herodotus (484–425BC), the Greek father of the study of history. Luke traces Jesus's human lineage back not to the patriarch Abraham, as does Matthew, but all the way back to the progenitor of the entire human race, Adam himself.

In both of these episodes or contexts—baptism and genealogy—Luke wants to anchor Jesus's arrival in history and his beginning / continued mission to the Gentile, Hellenistic world as inclusively as possible. It's no accident either then that Jesus's first order of business after baptism is to confront his primary rival or antagonist or enemy, his opposite in purpose, the prince of all evil, the devil or Satan himself.

It will be to our advantage here to consult with the late prominent anthropologist, Joseph Campbell (1904–1987 CE). This renowned scholar studies all human cultures beginning with the Neanderthals, seeking to identify and analyze the primary motifs, figures, and value systems which energize the human race so that we may understand ourselves better. His most famous scholarly work is *The Hero with a Thousand Faces* (1949) in which he catalogues the roles of the dominate figures who stand out for their exemplary, heroic deeds that reveal the heights and depths of both common and heroic human struggles with the powers, perils, and promises of spiritual experience across all cultures.

Jesus, of course, dominates much of Middle Eastern / Western culture with his prominence in biblical and even Koranic traditions. As Luke puts it, Jesus is filled with the Holy Spirit following his baptism. Baptism itself, of course, is more a Hellenistic ritual than a Jewish one. The Holy Spirit, however, is a Jewish concept, and so Jesus is primed with the best of both worlds—Jewish and Gentile. And the Holy Spirit leads him, guides him directly into the wilderness.

This soon-to-be-dramatic encounter is the Spirit's idea and plan. Every item in this narrative is pregnant with heavy symbolism—the wilderness, for example, being the raw reality of creation, ripe with dangers and enemies waiting to devour you. Forty days is the round number necessary to get the job done. What is the job ahead waiting to be tackled? Who or what lies ahead? Why, Satan himself, of course.

This will be the main-stage confrontation showdown between cosmic good and evil. These opposite powers are always in conflict across the universe, of course; but here, the two sides meet in a no-holds-barred, winner-takes-all contest for survival. Why does Jesus eat nothing at all during these forty days? To test whether his physical and/or spiritual strength endures.

And notice Satan is most polite and genteel in his demeanor. "Surely you are hungry and being the Son of God, why not command this stone to become a loaf of bread?"

Jesus has his answer ready: "It is written, 'One does not live by bread alone.'"

And Matthew quickly adds, from his own source, "But by every word that comes from the mouth of God" (Matt. 4:4). Jesus easily, it looks like, passes this—the economics test.

But Satan is learning. He can quote the Holy Scripture too. First, he takes Jesus to Jerusalem and places his rival on the pinnacle, the highest peak of Herod's magnificent temple complex. "Now, let's show 'em what you really got! Jump off here, for it is written, 'He will send his angels to protect you, to rescue you in midair, so you will suffer not one bit.' Unforgettable spectacle! Everyone will tell their grandchildren what they saw!"

Jesus now tells himself and his tempter, "Not good to test the Lord your God." Jesus is the hero when he refrains from acting like this kind of hero. He passes the "big splash" test.

Satan takes a rest; he turns his attention to other evil duties. But now he is biding his time, waiting for "a more opportune time." Interestingly, Joseph Campbell relied upon the work of Karl Gustav Jung (1875–1961 CE), an early psychologist and psychoanalyst. Jung was fascinated by the struggles between good and evil, Jesus and Satan, all across the human race and thought of these perennial struggles as the experience of inherited archetypes arising from within the collective human unconscious.

As we examine Luke's presentation of the three temptations of Jesus by the devil, we have the opportunity to learn from these three episodes spread over forty days—something more in depth, real, and true about ourselves, our human condition, and about the choices we face and must wrestle with as we seek to take advantage of these longer days we now enjoy in this approaching season of spring.

Lesson Fourteen: The Second Sunday in Lent; Read Mark 8:31–38

With this scenario, Mark signals that his document is now one half complete. Leading to this point, beginning with the introductory elements (1:1–15), Jesus brings the presence and work of the Spirit in opposition to Satan and the demons. Jesus calls disciples, teaches, exorcises demons, heals, and feeds the multitudes—all examples of the arrival of the Son of Man, the Jewish apocalyptic figure whose work brings to fulfillment the new age, *ho kairos* in Greek, already present and introduces the kingdom of God, already beginning to arrive and breaking into the present, and cataclysmically visible on the near horizon (8:38, 9:1, 13:3–36).

But Jesus knows his true identity is not clear although both welcomed by the poor, suffering, sinful crowds and resisted or rejected by the scribes and Pharisees, official guardians of the sacred treasures of Judaism. It is time to zero in on these ambiguities and bring more focus to the formal identity and specific roles or activities Jesus knows he must bring to fulfillment. Jesus takes a poll of public opinion (Mark 8:27–28). He knows his disciples represent a cross section of the common people they run into along the roads and among the villages where they find food and shelter. "I am curious," Jesus shares. "What are you hearing? Who do people say I am?" Not hard to answer. His disciples quickly report three possibilities: (1) John the Baptist, (Apparently Herod Antipas, tetrarch of Galilee, shared this conclusion (Mark 6:14–16). How frustrated he must have been having beheaded John the Baptist, now to have to put up with his resuscitation.); (2) Elijah, the proverbial forerunner of the Messiah; and (3) one of the prophets, there being a good many to choose from. Not a single slouch on this list of top candidates. But notice "Messiah" is not included.

So now Jesus is informed as to how the rumor mill is running. But Jesus needs to know, for his own satisfaction, what his own disciples think about his identity. After all, he has much more invested in them whom he has called to become "fishers for human beings."

Okay, Jesus thinks to himself. "But, fellows, I want to know about you." And so Jesus can wait no longer. "Do you agree? What about you? Just who do you say I am?"

Peter reads Jesus's mind; he knows his need to know. Peter blurts out, "Why you are the Messiah! [*ho Kristos* in Greek, which means *Mashiah*, anointed one, in Hebrew.]"

Surely Jesus hears what he wants to hear. Or would he rather hear "Son of God" or "Son of Man?" But wait, no high fives, no cheers. Instead, a very stern warning that they should say nothing to anyone about him. Paraphrase: "Do not use this title with reference to me under any circumstances." The implication is that such use will incur serious, dire, unwanted consequences. Why? Because the title *Mashiah* in Hebrew denotes ideas in the public mind, and in Peter's mind in particular, that are erroneous, distorted and that urgently need to be corrected.

The next Greek words, *kai erzato didaskein autous* (and he began to teach them), show a sharp shift in motivation, attitude, and language on Jesus's part aimed to oppose and correct what Peter has affirmed so vociferously. What is this new knowledge or truth? Note, Jesus does not repeat use of the title *Mashiah* but instead turns to the title "Son of Man." Translation: "It is absolutely necessary (imperative, no choice at all) that the Son of Man must suffer many things and be rejected by the elders and the chief priests and the scribes and be killed and, after three days, rise again from the dead. And he was speaking all of these words plainly." (The Greek language shows repetition or persistence on his part, as well as speaking openly, frankly, boldly, as if to include the listening public or anyone within earshot, although it is unclear whether Jesus speaks only to Peter and his other disciples or whether a larger crowd may be included.)

What is clear is that Jesus aims to correct how Simon Peter understands *Mashiah* and to do this by pointing directly to the title "Son of Man" and to his suffering, rejection, death, and resurrection. These words are too full of cognitive dissonance (contradiction) for Peter to hear and tolerate. Peter reacts viscerally without reflection. He grabs Jesus, pulls him aside, and begins to rebuke him for what he has just said. Peter is shocked, blown out of his mind. He scolds, orders, commands Jesus to show him his faulty thinking. How can Jesus possibly say such things about himself, preferring the title "Son of Man" instead of the better title *Mashiah*!

Jesus now turns away from Peter, taking note of his other disciples who are listening, and issues a counter-rebuke to Peter. "Get yourself behind me, Satan, for your mind is preoccupied not with the mindset of God but with human ways of thinking." (Note the dualism here, the two contrasting worldviews characteristic of the Jewish apocalyptic worldview.)

As Mark 1:12–13 makes clear, the Spirit propels Jesus forward into the desert to oppose Satan and the wild beasts; and now Jesus recognizes Satan's power at work in Simon Peter, who seeks to deny/correct Jesus's prediction of what the Spirit leads him to do. Peter here seeks to lead Jesus to confirm the divine power as he understands the role of the *Mashiah* (or if necessary, the Son of Man). Thus, Jesus has to order Peter, as Satan, to get behind him, in other words, to follow Jesus and thus not seek to lead Jesus, expecting Jesus to follow him.

As Mark recalls this narrative from the oral tradition and seeks to reconstruct it in order to have Jesus clarify who he is and what his role is as the Son of Man, there are two issues at stake. The first issue is the role and behavior of the Son of God (back to Mark 1:1–15). The question of best title is secondary, although Peter prefers *Mashiah*. When Jesus prefers "the Son of Man," Peter does not argue about title but is blown away by Jesus's vision of suffering, rejection, and death being necessary and inevitable in the behavior of Jesus, whatever title you give him. Apparently, the concept of resurrection after three days goes unnoticed. In other words, the first issue at stake is the balance between lowly servitude and exalted victory in the necessary work this Messiah / Son of Man must and shall perform. Peter can only repeat and defend the images of the Messiah he has learned and internalized from childhood as a loyal/faithful embodiment of the Jewish tradition. It will be helpful to check out the origin and development of this tradition of messianic leadership beginning with 1 Samuel 8:12 and the career of the first anointed monarch, Saul. Continue with the second monarch, David—the prototype for the ideal Messiah or anointed one—in 2 Samuel 7:1–17 and in 2 Samuel 12:1–15 as the prophet Nathan brings theological perspective to the historical and eternal dimensions of this anointed and thus charismatic ruler whose victories far overshadow his all-too-human frailties and whose popular messianic mystique and lore far exceed all other Jewish monarchs, even including his illustrious son, King Solomon.

An alternative vision of divine leadership occupies the so-called second Isaiah tradition (Isaiah 52:13–53:12) of the suffering servant who "pours himself out even unto death and is numbered with the transgressors in order to bear the sins of many." Written in the postexilic Persian Period of Israel's history, this strong interpretation does not include the title "Messiah" and is no doubt purposively ambiguous as to whether the suffering servant imagery refers to the behavior of an individual or to corporate social dimensions/descriptions of human behavior characteristic of Israel as a whole people.

The title "Son of Man" is even more ambiguous as a suitable title for Jesus, but he chooses to apply it to himself often enough so that we may conclude that this title was well enough established that Peter can accept it as a synonym for Messiah and rebuke Jesus for his predictions of suffering, rejection, and death ahead for the Son of Man. In other words, Peter envisions exaltation for Jesus, whether Messiah or Son of Man, but cannot hear and accept humiliation as coherent with his deeply ingrained Jewish mindset, which Jesus calls satanic when it excludes suffering servitude.

The second issue at stake in this scenario follows immediately upon Jesus's rebuke of Peter's inadequate vision of Jesus's impending behavior. Calling the crowd to join with his disciples, Jesus quickly cements the intimate connection between what lies ahead both for the Son of Man and for whoever aims to follow him. "If someone wishes to follow after me [implication: not after Satan], let him deny himself and take up his cross and follow with me."

Mark, the evangelist, has prepared his readers for this connection—for example, in Mark 1:17, it says, "Follow me and I will make you fish for people," and especially in Mark 3:13–19 where, having gone up the mountain, Jesus calls those whom he wants. They come to him, and he appoints twelve (i.e., the new Israel), names them apostles for three purposes: (1) to be with him, (2) to be sent out to proclaim the message, and (3) to have authority to cast out demons.

Then his chosen twelve were commissioned. Now (Mark 8:34), Jesus opens his invitation to anyone but makes more specific what "to be with him" includes: "If any want to become my followers, let them deny themselves, and take up their cross and follow me." Here Mark quotes Jesus so as to make him speak directly to the Gentiles in Rome when the destruction of Jerusalem by the Roman soldiers is imminent (ca. 70 CE). Perhaps we may quote the English-American patriot Thomas Paine (1737–1809) out of context to grasp the urgency that motivates Mark: "These are the times that try men's souls. The summer soldier and the sunshine patriot will, in this crisis, shrink from the service of their country, but he that stands it now, deserves the thanks of men and women" (quoted from *The American Crisis*, December 1776).

This is to say the second issue at stake in this scenario is whether whoever wants to follow Jesus, Peter of course included, will be with Jesus, identify with Jesus, and share Jesus's responsibility when he suffers, is rejected, and dies (and also rises from the dead). Mark no doubt poses this challenge both here in the honest audacity of Peter's rebuke and in the equally honest reaction of the disciples when Jesus is arrested and led away to his imminent crucifixion. "All of them deserted him and fled" (Mark 14:50).

Lesson Fifteen: The Third Sunday in Lent; Read John 4:5–42

It will be helpful to review contextual passages which precede this lesson. Jesus has concluded his discourse delivered both to Nicodemus and a wider inclusive audience (John 3:11–21) in which he explains the source of new birth from above, the love of God for the whole world, and the significance of this arrival of the Spirit into human life, with focus upon reconciliation with God and receiving eternal life. This new life in communion and fellowship with God takes shape in human works which no longer are hidden in darkness but which now, being eternal in quality and purpose, are clearly and openly performed in the light for all to see and glorify God.

John 3:22–24 says Jesus and his disciples have focused upon his signs, Jesus himself being the foremost sign who reveals and communicates God's love to everyone. Remember how God sent serpents as signs, and just as those signs had to be lifted up, so must the Son of Man be lifted up (on the cross) in order for salvation to arrive on behalf of God's suffering people (John 3:14–15). This time of emphasis upon Jesus's signs has been taking place in and around the city of Jerusalem.

Now it is time for Jesus and his disciples to leave Jerusalem and move out into the Judaean countryside. Perhaps this is because Jesus wants to point to water once again as a sign of his revelation of the love of God. We remember how at Cana, Jesus welcomed water used in purification rites as an opportunity to create a new sign, that of wine suitable for a feast of celebration (John 2:6–11). Now Jesus, and no doubt his disciples too, become involved in baptizing Jewish citizens because the water of purification helps to reveal the transition from birth in the flesh to new birth from above with the arrival of the Spirit who brings new life in the light instead of darkness.

Now, it turns out John, nicknamed "the Baptist" to recognize his occupation, was also baptizing nearby because there were abundant sources of flowing water. Neighbors nearby probably saw they had a choice: get baptized by John (or his disciples) or by Jesus (or his disciples). Confusion arises, and John's disciples confront him. "Teacher," they say, "what about this other teacher? What if he gets more customers than we get?" Rivalry between two camps in competition with each other! John reminds everyone of his previous repeated clarifications aimed to explain his modest role and magnify the expanding role of Jesus (John 1:6–34). As John puts it now, "He must increase, but I must decrease."

John, the narrator, now has John the Baptist deliver a discourse (John 2:31–36) for which Jesus has already established the model (John 3:11–21), concluding with this creedal doxology: "The Father loves the Son and has given all things into his hand. The one who places his trust in this Son enters eternal life. The one who opposes the Son, however, will not see life, but the displeasure [wrath, anger, judgment?] of God remains upon him."

It is time for Jesus to return to Galilee up north. That's his home territory but for another reason also. Jesus hears from some Pharisees that he is gaining attention because he attracts more baptism-seekers than John the Baptist. Jesus wants to squelch this apparent competition because it reverses their two roles. Scholars note that manuscript evidence shows a later editor has inserted these words, "Although it was not Jesus himself who baptized, but only his disciples" in order to stomp out the rumor altogether. We remember, of course, that according to Mark's narrative, John the Baptist was soon to be arrested and, sadly, eventually executed by King Herod Antipas (Mark 6:14–29).

Jesus and his disciples begin their journey northward, and of course, the territory of Samaria lies between Judaea and Galilee. Most travelers seek to avoid the most direct route, reflecting a, by this time, ancient and intense hostility between Jews and Samaritans. To spend much time in Samaritan neighborhoods made you ritually unclean and put you in danger of injury because of the disdain the Jews and Samaritans harbor for one another, which brings us to today's lesson: John 4:5–42.

Jesus has no hesitation to take the most direct route through this challenging Samaritan territory perhaps because he has not come into the world to protect himself but to risk contact with strangers who share the need of the entire human race for salvation from sin and evil. Traveling by foot is tiring, of course, and a half day's treading brings him and his companions to the city of Sychar. A good place to stop and rest because the sacred location known as Jacob's Well is prominent and beckons travelers who recall its historical significance.

Do not miss the ordinary human dimensions of Jesus's personality described here. Paraphrase: Half a day of treading dusty pathways with his disciples while the hot sun beats down upon them, Jesus is exhausted and spies a shady gathering place near the famous Jacob's Well where he can rest his weary bones for a while. His disciples make sure he is safe and comfortable and take off for the city in order to buy some food and put together a suitable lunch for them all. Jesus is about to doze off when he sees a Samaritan woman approaching the well with a container. Jesus is so thirsty he has no choice but to ask this woman, "Pardon me, Madame, can you share a drink of water with me?"

She stops, takes a good look at Jesus, and asks, "How can you, a Jew, ask me, a Samaritan woman, to give you a drink?" The narrator, John, inserts a parenthesis here: "You, my readers, must understand that Jews never share things in common with Samaritans." She is shocked that this Jewish man shows her respect and pleads for a drink from her water bottle, which will render him unclean.

Jesus responds to her question this way: "If you knew about the free gift God seeks to give you, and who this is who is asking you for a drink, you surely would have asked him and he would give you living water."

The woman is intrigued, fascinated by this interchange. She plows ahead. "My good man, you have no bucket, and the well is very deep. Tell me, just how do you intend to get that living water? Are you somehow greater than our ancestor Jacob who gave us this well, and with his sons and his flocks drank from it?" (Note the innuendo here that Jesus may presume to place himself above the patriarch Jacob in the history of salvation. Rhetorically, of course, Jesus is most certainly more important than Jacob.)

Jesus welcomes her honest questions and focuses his response this way: "Everyone who drinks of this water will soon be thirsty again. But all of those who will drink of the water I shall give them will never be thirsty, ever again. This is because the water that I will give will become in them a fountain of water gushing up into life eternal."

This woman is getting so turned on! She beams with enthusiasm. "Sir," she addresses him with respect and honor, "give me, please, this water you have to offer, so that I shall never be thirsty again and keep having to come here to draw water."

Jesus now wants to push her enthusiasm forward to include and involve her family. "Go call you husband and bring him back with you."

She is happy to oblige, but she must explain. "Sir, I do not have a husband."

Jesus wants to support and encourage her. "Yes, you speak correctly that you have no husband. And the truth is you have had five husbands. Also, your current partner is not your husband. So what you have said is true. You have no husband." (Notice that Jesus makes no judgment calls whatsoever about this Samaritan woman's history of behavior. He knows and accepts her and what he knows about her and exhibits a very open and positive, welcoming attitude toward her.)

This woman is awestruck. "Sir, I see now that you are a prophet. Help me to clarify my understanding. Our ancestors worshipped

God here on this mountain, but you say that the place where everyone must worship God is in Jerusalem."

Jesus sees the opportunity this Samaritan woman is giving him to share his divinely endowed Jewish heritage with her. "I am glad you ask me, because we Jews do indeed have a divine mandate to become a light to the nations. Trust me, woman, when I say the time is coming when you will worship in neither location, for the place for worship is not the issue. Rather, the time is coming, and indeed is already here, when the true worshipers shall worship the Father neither on this mountain nor in Jerusalem, but instead in Spirit and in Truth. For God is Spirit and worship means to connect with this Spirit of God when He moves into your heart and soul, and teaches you the Truth. Because God is Spirit those who worship God must worship in Spirit and in Truth."

This Samaritan woman responds this way: "I have been taught that the Messiah is coming, he who is called the anointed one, and that he will explain everything we need to know and understand."

Jesus responds to her, "I am he, the one who is now speaking to you."

It is important to recognize that Jesus in this dialogue replaces both the Samaritan worship on Mount Gerizim and the Jewish worship in Jerusalem, not with other locations nor with different physical facilities but with the concepts of spirit and truth. The Greek word for *spirit* is *to pneuma*, a neuter noun which closely duplicates *ruach* in Hebrew and means air, wind, or breath. We have cognates in English (e.g., pneumonia, a disease of the lungs; or pneumatic, as in tires or brakes). Like the air, wind, or breath, God is spirit whom you cannot see but whose presence is nonetheless powerful and indispensable.

The Greek word for *truth* is *he alethia*, a feminine noun which is actually a compound word—the Greek *he lethe*, a feminine noun meaning forgetfulness with the letter alpha as a negative augment, which thus means no longer forgetting but remembering. For example, in English, the word *agnostic* is the word for knowledge, gnosis being negated by the letter alpha, which turns knowledge into no knowledge. If *truth* means no longer forgetting but remembering, what is the object that is remembered? Turned from negative to positive—this means to remember who you are not only as a physical person but more importantly as a spiritual person created in the very image and likeness of God. This priority, of course, duplicates this Gospel's insistence upon the new birth from above of the Spirit and not of flesh, which is the first natural birth.

Jesus's teaching, prompted by his encounter and dialogue with this Samaritan woman, reaches its apex or climax when Jesus diminishes the rote of either orthodox liturgies (Jerusalem) or alternative heretical liturgies (Mount Gerizim) and instead points to the new birth from above as the gift of God made present and palatable by the Spirit of God who reveals and teaches the truth all humans need to embrace which enables them to know themselves honestly and realistically and thus become citizens of the newly arriving kingdom of God.

More paraphrase: Jesus's disciples return and are surprised that Jesus befriends this Samaritan woman; but no one questions him, perhaps indicating they are learning. This woman, at the same time, leaves her water jug behind and returns to the city. She has no more use for liquid water but is turned on to celebrate the spiritual water Jesus promises her. She shouts out, "Come and see a man who knows me better than I know myself. Could he possibly be the Messiah?" She is so persuasive the menfolk drop their work and form a pilgrimage out to Jacob's Well.

Meanwhile, Jesus's disciples have brought food and are concerned their teacher must be hungry. He replies by claiming to have food they don't know about just as he has water the woman did not know about, but when she listens, she perceives what he is talking about. Jesus launches into a teaching discourse in order to share his invisible food with them all. "My food is to do the will of the one who has sent me here and to complete the work given me to do. For example, natural farming means you plant seed and wait four months for harvest. The Spirit shows us the fields are already ripe all around us, begging for us to harvest. Some are sowers, who plant seeds. Others are reapers, who gather fruit ripe for eternal life. Both sowers and reapers are necessary contributors to the process that leads to eternal life."

Jesus smiles as he contemplates his ancestor, the patriarch Jacob, whose well still blesses pilgrims with liquid water while Jesus and his disciples now draw upon the new work of the Spirit here at the same well, where spiritual water is beginning to flow, where the ancient prophets are now bearing fruit in this harvest their one God is working also in and through these pilgrims, whether Jewish or Samaritan.

Meanwhile, back in the city of Sychar, the narrator John tells his readers, "Many Samaritans believed because of the woman's testimony." She keeps on saying, "He told me everything I have ever done, more than I knew about myself." This means that this Samaritan woman is the first female apostle sent by Jesus to proclaim to her neighbors in Sychar the good news of the arrival of spirit and truth as more important in the kingdom of God than the traditional locations of Mount Gerizim and Jerusalem.

Because of her testimony, menfolk and pilgrims from Sychar converge upon Jesus back at the well of Jacob. They extend to Jesus an official invitation, as it were, from their city to come and stay with them. This invitation, of course, could never come from a woman and be trustworthy even though her testimony makes it possible. And so Jesus and his entourage move into the city of Sychar and remain for a couple of days, and many more citizens come to know and trust Jesus because they hear him teaching firsthand.

At this point (John 5:42), John, the narrator, brings this episode to a celebrative conclusion when he makes sure the menfolk of Sychar honor and compliment the woman apostle. "No longer do we trust in Jesus because of what you told us, for now we hear him ourselves, and we now know that this is truly the Savior of the world." She has done her duty, her calling by passing the torch of evangelism away from herself and into the arms of the ruling gentry. But this Samaritan woman remains the center of attention in this episode and becomes such an effective witness to who this man, Jesus, truly is when she gets the central point of his message: "The time is coming, and indeed is already here, when true worshipers will worship the Father neither on Mt. Gerizim nor in Jerusalem, but in Spirit and in Truth."

Lesson Sixteen: The Fourth Sunday in Lent; Read Luke 15:1–3, 11b–13

Luke introduces this lesson with a summary of preceding narratives: more and more tax collectors and sinners (summary clichés for the cast-off, sinful losers condemned and abandoned by the entrenched officers/leaders of Judaism) flock to listen to and learn from Jesus. This makes the officials, of course—Pharisees and scribes—grumble and growl all the more against Jesus and his flagrant reversal of the values and expectations of Deuteronomic covenant theology. According to this (their system of priorities), sinners should be judged and condemned until and unless they first repent. And this rabbi, Jesus, practices the opposite system of priorities. Jesus seeks out and welcomes and encourages the tax collectors and sinners. He heals (works) on the Sabbath, and he shares fellowship and meals with the unclean and unwashed. How offensive and abrasive his behavior is to this self-righteous establishment!

How should Jesus confront and deal with this stiff opposition to his ministry priorities? According to Luke, Jesus launches into some sharply focused parables. Let us remember just what kind of oratorical (as well as literary) communicative device the parable was/is. The word *parable* in English derives from two Greek words: *para* (besides or parallel to) and *ballo* (to cast, throw, drive, or propel).

To speak a parable is to take seriously an idea, a teaching, a situation, or a proposition which needs examination, discussion, and explication. In order to clarify or to throw light on this inscrutable mystery, you throw (in Greek *ballo*) out a simple story which lands alongside or parallel (in Greek *para*) the teaching or situation which needs explanation. Because the narrative of the parable story is more simple and clear and, at the same time, parallel to or closely related to the mystery, this new story throws light on the first story and opens up possibilities for listeners to understand and learn what the original story or situation seeks to communicate.

This is to say, since your new teaching device, your parable, now lands or appears directly alongside or parallel with the problematic conundrum that needs clarification, listeners are invited to compare the known truth with the unknown truth beside it so that the known illuminates and clears up the unknown with the result that listeners may now understand their teacher.

The parable is usually best, most effective, when simple, short, and easily grasped in content. You should expect the parable to express or emphasize one central point of truth that needs to be heard and learned. And you should resist turning this teaching device into an allegory, as if each element or character carries its own meaning. The allegory is a separate teaching style or device.

Although the framers of the lectionary skip over the first two parables here (lost sheep and lost coin) in order to get immediately to the lost son, let's look briefly at these two examples of the parable. In Luke 15:3–7, Jesus draws upon the classical role of the shepherd as keeper/steward of the kingdom of God (Psalm 23). Although the role of shepherd had declined with respect to the arrival of Jesus in Judaism, Luke nevertheless makes the shepherds the first to hear the announcement of the good news of the incarnation (Luke 2:8–14).

This shepherd does his job so well. Ninety-nine percent of his flock are safe with him as they make their way toward the sheepfold. Taking inventory, this protector suddenly realizes one member of his flock is missing. Confident he is taking good care of the ninety-nine, he is crushed to discover he has failed to keep check on one who is lost. His responsibility is for the safety and well-being of all one hundred. And so he leaves the ninety-nine where they are, with some risk, as he goes to search for the missing one. When he finds his lost sheep, he does not spank him with rebuke or punish the little lamb but hoists him onto his shoulders and carries him safely to join the ninety-nine others so that all one hundred now arrive safely at home. Time for a party. Friends and neighbors—all the neighborhood—arrive to celebrate, give thanks for the safe homecoming of this one who was lost. "Just so," Jesus points out, "there is more joy in heaven over one sinner who repents than over ninety-nine righteous persons who need no repentance." Do we hear some irony here? Just who is there in Jesus's neighborhood with no need for repentance?

In the second parable (Luke 15:8–10), a certain woman has ten silver coins. She needs every cent she has, so to speak. She loses one of her precious coins. She drops every other task, lights her lamp, and combs through every nook and cranny in her one-room house until she finally discovers where she dropped this missing coin. She cries out with joy, and her friends come running. Hers are tears of joy. "Just so," Jesus smiles, "the angels in heaven rejoice whenever one sinner repents." Notice coins do not, cannot repent. The return of the lost coin depends solely upon the diligent search of the owner and the value the missing coin represents to her.

How does the parable work? What are the dynamics of effective parable teaching? Simply put, when the two stories are laid side by side, Jesus then invites you, the listener, to find yourself included and participating in the two stories in such a way that because you become an integral part of the narrative, Jesus stimulates you to discover the truth about yourself within the kingdom of God he is seeking to illuminate. Thus, it is that parables are appropriate for our study during this season of Lent when we seek to learn from Jesus's forty days in the wilderness more of what his call to repentance means for us.

The parable of choice and emphasis for this Sunday, Luke 15:11–32, has been called "the parable of the Prodigal Son" or "the parable of the Two Sons" or "the parable of Two Sons and Their Father." Paraphrase: The younger son of a wealthy landowner thinks of himself as Sylvester Stallone in the *Rambo* movie series. A young upstart, whippersnapper he is—bored, stiff, and tired with conventionality. This prosperity in the promised land is all well and good but too static, dull and offers no challenge or adventure. He's heard on the grapevine about other lands, other kingdoms out there free of Jewish restrictions and full of Hellenistic cultures and their allurements. Maybe he can get passage in a caravan and escape to Damascus, or Babylon, or even Persia—big cities where they say troops of dancing girls offer fantastic routines that transfer your heart, mind, body and soul to exotic, undreamed-of paradises.

He works hard for his father, behaves himself, always honors and respects his patriarch. He comes up with a proposition: "Hey, Dad, I know you have me set up in your will. But I've got a great idea. Give me 90 percent now instead of 100 percent then, and I'll go invest it in the market and repay you with interest. I've got some great tips where to invest, and we'll all come out way, way ahead!" His dad listens, a bit dubious, and waits a few days, but he loves his young son so much he decides to make him happy.

Soon, this young maverick gathers all he has, hops aboard a luxury caravan, and arrives in Damascus—too small, tame, and dull here. Back on the road again all the way to Babylon. "Wow, not a dull moment here." And the bankers and brokers welcome his money and set him up with companions who assure him "what happens in Babylon, stays in Babylon!"

This adventure continues for some weeks and months; and our hero settles in, confident he has found his hitch where life will only get better and better as far as he can see into the future. Then one day when he tries to collect some earned interest to send back home to his father, his broker sadly announces the stock market collapsed. Drought, famine, hunger, poverty, and destitution descend upon all of Babylon for as far as your eyes can see. The big party's over, and he begs for any job just to stay alive. He finds himself feeding pigs, eating what pigs eat, miserably destitute, and sadly, miserably all alone.

All he has is his memories, his knowledge of who he truly is, or was, but is no longer. But can he become once again who he was? Dying of hunger, he has no hope except the trust he once knew from his father. He realizes with remorse his father's slaves are alive, and maybe he can live too. Now a pauper, he has to beg and scramble and scrape and crawl his way inch by inch all the way back toward his birthplace. All he can do step-by-step is roll over in his mind what he can possibly say to his father, who has most certainly disowned him (and deservedly so), and, for all intents and purposes, cast him off into utter darkness.

Unbeknownst to him, however, his father has tapped into the rumor mill and hears word about how his delinquent son is headed home. His father spends his days out on the roadway, binoculars at work, straining, hoping against hope that his wayward son is still alive and somehow able to make his way back to his birth family.

One day, a speck on the horizon grows bigger, and this father can wait no longer. He begins running, leaping, humming, singing, shouting, "Come home, come home! You who are weary, come home!" As the young man limps his way along, dragging his feet in despair, his father grabs him; pulls him up to embrace him, with tears flowing; hugs and kisses him to express the love no words can express.

The weak, grubby, smelly young man, with his own tears flowing, begins to gasp and utter these words: "Father, my dear Father, I have sinned against heaven and before you and I am no longer worthy to be called your son. Treat me like one of your slaves."

His father turns to some slaves, who follow in support, and says, "Fetch the best robe, quickly now. Put a signet ring on his right hand, and new sandals on his feet. Get the fattest calf we have and prepare a feast. Call the musicians. Send out the call to everyone to come and join our celebration. For this son of mine was dead and is alive again! He was lost and is found!"

As neighbors begin to arrive from near and far, the strong smell of barbecue spreads across the hills and valleys. And now, as the older brother (son of the same father) comes home from the fields where he has been laboring, he hears music and dancing. He calls one of the slaves. "What in the world is going on?"

He replies, "Your brother has come home and your father has gone all out to prepare a huge feast, to celebrate the answer to his prayers. He has got him back home, safe and sound once again."

The older brother stops dead in his tracks, his anger sending smoke out his ears. He refuses to go in to join these festivities. His father comes out and pleads with him to come join the celebration. He gets redder and redder in the face, his pulse beating overtime. He raises his fist to his father. "For all these years I have been working like a slave for you and I have never disobeyed your command. Yet you have never given me even so much as a cold picnic so that I could celebrate with my friends. But look, when this selfish son of yours comes back, who has squandered your money and property on prostitutes, you kill the fattest calf for him. Aren't you ashamed, my father, to behave so disgracefully, to shame our family, your estate, to betray the loyalty of all our neighbors and friends, to behave so irresponsibly toward our God who has blessed us so bountifully?"

He reaches the end of his tirade and appears ready to leave his father, with deep disgust filling his demeanor and with frowns and groans.

His father raises his hands and answers his older son, "My dear son, you are always with me, and all I have is yours too. But don't you see, we must celebrate and rejoice, because this brother of yours, my son too, was dead and has come to life; he was lost and has been found."

Surely the best title for this parable is "The Waiting Father." He waited patiently, longingly, lovingly—never giving up hope that his errant younger son will wake up to his true self and reclaim his inheritance. And when this immature son does return, it is the father's patient waiting that makes all this development possible—the reunion on the roadside and the grand celebration of this homecoming.

But now, the father discovers he has been waiting even longer to hear his older son distance himself from his patriarch. He professes self-identity as a slave in his father's establishment. He does not claim his inheritance as an heir but sees himself as a slave. He has worked long, hard, and faithfully, but he does not acknowledge his father's love for him and his acceptance of that love. Thus, it is that both sons are absent or separate from their father and thus disclaim or reject their rightful heritage at one time or another.

There is finally reconciliation between the father and his younger son. Will there now also be reconciliation between the father and his older son? We do not hear whether or not the older brother decides to cease his boycott of the celebration and join the festivities. Thus, the father is still waiting. His patient waiting for his younger son paid him warm dividends. Will this older brother also allow his father such a blessing his father hopes to receive?

Perhaps Jesus tells this parable not only to counsel and to challenge those original Pharisees and scribes but also as an opportunity for all later generations to wrestle with how we find ourselves within this timeless but ever so timely story. If we listen carefully to the words Luke wants his readers to hear, perhaps we (you and I) will discover the same Spirit is still at work today as was the case then. Perhaps we will then recognize and claim our appropriate roles within this parable and accordingly grow in knowledge and practice of our faith during these forty days of this season of Lent.

Lesson Seventeen: The Fifth Sunday in Lent; Read John 11:1–45

It is customary to divide the Gospel of John into two major sections: chapters 1 to 12 as the book of signs and chapters 13 to 21 as the book of action (suffering, death, resurrection, ascension) when Jesus's hour has finally arrived (cf. John 2:4). Following this order, today's lesson centers on the seventh and last of Jesus's signs: the raising of Lazarus from the dead. Each of the seven signs, beginning with the new wine arriving in Cana, seeks to explain and points ahead to chapters 13 to 21.

Most of Jesus's seven signs begin with miracle, move to dialogue, and then to discourse. This lesson, however, much like John 4:4–42, presents dialogue, discourse, and miracle woven together rather than in separate episodes. The context for this lesson reaches back to the previous lesson, the sixth sign, when Jesus opens the eyes of the man blind from birth (John 9:1–41). The purpose of that lesson was to show Jesus as the Light of the World who opens the eyes of the physically blind to the new world of spiritual knowledge and who shows the physically alive how blind they are spiritually.

Jesus follows that miracle and extended dialogue with discourse using the metaphor of the shepherd and his sheep (John 10:1–18), showing the importance of intimacy between and among the shepherd and his sheep, including some who do not yet belong to this flock. This strong community bonding points to where all his signs lead—to chapters 13 to 21. "For this reason the Father loves me, because I lay down my life in order to take it up again. No one takes it from me, but I lay it down of my own accord. I have power to lay it down, and I have power to take it up again. I have received this command from my Father" (John 10:17–18).

This lengthy discourse serves to show division among the Jews—those who remember how he gave sight to the man born blind and those who are oblivious to that sign because they listen to his words, which are blasphemous to them, and ignore his signs and his works, which require new birth from above in the Spirit to which they are blind. When they seek to stone him, or at least to arrest him, Jesus once again slips away from them (John 10:19–39).

Jesus and his disciples take refuge across the Jordan in friendlier territory associated with John the Baptist. This brings us to today's lesson. Jesus has earlier developed a bonding relationship with a family in the village of Bethany, including two sisters, Mary and Martha, and their brother, Lazarus. Paraphrase: These two sisters send word to their friend Jesus. "Lord, Lazarus, he whom you love is ill. Please come at once."

Jesus now dialogues with himself. "Just like the man born blind showed forth God's glory (John 9:3), just so this illness does not lead to death, but rather to show forth God's glory, because the Son of Man shall be glorified through this sign." And this knowledge of how God works leads Jesus to decide to remain where he is for two days because his love for Mary and Martha and Lazarus motivates him to include them in any and every sign he shall work to show forth the glory of God.

Jesus's dialogue now extends beyond himself to include his disciples: "Hey, guys, let's get ready to return to Judaea."

They react. "Are you crazy? The Jews will stone you to death!"

Jesus replies, "What are a few stones when the Light of the World is ready to shine in order to expose such darkness?" Jesus continues, "But the real reason is our friend Lazarus has fallen asleep, and I am going to awaken him."

This double entendre falls on deaf ears. They insist. "Lord, if he is asleep, he will be all right."

Jesus has to put it plainly. "Lazarus is dead." Jesus continues, "For your sake, I am glad I was not there [to prevent him from dying], but let us go to him since the approaching sign will lead you to knowledge and trust."

His disciple Thomas, whose name in Greek (*Didumos*) means "twin," sees both sides of this exchange and mutters out loud and tongue in cheek, "Let's go so that we may die with him!"

When Jesus arrives near Bethany, he soon hears that Lazarus has already been buried in the tomb for four days. Now he has an exchange with both of Lazarus's sisters, first with Martha, who goes out to meet him while Mary stays at home. Martha greets him, "Lord, if you had been here, my brother would not have died! But still, I know God will bless whatever you ask him to do for you."

Jesus has words of comfort for Martha. "Your brother will rise and live again!"

Martha reacts as best she can. "I know he will rise again in the resurrection on the last day!"

Jesus now wants both to confirm her faith and to teach her the knowledge and trust she needs to hear and receive. "We do not need to wait to the last day. Listen to me now when I say this: I am the resurrection and the life. Those who trust in me, even though they die, will live. And everyone who lives and trusts in me, shall never die. Do you hear, understand, and trust what I am saying?"

Martha again responds as best she can, "Yes, Lord, I understand and trust that you are the Messiah, the Son of God, the one who is coming into the world!"

Martha goes quickly to call her sister Mary. When Mary meets Jesus, she kneels at his feet and cries out, "Lord, if you had been here my brother would not have died."

When Jesus hears her weeping and the Jews with her also weeping, he becomes disturbed in his spirit and troubled deep within himself. He asks, "Where have you laid him?" And Jesus wept!

Some of the Jews, looking on, observe. "See how this man loved our brother Lazarus!"

But other Jews remark, "Could not he who opened the eyes of the blind man (John 9:1–7) have kept this man from dying?"

As Jesus approaches the tomb, greatly troubled deep within his bowels, he sees it is a cave with a stone lying against it. Jesus directs, "Take away the stone, please."

Martha, the other sister of the dead man who is troubled herself, tries to be of help. "Lord, there is surely a strong stench because he has already been dead four days!"

Jesus pauses, smiles, and addresses both Martha and Mary, "Remember what I have told you, that if you trust in me, you shall see the glory of God!" They take away the stone. Jesus looks upward and begins to pray, "Father, thank you for hearing me now. I know that you always hear me, but I am speaking now for the benefit of all of these dear ones, who are with us now, so that they may come to trust that you have sent me to show forth your glory!" Having said this, Jesus cries with a loud voice, "Lazarus, come out!"

The dead man emerges from the cave with burial clothes still tightly bound to his hands and feet and his face wrapped in a cloth. Jesus says to them, "Unbind him and let him go!"

The outcome of this event is that many of the Jews, who are with Mary and Martha and who see with their own eyes what Jesus has done, trust in this person, Jesus, whose work shows forth the glory of his Father, God.

Thus, does this—the seventh sign which Jesus performs to show forth the glory of God—seek to make clear that the arrival of the kingdom of God does not wait for the last days. The glory of God is here and now, according to Jesus's words to Martha in John 11:25–26: "I am the resurrection and the life. Those who believe in me, even though they die, will live, and everyone who lives and believes in me shall never die."

It is helpful to quote a contemporary New Testament scholar who draws this conclusion from the witness, the editor John, seeks to present in this the fourth Gospel, and especially in this the seventh of Jesus's signs:

> "Eternal" does not mean mere endless duration of human existence, but is a way of describing life as lived in the unending presence of God. To have eternal life is to be given life as a child of God. To speak of the newness available to the believer as "eternal life" shifts eschatological expectations to the present. Eternal life is not something held in abeyance until the believer's future, but begins in the believer's present. (Gail R. O'Day, *The New Interpreter's Bible*, vol. 9, p. 552)

Lesson Eighteen: Passion/Palm Sunday—Holy Week Begins; Read Mark 14:1–15:47

Perhaps this lengthy narrative can be divided into sections to use for Palm/Passion Sunday, as well as on Maundy Thursday and Good Friday. This may be the only occasion when congregations hear the passion narrative read in its entirety. This opportunity calls for strong readers, perhaps with dramatic flair, who have studied/pondered the deep ironies and subtle nuances the first Gospel writer/editor, Mark, puts forth in these two chapters.

Begin with the recall of how Mark structures three predictions of the passion (8:31–33, 9:30–32, 10:32–34), each with increasing intensity focused upon two themes. First, what is going to happen to the Son of Man each time he seeks to drive home that the Son of Man will suffer, be rejected, be killed, and rise again from the dead? The disciples' inability, slowness, or outright refusal to hear and take these predictions seriously is closely intertwined with the second theme that "if any want to become my followers, let them deny themselves, take up their cross and follow me. For those who want to save their life will lose it, and those who lose their life for my sake and for the sake of the Gospel will save it" (Mark 8:34–35).

The second theme Mark made clear earlier in Mark 3:13–15 when Jesus chose and appointed twelve whom he wanted (1) to be with him, (2) to be sent out to proclaim the message, and (3) to have authority to cast out demons. In other words, Jesus, the Son of Man, is calling together this team of twelve disciples/apostles, the new Israel, to participate in and share the work and responsibility the Son of Man has first been called, anointed, equipped, and sent forth to announce and to inaugurate (1:1–20).

Notice how the providential provision of the colt for Jesus's triumphal entry procession signals divine control of decisions and choices (11:1–11) so that loud shouts of "Hosanna" and "Blessed!" are appropriate, and it appears the disciples can endorse and participate in this upbeat, over-the-top victory parade. The destiny of the Son of Man is going to happen as predicted, Mark assures his readers. But the great drama awaits our contemplation because the looming question is how these twelve chosen and appointed apostles (plus some others as we know; for example, some women and unnamed men) will behave under intense pressure when this hoopla fades and the chips are down.

As if Jesus has not brought enough controversy with the Jewish authorities with him from Galilee, his confrontations in Jerusalem soon convince the chief priests and the scribes "to take Jesus by stealth and kill him," keeping their plot out of public eyes because of the Feast of Unleavened Bread, or Passover (14:1–2).

The woman who arrives with her alabaster jar of very costly ointment of pure nard performs an aesthetic act of devotion. "She anoints my body for burial beforehand," Jesus acclaims in recognition and defense of her initiative. Mark includes her story and thus fulfills Jesus's promise that "wherever the good news is told across the whole world, her part will be included"(14:3–9).

It is probably divine wisdom that no Gospel writer attempts even a single description of Jesus's outward physical appearance. He must have looked very ordinary with no distinctive characteristics—probably one who blended in well with whatever crowd of ordinary folk he fell into. This opens up a job for Judas Iscariot, who finds eager buyers for his service of crafty betrayal (14:10–11).

The preparations for the festive Passover meal are divinely established (14:12–16). Sharing the ritual Passover nourishment, Jesus drops the bomb: "One of you, dipping bread with me into this bowl, will betray me."

"Surely, not I?" each one asks incredulously.

"The Son of Man fulfills what is written of him, with or without my betrayer," Jesus affirms, "but even so this one will bewail the day he was born."

Again, he goes away from them and prays the same words. And once more, he comes and finds them sleeping. For their eyes are very heavy, and they do not find words to reply. Then Jesus departs again and returns a third time. He speaks to them, "Are you still sleeping and taking your rest? Enough of all this! The hour has arrived, and the Son of Man is betrayed into the hands of sinners. Get up, let us be going. Look, my betrayer is at hand" (Mark 14:37–42).

As Jesus speaks, Judas Iscariot arrives with a mob armed with swords and clubs sent from the chief priests, scribes, and elders. Having given them his method of betrayal, Judas goes up to Jesus, addresses him as "Rabbi," and kisses him. They seize Jesus and arrest him. Before they can move, someone swings his sword and strikes the slave of the high priest, cutting off his ear.

Jesus speaks up, "Why all this violence? Day after day I was teaching in the temple and you did not arrest me. Now you come with swords and clubs, as if I were a bandit. But let the scriptures be fulfilled." Without any hesitation, all of Jesus's disciples desert him and flee (14:43–50).

An unnamed young man was among those following after Jesus, wearing nothing but a linen cloth. They seize him, but he leaves the linen cloth in their hands and runs away naked (14:51–52). No scholarly consensus explains this cameo appearance of an anonymous member of the deserters except that he is exposed for the coward he is. One theory is that this is Mark himself, reporting his own guilt as a deserter but revealing that even so he was an eyewitness of these events.

An aside: When I was teaching college students during the years of the hippie movement, I explained that this was actually the first "streaker," who thus provides biblical precedent for the flower children phenomenon.

In Mark 14:66–72, this scenario first establishes Simon Peter's presence, safely at a distance, and then the drama of the mock trial of Jesus before the Jewish authorities. Spurious and conflicting testimonies neither warrant nor receive Jesus's reply. But when the high priest asks him, "Are you the Messiah, the son of the blessed One?"

Jesus tells the truth. "I am, and you will see the Son of Man seated at the right hand of the Power, coming with the clouds of heaven."

The high priest tears his clothes and bewails, "This blasphemy needs no other witnesses. He condemns himself. What shall we do with him?" No vote is needed, but a unanimous roar bellows "Death to this blasphemer!" No shortage of commands to kill blasphemers in the Torah! Finding no stones nearby, everyone can rant and roar, spit and beat this heretic as mob violence takes over. Mark shows how his predictions that the Son of Man will suffer and be rejected come true.

Meanwhile, Mark 14:66–72 summarizes Simon Peter's three denials and flowing tears, his self-exposure being facilitated by a young maiden. So much for pious bravado from the chief spokesperson of the disciples, who are not with Jesus (cf. Mark:13–15) from Gethsemane onward. Will there be any restitution for these disciples, including Judas Iscariot? Perhaps so because Jesus has promised to reunite with them after his resurrection in Galilee. How the plot does thicken! Which means we have to stay tuned.

In Mark 15:1–20, the Jewish council can punish Jesus for blasphemy through their mocking, taunting, flogging, spitting, beating, but only the Roman procurator can carry out crucifixion. Pontius Pilate asks Jesus about the Jewish charges, "Are you the king of the Jews?"

Jesus answers, "This is what you say."

Pilate listens to the Jewish charges of impiety, abandonment of the Torah, heresy, and blasphemy, but Pilate sees all this as a Jewish intramural squabble. Pilate is, as always, amazed at what tedium motivates these self-appointed Jewish functionaries to harbor such animosity against such an innocuous and obviously innocent rabbi and prophet.

But aha! Pilate thinks maybe he can orchestrate a pathway through this malaise. Everybody knows Barabbas is guilty as hell, having committed murder during the recent insurrection. Pilate has up his sleeve his custom during the festival to release a prisoner, whomever the crowd point to, as a gesture to improve relations between Jews and Rome. Surely the crowd, Pilate plots, will recognize the trumped-up charges against Jesus, who after all is popular with certain segments of the population, and choose justice—that is, choose to execute Barabbas who is guilty, and ask Pilate to release Jesus with nothing more than a rebuke for impiety. Pilate, however, is amazed and aghast when the crowd calls for the release of Barabbas and the crucifixion of Jesus. Expediency prevails. Justice be damned! Wishing to satisfy the crowd, Pilate releases Barabbas and delivers Jesus to be crucified. Talk about "political correctness," to use today's language.

In Mark 15:21–34, who are Alexander and Rufus? Maybe citizens in Rome whom Mark knows; and here he can connect them with Jesus through their father, Simon of Cyrene. The Roman crucifixion goes according to standard protocol, with the single exception of the inscription proclaiming the condemned man's guilt: "The King of the Jews." Talk about the height of irony!

They taunt him to save himself so that he can then save others when, of course, Marcan theology seeks to show he can and will save others precisely because he will not save himself in this circumstance. Why darkness over the whole land from noon to three o'clock when Jesus cries out, "Eloi, Eloi, lama sabachthani?" Why does Mark first quote Jesus's Aramaic words and then translate them to "My God, My God, why have you forsaken me?"

Compare Jesus's moment of death here (15:37) with the other three Gospels' versions, as well as their depictions of Jesus's time alone agonizing in the Garden of Gethsemane. Why does Mark tell us that precisely at the moment of Jesus's death, "the curtain of the temple was torn in two from top to bottom"? And right here, (15:30) Mark's entire Gospel narrative reaches its climax with the Roman centurion's observation and recognition that "truly, this man was God's Son." Mark has searched from the beginning (1:1–20), hoping that someone, some Jewish disciple, will recognize that this Jesus of Nazareth was and is the Son of God. This very first recognition comes not from a fellow Jew but from a Gentile—a Roman military officer. Mark reluctantly admits and portrays the future for the early Christian movement to be moving away from Jesus's own family, neighbors, and countrymen, and abroad, outward across the Hellenistic world.

But wait. In Mark 15:42–47, a member of the council and some women have not deserted Jesus through his arrest, suffering, rejection, and crucifixion. Not one of Jesus's official disciples, but perhaps these women will be ready, waiting to see Jesus alive on the third day.

CHAPTER FOUR

The Season of Eastertide

Lesson Nineteen: Resurrection of the Lord / Easter Sunday; Read John 20:1–18

This, the fourth Gospel, the Gospel of John, presents three versions of the resurrection appearances of Jesus. Today's lesson is the first version (John 10:1–18) set early on the first day of the week outside the empty tomb. The second version, one week later, behind closed/locked doors, includes all the disciples except Thomas (John 20:19–25). The third version transpires still a week later and this time includes Thomas (John 20:26–29). Notice the progression, from initial appearance of the risen Jesus to one of his disciples, Mary Magdalene, and his instruction to her to share his announcement with his other disciples. Next, she has prepared them, and they wait for his arrival before them all, minus Thomas. And third, Thomas is included, and Jesus's confrontation with Thomas makes his appearances complete.

This lesson is limited to the first version (20:1–18), although we may need or wish to connect this narrative with previous episodes and look forward to Jesus's long-range vision and expectations. For example, the lead character in this plot sequence is a woman, Mary Magdalene. Interestingly, Mark, followed by Matthew, lists her first in the names of persons from Jesus's entourage who observe his crucifixion and death (Mark 15:40–41 and Matthew 17:55–56). Luke mentions no names but agrees that there were women there who followed him from Galilee (Luke 23:40). We recall, of course, that according to Mark 14:50, all of Jesus's male disciples deserted him and fled when he was arrested. And so the Synoptics mention no male disciples, although one or two of their mothers were there.

John, however, tells a different story. This scenario (John 19:25–27) is worth quoting: "Meanwhile, standing near the cross of Jesus were his mother and his mother's sister, Mary, the wife of Clopas, and Mary Magdalene. When Jesus saw his mother and the disciple whom he loved standing beside her, he said to his mother, 'Woman, here is your son.' Then he said to the disciple, 'Here is your mother.' And from that hour, the disciple took her into his own home." And so according to John's Gospel, at least one male disciple was present. No name is given, but a relationship is described—this is the disciple Jesus loved. And Jesus gives him to his mother as her son and gives her to him as his mother, establishing a new family relationship such that he becomes her guardian.

It is certainly no accident subsequently that both Mary Magdalene and this enigmatic beloved disciple figure prominently in John's first version of Jesus's resurrection appearances. In fact, there are only two other characters, Simon Peter and Jesus himself. (The angelic messengers, of course, are only a necessary component of the empty tomb scenario.) Simon Peter and this beloved disciple seem to hang together as comrades in this narrative (John 20:1–10). Mary Magdalene is the first disciple to venture forth while it is still dark, early on this first day of the week. As she approaches the tomb, she is startled to see the stone has been removed from the entrance. This means only one thing to her. Jesus's body is gone, removed, stolen. The possibility that Jesus himself is alive, has risen, and removed himself from the tomb never crosses her mind.

She hastens back home to tell the other disciples what she has discovered and runs into Simon Peter and the other disciple, the one whom Jesus loved. (Notice again, no name, only a relationship described.) They apparently hang out together. No one else is available. Mary frantically cries out, "They have taken the Lord out of the tomb, and we do not know where they have laid him." The pronouns *they* and *we* serve to bring substance to her suppositions growing out of her shock, fear, and ignorance.

Simon Peter and the other disciple take off running to check out Mary's reports. The other disciple outruns his companion and gets there first. He stoops to look inside the tomb and sees linen wrappings but no body. Perhaps out of reverence, he is awestruck and does not enter. Simon Peter, following, barges right into the tomb. He sees the linen wrapping lying in a heap and the cloth that had covered Jesus's head lying not with the other wrappings but rolled up in a place by itself. Now the other disciple enters the tomb also and sees exactly what Peter sees. They are both stunned.

Mary's assumptions/fears are wrong. The body has not been stolen. Something else has happened. The body must have unwrapped itself and walked out. Peter is silent. But when the beloved disciple enters and sees this reality, his mind and heart are not silent. Only of him does the narrator say, "He believed." Actually, the Greek verbs are *eiden* ("he saw") and *episteusen* (not "he believed" but "he trusted"). *Believe* implies some knowledge, vision, or rationale, and the next sentence explains why this translation is wrong. They, both of these disciples, "did not yet understand the scriptures, that he must rise from the dead." In other words, this is not a matter of head knowledge but of heart knowledge.

What the beloved disciple sees moves, inspires, motivates his heart and soul to trust this new reality of Jesus becoming alive, when his mind, reason, logic, information do not yet provide him with any such solutions. Here, the Gospel writer John's theology emerges. Salvation is a matter of relationship, not of reason or information that removes all questions and proves truth beyond doubt. Simon Peter has no such response, still struggling to cope with his basic, problematic relationship to Jesus as the "Son of Man."

The two disciples return home. Apparently, both do not yet understand what the scriptures mean and teach about the urgency and necessity for resurrection. For Simon Peter, this stymies or prevents his recognition and acceptance of this new reality Jesus brings. He insists upon evidence or proof. The beloved disciple, however, welcomes, cultivates, enjoys the personal, spiritual, trusting, intimate relationship that does not demand security but acknowledges great risk as necessary and even positive in value and purpose. Simon Peter holds out for more evidence and explanation. The beloved disciple sees the evidence before him but leaps to affirm how this confirms his already warm, trusting relationship with this rabbi he has grown to love as his teacher and Lord.

It is intriguing to trace earlier descriptions of the relationship between these three characters: Simon Peter, Jesus, and his beloved disciple. In John 13:1–38, when Jesus celebrates Passover by washing his disciples' feet, Simon Peter shows his usual shallow grasp of just what Jesus is up to. But he is reclining with this "disciple whom Jesus loved" and calls upon him to ask Jesus for teaching. Later, when Jesus raises the meaning of love for one another to be the one necessary ingredient for their fellowship, perhaps pointing in some way to the disciple whom he loved, Simon's rash but serious profession of absolute love for Jesus prompts Jesus to predict his denial three times in the near future.

After Jesus is arrested, Simon Peter follows Jesus and calls upon "another disciple" with inside connections to smooth the way for his entrance into the courtyard of the high priest. Could this be the same beloved disciple continuing his friendship with Simon Peter? At any rate, this connivance seems to promote the fulfillment of Jesus's prediction when Peter makes his three denials just before the cock crows (John 18:15–27).

There may be an oblique reference to this beloved disciple in John 19:34–35. After Jesus has died on the cross, "One of the soldiers pierced his side with a spear, and blood and water came out." The narrator interjects these words, "He who saw this has testified so that you also may believe. His testimony is true, and he knows that he tells the truth." Since the beloved disciple is the only male disciple John records as having watched Jesus's crucifixion, these words may be John's assurance of the integrity of his own witness throughout his Gospel.

By carefully slipping this beloved disciple into his narrative, with no name but with a strong yet mysterious and oblique spiritual relationship with Jesus, John seems to call attention to the fragile nature of human participation in the dynamics of covenant sensitivity, knowledge, understanding, and commitment.

For example, when Jesus is arrested and finally brought before Pontius Pilate, this Roman procurator tries every way he can to resist his Jewish accusers' demands for Jesus's execution. Jesus gives him his opportunity to ask the bedrock question that worries this one-man judge and jury. "'For this I was born and for this I came into the world, to testify to the truth. Everyone who belongs to the truth listens to my voice.' Listening to his Jewish prisoner very carefully, Pontius Pilate asks him, 'What is truth?'" (John 18:37–38).

Here is the narrator John's placement of the big truth question not in the mouths of Jesus's disciples but with Jesus paving the way, right up front in the mouthpiece of the archenemy, the Roman Empire. And this procurator asks this question, the central focus of the Roman philosophy of Stoicism, to challenge both his Jewish antagonists and his Roman henchmen who pledge allegiance to and worship the emperor himself. In other words, this is John the narrator's big question also: "What is truth?"

For we must remember this Gospel writer begins his Gospel with the question of the origin and meaning of the cosmos, the entire universe, all of creation and makes it very clear the answers to these questions lie in the reality of *Ho Logos*, the *Truth*, who is the one God himself, who becomes flesh, incarnation, in the arrival of Jesus of Nazareth, the light that shines in the darkness, full of grace and truth (John 1:1–51). And this same source of all truth is now on trial for his life before Pontius Pilate. Good time to remember the disciple Nathaniel's honest question, "Can anything good come out of Nazareth?" (John 1:46).

In other words, is truth to be discovered outside the human mind, in which case objective evidence must be accountable for the truth or not of Jesus's resurrection from the grave? Or does truth, at least in some large part, arise from within the need and promise of human consciousness to respond to sacrificial love as the truth Jesus's resurrection offers, affirms, and provides in reality?

Back to John's first version of the resurrection appearances of Jesus (John 20:1–18). After Simon Peter and the beloved disciple see and respond to the linen wrappings lacking a body, doing the best they can without the knowledge and understanding they still need, they return home. Mary Magdalene, however, has made her way back to the tomb and stands outside weeping, disappointed her two cohorts offer no help to find the body. She needs help. She bends over to look in the tomb, and lo and behold, two angels (messengers) now occupy the very spot where Jesus's body did lie. They ask, "Woman, why are you weeping? Who are you looking for?"

Mary replies, as best she can, "They have taken away my Lord, and I do not know where they have put him." Mary hears a rustle behind her, turns around, and finds Jesus himself standing there. But she does not recognize him and assumes this person is the caretaker of the garden.

Jesus speaks to her, "Woman, why are you weeping? Who are you looking for?"

Assuming this man knows his business, Mary replies, "Sir, if you have carried him away, tell me where you have laid him, and I will take him away." Her eyes glance away, expecting him to direct her to her requested destination.

Instead, Jesus calls out to her, "Mariam."

Startled, Mary swings toward him and replies in Aramaic, "Rabbouni," which means "My very own dear teacher."

This exchange brings to life Jesus's teaching on his role as the good shepherd and the response of his flock of sheep (John 10:1–18). To paraphrase, "I am the good shepherd. My sheep will follow me because they know my voice. They will not follow a stranger, but they will run from him because they do not know the voice of strangers. I am the good shepherd, who lays down his life for his sheep. I know my own and my own know me, just as the Father knows me and I know the Father. And I lay down my life for my sheep."

In other words, without her brain's frontal lobes providing reason, Mary responds subliminally, out of her gut, her heart and soul, her bowels, to participate once again in the personal intimate, warm, embracing covenant relationship she has known as a disciple of this rabbi from Nazareth in Galilee. She bends her knees and, without thinking, cannot resist reaching out to embrace her dear Lord.

His love for her overflowing, Jesus cautions her, "Do not seek to hold me here. I must not linger, for I am even now moving forward to ascend to the Father. But go quickly and speak to my brothers and assure them I am ascending to my Father and your Father, to my God and to your God."

And now Mary Magdalene, the first of the disciples to meet the risen Jesus face-to-face, hurries to announce to all her "brothers," "I have seen the Lord." And she shares all the risen Jesus has explained to her.

Considering that the testimony of a mere woman was neither respected nor allowed in a court of law in those times, of what worth will her witness prove to be? Perhaps this open-ended question invites John's readers to move onward to the second and third installments in this same chapter (John 20:19–29), where human fears and the physical barriers of locked doors and windows shall not prevent Jesus from his appearances to his startled disciples and his announcement, "Peace be with you."

Lesson Twenty: Second Sunday of Easter; Read John 20:19–31

It is now evening of the first day of the week, meaning before sundown. The disciples of Jesus are meeting. Why? One big reason: for fear of the Jews. But we understand they all deserted Jesus and fled soon after his arrest. Only a few disciples, John reports, were present with him at his crucifixion (John 19:25–27). Could they not be safer hiding out each one alone or in small groups? Uniting surely calls attention to them, so they must rally together for another reason, hoping the locks and chains on the doors will protect them.

Probably, they are united once again, despite all risks in doing so, because Mary Magdalene did exactly what the risen Jesus told her to do earlier that day: "Go to my brothers and say to them, 'I am ascending to my Father and your Father, to my God and your God'" (John 20:17). Mary obeys Jesus. Why? Because Jesus calls his disciples "my brothers." The Greek words for "my brothers," *tous adelfous mou*, do not denote gender, males, but "members of my family." Jesus affirms his disciples are now members of his family, not lapsed or failed companions tainted forever by their disloyalty or fearful behavior. Mary hears this good news of Jesus's love, blessing, and restoration. She hears all the disciples are included in Jesus's process of glorification, especially his imminent ascension: "I am ascending to my Father and your Father, to my God and your God." The pronoun *your* in Greek, *humon*, is plural and, in this case, strongly gender inclusive.

Mary was quick to announce to the disciples, "I have seen the Lord." And she repeats what Jesus has told her to be sure they hear (John 20:18). Now scholars agree that in all ancient cultures, women in general were not respected as witnesses in serious deliberations. But these disciples rally together, despite putting themselves at greater risk by doing so, because they listen, they hear, they accept, they trust the truth Mary obediently delivers to them. If Jesus calls them his brothers, his family, then the message is loud and clear: Jesus is alive and announces on the lips of his witness, Mary Magdalene, that he includes all his disciples as members of the new family of humanity, this new creation God their Father is working out through the glorification of Jesus, still in progress.

The locks on the doors address the reality of their fears. But the locks also show that what provokes their fear is not a serious obstacle to the risen Jesus who seeks reunion with them. Without benefit of doorkeeper or locksmith, Jesus suddenly joins them. He stands squarely in the midst of them. Not above them or over them but as one of them, a family sharing reunion. What do they expect from him? If fear for their lives is their motivation, then surely they must fear Jesus will chastise them, blame them, judge them, hold them guilty of desertion and betrayal.

But what does Jesus say? "Peace I bring to you." He repeats the same theme he has shared with them often during the long Farewell Discourses (John 13–17). Specifically, Jesus promised his own very special peace (John 14:25–27), and now he delivers on his promise. Despite their guilt, their fear, their locked doors, he stands among them and brings his peace to them. Jesus has promised, "On that day, you will know that I am in my Father and you in me and I in you" (John 14:20). The Greek word translated *peace* is *he eirene* (feminine) and means "harmony," as opposed to disharmony or chaos, or "order," as opposed to disorder. The risen Jesus is the arrival of the new creation, and Jesus, whom neither fears nor locks can inhibit, personally brings this new creation, peace, and presents it to his gathered brothers or to the members of his new human family.

When Jesus shows them his hands and his side, he reminds them he is the same Jesus from whom they fled when he was arrested, and there is continuity with his former self, through the movement of his glorification, his suffering, his death, and his burial in the tomb. His former body has now been raised from the dead, made new, and this new creation leaves behind what has now been overcome and brings the new reality, which the word *peace* summarizes. The disciples make the appropriate response. They rejoice!

Jesus repeats his proclamation, "Peace be with you." And he begins to define what this new reality of harmony and order or unity shall mean, "As the Father has sent me, so I send you." Recall the initial appearance of Jesus in this Gospel document attracted potential disciples, whom Jesus welcomed, cultivated, and nurtured to become his chosen band (John 1:35–51). And there were obstacles to be overcome. One of those early disciples, we should remember, Nathaniel, focused a metaphor for Jesus's entire career when he makes this observation, "Can anything good come out of Nazareth?" And Jesus then had the audacity to promise, "Very truly I tell you, you will see heaven opened and the angels of God ascending and descending upon the Son of Man" (John 1:51).

Jesus now delivers on the answer to Nathaniel's question when he greets his disciples in his resurrected body and welcomes or, better still, commissions them to come aboard this newly born and newly christened ship about to leave the harbor. Indeed, as Jesus shows these disciples his hands and side, so they must have ringing in their ears Jesus's unforgettable promises from his Farewell Discourses: "Very truly I tell you, the one who believes in me will do the works that I do and, in fact, will do greater works than these because I am going to the Father" (John 14:11–14). And how shall they do these works? Jesus literally spews forth the powerful force necessary to drive this anticipated new movement. Jesus breathes upon them, saying, "Receive the Holy Spirit."

Many scholars recognize that this moment is John's version of Pentecost. Not the public, boisterous festival portrayed by Luke in Acts 2 but this subdued, private, intimate moment of communion, personal bonding between Jesus and his disciples, all of them merging together into the new family of God the Father, the first fruits of the new creation, blessed, called, commissioned, and empowered by the newly risen Jesus as he breathes out of his own lungs the Holy Spirit who will circulate through their respiratory systems and enable them to trust and to welcome the anointing/commissioning Jesus calls them forward to accept and to express.

Let us not miss the parallel here between this divine breathing event/occasion and the first such creation event portrayed in Genesis 2:7, also Genesis 1:26–28. The first creation or covenant moves along through history (modern science would suggest through eons and eons of natural evolution), and now in the Creator's good time, we arrive at the occasion of the second or new creation. The Creator (God the Father) and the Redeemer (God the Son) now present a new role for God the Holy Spirit. And just what is this new role God the Creator will soon be fulfilling as Jesus commissions his disciples to go forth, as he himself has already gone forth?

A very specific ministry: "If you forgive the sins of any, they are forgiven. If you retain the sins of any, they are retained." Notice carefully, the destiny of the human race begins and depends upon the initiative and work of the Creator himself, who sends Jesus, who brings the Holy Spirit, who commissions human disciples whom Jesus entrusts with bringing forgiveness of sins to those whose fallen nature waits, in need of redemption. This new creation begins with the great love of God the Father (John 3:16), expressed in Greek as a noun, *he agape* (feminine), or as a verb, *agapao*. This new creation does not begin with cataloging the sins of humankind. Presumably, there are plenty of sins in need of and/or waiting for forgiveness. The disciples are not called and commissioned to scrutinize and make judgment calls as to which sins are forgivable, which are not, etc. Forgiveness is active and aggressive. Sins are forgiven when the forgiver gets busy and decides to forgive. When you forgive, as the servant of God you are called and equipped to be, sins are forgiven. Plain and simple.

If you should refuse or refrain from forgiving, you make the choice; the character or nature of the sins in question does not decide for you. Unforgiven sins, therefore, hang around and mess everything up, not because the sins are there but because you neglect to express/communicate/deliver your forgiving opportunity and responsibility. If this arrangement sounds contrary to normal thinking, or common sense, this is because this is the goal of the new creation, empowered by the Holy Spirit, not driven as in the former/old creation, by unrepentant human values and reasoning. When Jesus breathes the Holy Spirit upon and into these waiting disciples, Jesus shares his Father and their Father, his God and their God with them, and Jesus trusts they will trust his promises.

Notice Jesus's disciples here are an anonymous bunch. Presumably, Simon Peter and the beloved disciple are present. Are Mary Magdalene and other women also here? What we hear is not the names of those present but instead who is not here. Thomas is absent, one of the original twelve. He misses out on Jesus's initial appearance, his blessing with peace, his breathing upon them, and his commissioning. In the days following, the disciples who were there are excited and cannot keep silent, and so they regale Thomas with everything he has missed. Thomas is remembered as a curious individual not afraid to raise his hand to demand explanations (John 14:5–7). He is no doubt fascinated with everything they tell him about Jesus's visit with them. But then Thomas insists, "Unless I see the mark of the nails in his hands and put my finger in the mark of the nails and my hand in his side, I will not believe."

Now the name Thomas (*Thomas* in Greek) is derived from an Aramaic name, which means "twin" or *didumos* in Greek. As this name became popular in Greek, it apparently carried along this connotation that the bearer was split into two halves, or double-sided in personality. If one side of Thomas is his discipleship, one of Jesus's steady, loyal twelve, what was his other side, the other half of his split personality? Or to put this question this way, Why was Thomas absent when all the other disciples were gathered together behind locked doors when Jesus made his first appearance? A good supposition is that he was of two loyalties, both a participant in Jesus's disciple band and, let's say, a neophyte or new initiate member of the local philosophy club or the Aristotelian society or the Stoics' fraternity.

Now like thinkers with this side of Thomas's persona are somewhat scarce in Judaea, mostly Roman members of Pontius Pilate's brigade, or Hellenes, Greeks attracted as new, experimental monotheists to the Passover Festival. Once the festival has passed, they schedule a retreat, a working seminar to fraternize and to ponder the latest developments in scientific or critical-thinking techniques. You might say a branch of classical Athens has been on holiday in Jerusalem. Thomas is getting his batteries charged.

Now Jesus has already presented empirical, physical evidence of his resurrection to the other disciples. They have seen his hands and his side. When Thomas hears their report, he leaps with excitement, because Jesus uses evidence, which makes his disciples rejoice with their discovery. Thomas is eager to bring his need for evidence to receive the same kind of experience and blessing his fellow disciples have already received. But to be true to both sides of his twin personality, he insists upon his own opportunity to see and examine Jesus's hands and side as his colleagues have already done.

This opportunity does not occur until a week later when the disciples gather again and Thomas is with them this time. Doors locked again, and Jesus appears and repeats, "Peace be with you." Now Jesus knows Thomas well and offers himself for Thomas to see and to examine. In other words, Jesus has no objection to Thomas's skepticism. He does not chastise or criticize Thomas. He welcomes Thomas's need to see and touch. He encourages Thomas to do what he insists he must do—that is, to give his five senses a full workout. The NRSV translation reports Jesus's only instruction to Thomas is, "Do not doubt but believe." A better translation is, "Do not become faithless but become faithful." Notice, Thomas does see but does not touch Jesus. Instead, Thomas's quick and only response is, "My Lord and my God." This direct address is the most emphatic and powerful profession of faith by a human being in the entire Gospel of John.

Jesus, ever the teacher, wants to summarize the lasting lesson, the truth, the living reality all future generations should receive and put to practice from this scenario: "Because you have seen me, you now believe? Blessed are all the ones who never see me but who come to believe!" Humanistic culture, knowledge, wisdom, modern scientific theory or method, empirical proof are here recognized and affirmed but also placed in perspective. Thomas believes in Jesus, now as his Lord and his God, not because he gains intellectual, rational knowledge that convinces his skeptical mind's need for empirical evidence. Thomas believes because he now trusts Jesus who gives himself in his crucifixion and trusts Jesus whom God the Father raises from the grave. Once again, as with the beloved disciple's earlier experience (John 20:8–9), heart and soul, the reality and experience of covenantal bonding take precedence over the rationality of the human mind.

Reliable scholarship concludes that the writer of this Gospel, John, has now shared his strongest narratives with his readers and that he draws his efforts to their conclusion: "Now Jesus did many other signs in the presence of his disciples, which are not written in this book." Wow, this truth begs so many questions: Where and what are all these many other signs? Why does John choose some and keep others to himself? How can we get ahold of them? Only one answer: "These are chosen and written so that you may come to believe Jesus is the Messiah, the Son of God, and that through believing you may have life in his name."

In other words, John, this writer, identifies his labor with the blessing and the challenge Jesus brings to his disciples in 20:19–23: "Peace be with you. As the Father has sent me, so I send you. Receive the Holy Spirit. If you forgive the sins of any, they are forgiven. If you retain the sins of any, they are retained." Thus John, through his labors as Gospel writer, participates in the arrival of God's new creation, Jesus's resurrection, which includes the disciples and their sharing of Jesus's peace with the whole world and John hopes will include all readers of his carefully constructed and edited tome.

If you wish to do some serious in-depth study on this theme of the new creation, I recommend the work of British scholar N.T.

Wright, especially his recent book, *Surprised by Hope*, and a second book, *Surprised by Scripture*.

Lesson Twenty-One: Third Sunday of Easter; Read John 21:1–19 (20–25)

Scholarly consensus points to this material (John 21) being an addendum to the original text (John 1–20). John 20:29–31 is such a strong, appropriate climax to the project of this Gospel that it must have been the original conclusion. This does not minimize in any way, however, the value and contribution that 21:1–25 makes to this project. This recognition has strong support in the fact that all ancient manuscripts include this material. This chapter was valued as necessary and appropriate as soon as this fourth Gospel was accepted into the canon, according to the evidence.

This is not true for John 7:53–8:11, the story of the woman caught in adultery, which is missing from many early manuscripts. This story became a valuable and necessary part of the fourth Gospel, however, as transmission proceeded through the centuries, because it was assessed to be strongly consistent with the portrait of Jesus presented throughout this document.

Likewise for 21:1–25. Although 20:1–31 appears to be highly sufficient as the original official conclusion to the career of Jesus, the contents of 21:1–25 in no way detract from but are consistent with and contribute to the portrait of Jesus in John 1–20. Furthermore, the location of Galilee occupies strong reality in the post-resurrection meetings of Jesus with his disciples, expected in Mark (Mark 16:1–8) and reported in Matthew (Matthew 28:16–20), and this tradition probably strengthens the witness to Jesus who does not conclude his glorification in the capital city of Jerusalem but reunites with his disciples in the rural neighborhood where their project begins and develops.

Notice the transition this new writer provides, "After these things," meaning after Jesus's appearance twice before, reported in 20:19–29. To paraphrase, do not separate what I report here from the two appearances of Jesus to his disciples when they huddled behind closed doors. Here, we have the same resurrected Jesus, but only some seven of his disciples, some mentioned by name, including the "disciple whom Jesus loved," but apparently no women. If we take this fishing scene to be symbolic of the by now well-known call of Jesus to his first disciples "to become fishers for people" (Mark 1:16–20), we may recall women were not part of the fishing industry but more confined to domestic duties.

True to his persona described in all four Gospels, Simon Peter takes initiative to call his colleagues to their mission, and they finding themselves back in Galilee, where they were first confronted and called by Jesus to leave their service to John the Baptist and follow him (John 1:35–51). Simon Peter says, "I am going fishing." His colleagues reply, "We will go with you." They are in home territory, where they know which waters are best and whether it is advisable or not to fish after dark. They stick to this task all night long but catch nothing. Experts at fishing as they are, what is wrong? What is missing?

Dawn arrives. Sunlight begins to replace the darkness. Suddenly, Jesus stands on the shore. His disciples out in the boat do not recognize that this person is Jesus. Jesus speaks to them, "Children, you have no fish yet, have you?"

Grudgingly, they reply, "No, none at all."

He says, "Cast the net over the other side of the boat, and you will find some fish."

They do as he directs, and before long, the net is so heavy with fish they can hardly haul it in. Only now does one of the disciples recognize who this visitor is. The narrator says, "That disciple whom Jesus loved says to Peter, 'It is the Lord.'" Thus, this reporter connects his narrative with that elusive, mysterious, but major character in the Gospel identified by the special love Jesus has for him.

Simon Peter now hears who this visitor is and realizes he is naked. He puts on some clothes and jumps into the sea to reach the shore. He is naked when Jesus is not present or, being present, is not recognized by Simon Peter on his own cognizance. Realizing who Jesus is, this disciple discovers suitable clothing is available to him and much more appropriate than nudity. Suitably attired, this still impetuous disciple jumps into the sea and headed to the shore. The other disciples bring the load of fish.

This visitor to their shore, Jesus himself, prepares to host breakfast. He has a charcoal fire ablaze, with both fish and bread ready to serve. He asks for some of the fish they have just caught, and Simon Peter responds by bringing some of the large fish, there being 153 of them from which to choose. Jesus is ready. "Come and have breakfast," is his invitation. Speechless, his disciples are now fully aware this is their Lord. Jesus now takes the bread and the fish from the fire and serves them. This is a eucharistic event that the narrator presents fully parallel to the fourth sign in John 6:1–15, when Jesus feeds five thousand with bread and fish.

Jesus teaches and explains his understanding of the presence of the bread of life in himself in John 6:35–71. And just as the Passover Feast was new and different in John 13:1–30, with the washing of feet, so this eucharistic feast at the seaside is different but powerful, with the sharing of bread and fish. The narrator now identifies this event beside the sea as the third appearance of Jesus to his disciples after he has been raised from the dead. Thus, he places this event in sequence with the earlier two appearances behind shut doors (John 20:19–29).

It is important that this narrator continues to stress how Jesus presents himself to his disciples but they do not recognize him by sight. They recognize him only by hearing about him or from him. As John made so clear in 20:1–29, response with recognition and trust arrives as a gift of the Holy Spirit, never as a piece of work the human mind achieves from empirical evidence. This emphasis upon divine initiative rather than human work is strongly expressed here in 21:14, when the Greek verb *phaneraw* ("reveal, show, manifest") appears in the passive voice. Thus, Jesus makes his universal proclamation, "Blessed are those who have not seen and have come to believe" (John 20:29).

This narrator has presented this scenario (John 21:1–14) as a symbolic portrayal of discipleship in the new covenant ministry the risen Jesus provides. It is appropriate to review John 13–16, the Farewell Discourses of Jesus with his disciples, and John 17, the High

Priestly Prayer, in order to recognize how the promises Jesus makes and the concern he has for his disciples connect with this eucharistic meeting they share in Galilee on the shore of the Sea of Tiberias.

And now, having finished their breakfast time together, Jesus takes Simon Peter aside for a private exchange. Three times Jesus asks Simon Peter, "Do you love me?" Each time, the disciple answers, "Yes, I love you." Two Greek verbs are used in this dialogue. Jesus uses *agapao* two times and *fileo* one time. Simon Peter uses *fileo* all three times. Since the Greek verb *agapao* means "sacrificial love" and the Greek verb *fileo* means "friendship," some English translations have Simon Peter answer, "I am fond of you," not "I love you." Of course, this conversation originally did not occur using Greek language but Aramaic, as far as we know. All of Jesus's original Aramaic words are written in the Gospels using Greek, and thus, the translators choose which Greek words to use, seeking to be accurate or faithful to what Jesus and this disciple intend to say.

The best interpretation of what is going on here rests upon Jesus's instructions to Simon Peter following his affirmative response to Jesus's three questions: (1) "Feed my lambs," (2) "Shepherd my sheep," and (3) "Feed my sheep." Here, the risen Jesus, Lord and Master for these disciples, commissions his disciples, speaking to this one disciple, to share the saving love of God his Father with the human race.

This means the Greek verb *agapao*, "sacrificial love," is the motivating force and blessing being bestowed upon the sinful humankind through this risen Jesus who trusts his disciples, who, of course, now trust him when he promises they shall "do the same works Jesus does and do even greater works than these" (John 14:12–14).

Since this commissioning process necessitates three versions of the same question, and includes Simon Peter's hurt and remorse during the third repetition, scholars conclude that this exchange represents this disciple's reversal or repentance for his three denials of Jesus before the Roman accusers (John 18:15–27). In this exchange, Jesus forgives the guilt Simon Peter acquired in his three denials and newly commissions him to now "deliver the goods," to bring forgiving love and salvation to Jesus's lambs and sheep, including all of suffering humanity.

It is important to recognize how closely and smoothly this addendum (John21:1–25) follows upon all the major themes and concerns repeated over and over in John 1–20. This writer agrees with and seeks to confirm the first writer's precedents and hopes to contribute wisely and positively to the role this Gospel plays in the early decades of this still embryonic Christian movement.

And thus, the dialogue of John 21:18–19 reflects the prominent and effective leadership of Simon Peter in the early developments of this movement from Jewish origins to more Hellenistic, Gentile contexts. In particular, this exchange probably reflects the strong tradition that this disciple, Simon Peter, became a powerful leader in the church in Rome and, as legend reports, achieved martyrdom as his final and valedictory act of love (Greek verb *agapao*, "sacrificial love") and witness to the risen Christ. In order to encourage and instruct Simon Peter to continue his witness, which will lead to his martyrdom, Jesus simply says, "Follow me."

In John 21:20–23, the dialogue now shifts to emphasis upon "the disciple whom Jesus loved." Simon Peter, having heard of his own future climactic witness, now asks whether some such honor also will include this other notable disciple. Perhaps there is a connection between Simon Peter's curiosity about this beloved disciple and Jesus's first question posed earlier to him, "Simon, son of John, do you love me more than these?" (John 21:15).

Jesus has a rather sharp reply to Simon Peter's curiosity about this beloved disciple's destiny: "If it is my will that he remain until I come, what is that to you?" Jesus here suggests that God the Father, acting through Jesus, Son of God, may indeed call and inspire different disciples to different contexts and different roles and responsibilities. What is more important than competitive levels of knowledge and roles vis-á-vis each other is the simple command from Jesus, "Follow me!"

This narrator notes these exchanges are reflected in the early developing history of Christianity, when rumors may abound and spread, which fail adequately to reflect the subtle nuances in Jesus's counsel and guidance.

In John 21:24–25, finally, the writer of this addendum interjects himself into the narrative in order to provide his own conclusion to the now amended Gospel: "This is the disciple who is testifying to these things and has written them, and we know that his testimony is true." And as if to gain the upper hand in a benevolent game of one-upmanship, this writer has a much larger claim to knowledge about Jesus than was earlier expressed in John 20:30–31: "But there are also many other things that Jesus did. If every one of them were written down, I suppose that the world itself could not contain the books that would be written."

And so John 21:1–25 is appended to John 1–20 in order to move ahead to show continuity from chapters 1 through 20 and the newly developing Christian movement, which extends the same Gospel message into the future. Interestingly, one connection is missing—the role of women, which, to some notable extent, belonged to the band of disciples and even Jesus's new family of "brothers" in John 1–20 but are missing here. This change probably honestly reflects the reality of how Christianity developed as it moved out across the Gentile world and came under pressure to respect and to conform to local cultural mores.

Lesson Twenty-Two: Fourth Sunday of Easter; Read John 10:22–30

During these seven Sundays of the season of Easter, the lectionary first calls us to study the resurrection narratives themselves (John 20–21) and now calls us to return to some selected preglorification passages in Jesus's life. This is a highly desirable procedure because this choice of passages for study and proclamation reminds us that the resurrection of Christ Jesus from death and the grave is the pivotal incident/occasion/event/development in covenant history that illumines all the previous narratives that present the career of Jesus to us all.

As we move backward, so to speak, from the climax to the pre-climactic episodes in Jesus's biography, we can investigate and learn their revelation for us as we allow the resurrection to open up for us clues and dimensions that without or before the resurrection were partial or incomplete in presenting the truth of just who and what was/is going on in this sacred history.

Let's see how this works in this passage (John 10:22–30) assigned for the fourth Sunday of Easter season. Jesus is visiting Jerusalem, one of his several visits to the capital city, according to this Gospel, but before his triumphal entry (John 12:12–19), he is busy teaching and interacting with the Jewish authorities. This was the time of the Feast of Dedication, and although this feast was not a feast of obligation, as was the Feast of the Passover, as an educated rabbi, Jesus knows the history of its significance and was probably motivated to participate and to draw his disciples/listeners/onlookers into dialogue on the history of sacred Judaism included in this festive but solemn celebration.

It may be helpful to recall the meaning of this Feast of Dedication. Following the return of faithful Jews to Jerusalem after the Babylonian exile (587–537 BCE), the remnant of Israel was first ruled by the Persian Empire (537–300 BCE) and then by the Hellenistic Empire (300–165 BCE). After the death of Alexander the Great (356–323 BCE), his empire was divided up among his ruling generals, and Judaea fell under the control of the Seleucid Dynasty of Syria. Although resented and resisted passively by the Jews, this dynasty was basically benign and allowed the Jews to run their own affairs unmolested. That is, until the arrival of Antiochus IV Epiphanes (175–164 BCE). This despot launched an aggressive campaign to eradicate Judaism as an inferior detractor from the cosmopolitan, enlightened Hellenistic culture destined to rule all the world. Popular culture reports that the Gentiles generally looked down on the Jews as atheists because they insisted no one could see their God. Gentile culture liked multiple gods, and the more visible, the better.

Antiochus IV Epiphanes's eleven-year rule was marked by his dedicated attempt to Hellenize the Jews. He meddled in the appointment of high priests, forced Greek customs upon the Jews, looted the temple, defiled the altar, and cruelly persecuted the pious Jews who devoutly wished to observe their own revered religious laws and customs. When he decreed that every Jewish city and village must sacrifice to the Greek gods, a family of pious former priests, the Hasmonaeans, rebelled, and their leader, Judas, led a violent revolution that successfully drove the Seleucids out of control. Judas was given the title Maccabeus (hammer), and what he began as a guerilla war became a full-scale military engagement in which smaller Jewish forces defeated larger Syrian armies.

Finally, Judas Maccabeus recaptured Jerusalem, cleansed the temple, and rededicated the altar (164 BCE). Legend says that there was only enough oil in the sacred fire (menorah) to last one day, but miraculously, it lasted eight days. This eight-day celebration continues annually to this very day, known as Hanukkah, or the Feast of Dedication. Thus, Israel enjoyed a period of political, social, and religious independence from 164–63 BCE—that is, until the Roman general Pompey arrived to annex this new colony to his already conquered territories.

Scholars conclude that the Old Testament book of Daniel was actually composed during this stressful but victorious time, although narratively set in the time of the Babylonian exile. For example, the "abomination that makes desolate" reference in Daniel 11:21, and 12:11 actually refers to the Syrian building of a pagan altar upon the high altar of Judaism in the temple. Refer to the Old Testament apocryphal books of 1 and 2 Maccabees to discover a more detailed description of this eventful time in the history of Judaism.

Back to our lesson (John 10:22–30). To paraphrase, out of respect and enjoying spiritual meditation on the mystical dimensions of the theme of dedication and commitment following persecution and desolation, Jesus was walking in circles within the temple walls, genuinely seeking to merge his prayer life with the inspiring story of Judas Maccabeus and his heroic witness to the mission of this his ancestral nation of Israel.

Committed as he is to his mission to show forth the grace and truth of his Father God's love for his creation, Jesus ponders his options for faithful and effectual bonding with this community, with his neighbors who are also his family in inherited faith and who, like him, express their own wonder and vision of the reality emerging every year in their faithful observance of this Feast of Dedication.

Suddenly, Jesus finds his reverie interrupted. He realizes he is being encircled by his fellow meditators whose minds and souls are also deep in contemplation. They are genuinely drawn to him, and their voices begin to reach him and beckon him from his quietude. Not once, not twice, but slowly and repeatedly he becomes aware of their needs, their consternations, their weariness, their puzzlement.

They experience separate musings and questions arising out of themselves, seeking him to hear and answer, seeking to reach far beyond him to their common spiritual parent, their Father God. Gradually, their tones and gestures, their breaths and sighs begin to coagulate into a plea too deep for words and yet a plea needing, demanding, begging to be heard and taken seriously.

The Greek language here is notoriously difficult, if not impossible, to translate, but here goes a try: "Altogether there arises a cry of anguish, of desperation, of suffering curiosity so painful Jesus is both overwhelmed and speechless as he realizes their longing." In literal translation, "How long will you keep holding our lives in the palm of your hand, our souls in agonizing suspense? If you are the Messiah, the savior and deliverer of Israel, please, please why don't you tell us openly and plainly?" This is a cry of desperation, so hopeful and yet so longingly suspicious, so fearful of an answer they will be unable to assess and assimilate positively. And so they wait, eager yet fearful of Jesus's reply.

Jesus cannot smile or frown or weep or remain silent. He sits down, in his teaching mode, and gradually constructs his words. Cautiously but sincerely, they emerge, "I have already told you. I have been telling you. Over and over I have told you, but you do not hear. Why do you not hear? Because I speak through the works that I do, and you do not trust what you hear in my works. Do not listen to what comes out of my mouth. Listen to the works I do in the name of my Father, because these works point away from me and to my

Farther. And this is how I tell you who I am, when I show you my Father who sends me here so that I do his works."

At this time, it may be helpful to review the subject to which Jesus points his listeners here—his works. John, the Gospel writer, presents Jesus's works in the form of seven or eight signs, which do not call attention to the signs themselves or to Jesus himself but which point away to the one who initiates and works through Jesus, God the Father. Recall this list of signs:

1. John 21–11—In Cana of Galilee, Jesus turns water into wine.
2. John 4:46–54—Jesus heals the royal official's son.
3. John 5:1–18—Jesus heals a lame man.
4. John 6:1–14—Jesus feeds five thousand with loaves of bread and fish.
5. John 6:16–21—Jesus walks on the sea.
6. John 9:1–41—Jesus heals a blind man.
7. John 11:1–44—Jesus raises Lazarus from the dead.
8. John 21:1–14 (epilogue)—Jesus engineers the miraculous catch of fish.

Why do Jesus's listeners not trust his works to provide the answer they seek? Why when he gives them the answer he has ready for them do they not trust in his works, these signs to serve as his best answer? He says the reason they do not trust is because they do not belong to his sheepfold. It will be helpful here to review the larger context for Jesus's words here (John 10:1–21). Using the metaphor of the shepherd and his sheepfold, Jesus describes the intimate, trusting relationship the sheep have with their shepherd because of the shepherd's ownership of his flock and his commitment of his own life, if necessary, to ensure his flock's health and well-being. This is a good, strong example of the Gospel writer John's smooth integration of theology, Christology, and ecclesiology. All the Gospel message is summarized in this passage, and this message originates and flows out of the prior initiatives of God the Father who sends Jesus the shepherd to do God's works. This is the answer Jesus's hearers should accept, absorb, and trust.

But they, Jesus's listeners, are preconditioned, for whatever reasons, probably cultural, social, and ethnic environmental forces, as well as false spiritual influences. And thus, they insist on hearing Jesus give them the kind of answer that will satisfy their already deeply engraved expectations and demands. They trust what they normally, naturally expect and demand to hear, not what God the Father is sending to them in his Son, Jesus of Nazareth (cf. the disciple Nathaniel's sarcastic question in John 1:46).

In this standoff, of course, we should be prepared to anticipate the parallel dilemma of the disciple Thomas (John 20:24–29). Thomas demands the evidence his eyes and head are prepared to accept and none other. Jesus does not reprimand Thomas for his self-centeredness but instead offers Thomas himself and the prior knowledge of his having been chosen and endowed with the grace and truth, which he is called to embrace and to trust. Thomas responds not with persistent demands that Jesus meet and deliver on his terms but instead with the strongest and most emphatic profession of faith in all the four Gospels: "My Lord and my God!" Thomas remembers he belongs to Jesus's sheepfold and, above all other influences, trusts his shepherd's lordship, which he recognizes in Jesus's works, that is, in his evidences of his crucifixion. This shepherd has indeed laid down his life for his sheep.

The context provides hopeful ambiguity. In John 10:19–21, to paraphrase, Jesus's use of the shepherding metaphor is powerfully ringing in some ears. After all, rural, agricultural images pervade the Bible from one end to the other. Why? Because with all the difficulty Jesus has in penetrating his listeners' dull and rigid minds, he is God the Father's spokesperson knows and is equipped to speak with simple, down-to-earth references and involvements, which are normally and inevitably inclusive of their milieu and spiritual dimensions of experience. We read that the Jews, his listeners, are divided on their response. Some accuse him of being obsessed by a demon, to them a suitable explanation of why he does not say and show what they are prepared to receive. Stuck in their intellectual and spiritual fossils, they utter, "He is out of his mind. Why listen to this false prophet?"

Others, however, conclude, "These words cannot possibly come from one who has a demon. Can a demon open the eyes of the blind?" In other words, some of the Jews do indeed pay attention to Jesus's works and find them trustworthy, which means some of them do indeed belong to the flock that knows the voice of their shepherd and trusts this shepherd will lay down his life if necessary to save them from the ravenous wolves. Jesus explains his works testify to him, communicating who he is, and these works invite and call for trust. Not for proof or evidence or report or description that removes human life from the central relationship of belonging to the sheep-fold and trusting and benefiting from the shepherd's ownership and protection from all danger. No shortcuts, please.

This is why Jesus promises, "My sheep hear my voice. I know them, and they follow [trust] me. I give them eternal life, and they will never perish. No one will ever snatch them out of my hand. This is because what the Father gives me is greater than all else, and no one can snatch it out of the Father's hand. The Father and I are one."

The Greek word for *one* is not in the masculine gender, which you might expect if Jesus is arguing issues of identity as a suitable answer his listeners demand to get him to prove to their satisfaction of just who he is, especially that he is the Messiah. The Greek word for *one* (*hen*) here is neuter in gender. This means Jesus is stressing that he and his Father God are united in purpose, program, and mission.

Every listener is called and invited to trust that who God the Father is and what he is doing and aims to achieve in his creative powers and works is exactly the same for his Son, Jesus, who, for this reason, is indeed the Messiah, the anointed one whom to know is to know God the Father, and vice versa.

And when we truly seek to trust this is the truth, we are invited to listen to what God the Father is communicating when we hear, see, recognize the works his Son, Jesus, does, both in the seven (or eight) signs Jesus works prominently in this Gospel and, even more, especially in Jesus's glorification works (suffering, rejection, crucifixion, resurrection, and ascension). We are all, every one of us, invited to hear, welcome, and trust this great, good news of the love of God the Father, who, in Jesus's works, showers upon his creation new life that has overcome all death, all suffering, and all warfare for all eternity.

Lesson Twenty-Three: Fifth Sunday of Easter; Read John 13:31–35

This lesson appears in the fourth Gospel narrative early in these five chapters when Jesus's struggles with the Jewish authorities in Jerusalem have subsided somewhat and Jesus takes his disciple band aside to counsel them, teach them, and pray for/with them (John 13–17). Earlier, Jesus was under attack because he would not use the words his opponents demanded to hear in order to prove he was the Messiah. Instead, he pointed to his works as more expressive than his words, but his opponents do not hear because they do not belong to his sheepfold, do not know his voice, and have no trust in his role as shepherd to suffice for his role as Messiah (John 10).

Since this was the arrival of the Feast of Dedication, we may assume his detractors expected/demanded Jesus to portray himself along the lines of a Judas Maccabeus, the military general who repelled the Seleucids and brought political/social peace to Judaea through militaristic success. Since Jesus does from time to time refer to himself as the Son of Man (apocalyptic military victor), Jesus may actually contribute to the ambiguity concerning his role/responsibility. When he minimizes his words that he will not deliver and puts emphasis upon his works, which he insists show forth all they need to know about him as the Messiah, Jesus, of course, is trying to show forth his new different role and function as the Messiah, who most certainly does not fit his opponents' fossilized images of themselves, their nation as God's chosen people, and their promised Messiah.

Jesus, of course, throughout this fourth Gospel, brings a shockingly new reality to work among his Father God's chosen people, exactly when the eternal Logos, God himself, becomes human flesh and moves in to live and work in order to show the grace and truth God's people lack and need (John 1:1–18). It is no accident then that Jesus saves his seventh and final sign to show his work as Lord and Savior of all humankind during this time of his teaching and counseling in Jerusalem. This seventh sign is the raising of his friend Lazarus from the dead (John 11:1–44).

Jesus explains the significance of this work to Lazarus's sister Martha, "I am the resurrection and the life. Those who believe in me [who belong to my sheepfold], even though they die, will live, and everyone who lives and believes in me will never die. Do you believe this, Martha?"

Martha answers, "Yes, Lord, I believe that you are the Messiah, the Son of God, the one coming into the world."

In other words, Jesus speaks a few words (e.g., "Lazarus, come forth!"), but he speaks loudly with his work, his behavior, his love, which his Father God sends forth and shares with his son, who brings new life where there has been death.

This new persona and love bringer is a far cry from the models of the Messiah Israel inherits from the legendary, charismatic, yet limited figure of King David and, more recently, the spectacularly victorious Judas Maccabeus. Bound as these Judaeans are to subservience to the Roman Empire, it is understandable they recall King David and King Solomon's victories against their enemies. But they are unprepared to loosen up, wake up, repent, recognize, and welcome the love of their same ancient Creator God, who is taking great leaps forward to offer them and work among them to shower them with deliverance from evil and with salvation and to bless them with resurrection to eternal life.

It is appropriate to look ahead to Jesus's definition of eternal life: "And this is eternal life, that they may know you, the only true God, and Jesus Christ, whom you have sent. I glorified you on earth by finishing the work you sent me to do." Notice there is no reference here to calendar time or quantifiable measurements of chronology, but there is a huge focus upon the quality of life raised from death and described as intimate knowledge and relationship centered upon the Creator's faithful fulfillment of all his promises and the response and participation in this relationship based upon the human creature's trust and love joyously received and returned to the Lord and Savior of all the world (John 3:16).

With these contextual preparations in mind, we turn to this lesson (John 13:31–35) assigned to the fifth Sunday of the Easter season. Jesus is celebrating the Feast of Passover with his disciple band. It is no accident that the Gospel writer John deviates from the Synoptic Gospels' emphasis upon the bread and wine, keeping Jesus's glorification closely aligned with the ancient Jewish liturgy based upon sacrifice.

Here, Jesus recognizes that his glorification begins and is taking place, not with the traditional Passover liturgy that celebrates the deliverance of Israel from Egyptian slavery but with an entirely new liturgical activity, gesture, behavior that presents the Lord and Savior of all humankind as a humble servant. No doubt Simon Peter is not the only disciple present who is amazed, aghast, and blown away by the sight of his rabbinical master, his Lord and Savior, stooping down to wash his disciples' dirty feet. This was a role reserved for the lowest servant or slave in the household. Jesus's attempt to explain and counsel his fellow worshippers may do little to assuage his disciples' surprise and consternation. But they, after all, are members of his sheepfold who know his voice and trust his protection of them from all the ravenous wolves and other enemies whom they must face now in this process of glorification and far beyond.

And so after the departure of Judas Iscariot, Jesus begins to counsel/teach his disciples, seeking both to comfort them, to allay their anxiety, and to challenge them to open up to Jesus's works (e.g., his washing of their feet) rather than remain stuck in expecting his words to suffice. The Greek verb *dokxazo*, "to glorify," is used here both in the passive voice and in the active voice. To paraphrase, "We are witnesses to God's eternal decrees, as if to say, God has planned from before creation to send his Son in the flesh who will love this human race through his humble service. This is a necessary and eternal dimension of who God is and how much God loves his entire creation."

At the same time, however, to continue this paraphrase, "God is alive and his Son is alive, and what transpires in this narrative involves the free, spontaneous decisions and actions of all the participants. Jesus's glorification begins here with his farewell process of both leaving and supporting his disciples and proceeds to this personal suffering and agonies, his arrest and persecutions, his crucifixion and burial, and his resurrection and ascension."

Jesus turns to his disciples. "Little children," he addresses them, probably recognizing in them both affection and family dependencies and reminding them of their need to always think of themselves as humble servants, never as superior, cruel despots, in their mission responsibilities. Although he has tried to prepare them along the way for this moment of glorification, he knows all too well how much they are experiencing anxiety and even trauma in their sincere yet awesome awareness of what lies ahead.

"Little children, I shall be here with you only a short time. You will be searching for me, and as I told the Jews and now I tell you, where I am going you cannot go." To paraphrase more, "But there is something very important and helpful I can leave with you. Listen to me now. I want to leave a new commandment with you. This is my new commandment—that you love one another. Just as I have loved you all, so my love means for you that you must love one another. I know you love me, but I am going away. Now you must love one another, all of you, sisters and brothers. When you do this, obey my commandment and love one another, guess what? Everyone will see and know you love one another, and this will show them that you are my disciples. This way, you will witness to me and my love for this world, when you love one another. This, my love, will merge with your love, and all together we shall share our great Father God's love with his entire creation and especially with all of us, human beings, whom he creates in his very own image and likeness."

Notice, Jesus does not command his disciples to pay their taxes, to keep the Sabbath holy, or to bring their sacrifices to the temple as expected. He does not command them to pay their temple tax. He does not command them to be regular in synagogue attendance. He does not command them to honor their father and mother. He does not command them to be loyal to the Jewish officials, priests, and Sadducees. He does not command them to feed the hungry, heal the sick, welcome the stranger, visit the prisoner, clothe the naked, or give water to the thirsty.

And Jesus continues to counsel his disciples. Moving beyond this lesson alone, we hear him speak this way, "As the Father has loved me, so I have loved you. Abide in my love. If you keep my commandments, you will abide in my love, just as I have kept my Father's commandments and abide in His love. I have said these things to you so that my joy may be in you and that your joy may be complete" (John 15:9–11).

And Jesus has still more encouragement, "This is my commandment, that you love one another as I have loved you. No one has greater love than this, to lay down one's life for one's friends. You are my friends if you do what I command you. I do not call you servants any longer because the servant does not know what the master is doing, but I have called you friends because I have made known to you everything that I have heard from my Father. You did not choose me, but I chose you. And I appointed you to go and bear fruit, fruit that will last, so that the Father will give you whatever you ask him in my name. I am giving you these commandments so that you may love one another" (John 15:12–17).

Lesson Twenty-Four: Sixth Sunday of Easter; Read John 14:23–29

This short lesson highlights two foundational realities that permeate chapters 13–17, the extended Farewell Discourses between Jesus and his disciples. The first issue arises in the question of Judas (not Iscariot) in 14:22: "Lord, how is it possible that you say you are about to reveal yourself to us and not to the world?" As is usually the case in these discourses, one disciple speaks for all disciples. These disciples are finally beginning to understand the reality of their Father God's eternal Logos becoming flesh, living with and among the human race in order to reveal the eternal grace and truth (John 1:14–18). And this means this revelation is aimed at and for the whole world (John 3:16–21).

Now when Jesus speaks of going away, leaving them, and returning to live and be with them, it sounds as if this new future presence will be some kind of esoteric, gnostic-style, secretive reality, aimed not at the world but at a restricted enclave of privileged spiritual aristocrats who alone will receive, possess, and control the great love of God. In other words, these disciples are gradually catching on, hearing, and understanding the reality and meaning of Jesus's glorification, his career, including his incarnation, healing/teaching ministry, arrest, suffering, trials, crucifixion, resurrection, ascension, and now strong emphasis upon his return to be with them in the Pentecostal presence of the Holy Spirit living and working in, among, and through them.

It is growing from and out of this realization and understanding that this gut-wrenching question cuts through their minds and hearts and pleads for attention and for an answer that relieves their anxiety, comforts them in their ignorance and doubt that threatens trust, and reassures them that their calling and now promised continued discipleship will fulfill all of Jesus's promises to them. There are three answers or solutions to their dilemma that John, the narrator, provides in the teaching and counsel Jesus offers in this chapter (John 14:1–31).

First is the serious and profound demonstration that Jesus speaks and teaches them from out of his deeply spiritual worldview, full of symbolism and double, if not triple, entendre, while his disciples operate out of an empirical, temporal, simplistic milieu of normal, everyday experiences and expectations. Thus, Jesus begins his counsel with this story line: "Do not let your hearts be troubled. Believe in God, believe also in me. In my Father's house, there are many dwelling places. If it were not so, would I have told you that I go to prepare a place for you? And if I go and prepare a place for you, I will come again and will take you to myself so that where I am, there you may be also. And you know the way to the place where I am going" (John 14:1–4).

Now Thomas (Greek translation of an Aramaic word meaning "twin"), he of two personalities united in one body, speaks from his natural, skeptical curiosity, "Lord, we do not know where you are going. How can we know the way?"

Jesus answers Thomas this way, "I am the way and the truth and the life. Everyone who comes to the Father, without exception, comes through me. If you know me, you will know my Father also. From now on, you do know him and have seen him." Does this answer satisfy Thomas?

The disciple Philip now joins the interrogation panel. "Lord, show us the Father, and we will be satisfied."

Jesus replies, "I have been with you all this time, Philip, and you still do not know me? Whoever has seen me has seen the Father. How can you say 'Show us the Father'? Do you not believe that I am in the Father and the Father is in me? The words that I say to you I do not speak on my own, but the Father who dwells in me does his works. Believe me that I am in the Father and the Father is in me, but if you do not, then believe me because of the works themselves" (John 4:8–11).

This movement from words to works grows out of Jesus's earlier words: "I give you a new commandment, that you love one another. Just as I have loved you, you also should love one another. By this, everyone will know that you are my disciples, if you have love for one another" (John 13:34–35). Jesus now connects with his earlier commandment: "Those who love me will keep my word, and my Father will love them. And we will come to them and make our home with them. Whoever does not love me does not keep my words, and I remind you what I say to you does not originate with me but comes to you through me from the Father who sent me" (John 4:23–24).

In other words, John, the narrator, makes sure Jesus invites his disciples to continue to struggle with the deep symbolism and linguistic complexities in their time of transition, as Jesus and they together move into and through Jesus's glorification here on this earth. But this process of participation in Jesus's glorification is not primarily or only a struggle going on within the head and heart, as important as spiritual communion is to the mutual bonding and commitment taking place and continuing to grow between Jesus and his disciple band.

And so the second part of Jesus's answer to his disciple Judas points strongly to the new commandment to love one another, even and especially when this means to lay down your life for another. Words may be the first contacts between Jesus and his disciples, but their behavior, their works, their witness, and their obedience in work as well as intention will prevent this new movement from atrophying or shrinking itself into a private, self-centered, isolated spiritual movement. Jesus puts this second part of his answer this way, "Very truly I tell you, the one who believes in me will also do the works that I do and, in fact, will do greater works than these because I am going to the Father." (This strong affirmation assumes the challenge or dilemma with words—that is, Jesus's two-level or multilevel process of communication has been smoothed out and his disciples are understanding his teachings.) Jesus continues, "Because I am going to the Father, I will do whatever you ask in my name so that the Father may be glorified in the Son. If in my name you ask me for anything, I will do it" (John 14:12–14).

This promises of works and even greater works means that Jesus's disciples are indeed obeying his new commandment, that they love one another just as he has first loved them. "They who have my commandments and keep them are those who love me, and those who love me will be loved by the father. And I will love them and reveal myself to them" (John14:21).

This means it is time for the third dimension of Jesus's response to Judas's question.

"And I will ask the Father, and he will give you another Advocate, to be with you forever. This is the Spirit of truth, whom the world cannot receive because it neither sees him nor knows him. You know him because he abides with you, and he will be in you" (John14:16–17). "But the Advocate, the Holy Spirit, whom the Father will send in my name, will teach you everything and remind you of all that I have said to you" (John14:26).

The word translated *advocate* or *encourager* here in English is *ho parakletos* in Greek. This is a compound word, first the prefix *para*, which means "alongside or parallel or beside or adjacent to or in tandem with, as in a partnership." Then the suffix *kletos*, from the verb *kaleo*, which means "call, beckon, invite, encourage, comfort, promote, or advocate." Jesus assures his disciples, "I will not leave you orphans. I am coming to you" (John 14:18). Then he promises this, "The Advocate, the Holy Spirit, will be forever with you." And this means, to paraphrase, "Peace I leave with you, my very own peace I give to you. And note well, I do not give you the same kind of peace the systems of this world give you. My peace is the presence of God our Father's love, which invites your love in response for each other and for the love giver. This means you should not let your hearts be troubled or let them be afraid. Because you love me, you should now rejoice because I am going to the Father" (John 14:26–28).

The Greek word here translated *peace* is *he eirene* (feminine) and points to harmony instead of disharmony, order rather than chaos, or resolution of conflicts such as those which agitate Jesus's disciples throughout his Farewell Discourses (John 12–17). In this context, however, this promised peace does not mean an end to the serious implications of tough love or an end to costly obedience or an end to the realities of Jesus's glorification—teaching/healing, arrest, suffering, trials, crucifixion, resurrection, ascension, etc., including the promised soon arrival of the Holy Spirit, who will move and dwell within and among these all-too-human disciples, now called to discipleship in new and challenging venues.

Lesson Twenty-Five: Seventh Sunday of Easter; Read John 17:20–26

This lesson consists of the concluding statements of Jesus's Farewell Discourses with his disciples, beginning with chapter 13. Let's check out the context the narrator provides in 17:1–19. Here, Jesus enters deep and profound prayer on behalf of the world and his disciples. This chapter in popular parlance is referred to as Jesus's High Priestly Prayer. Jesus seeks to describe the tension between himself and his disciples and the world, creation, which provides the universal context for his career on earth (his glorification). Perhaps a glance back to the prologue (John 1:1–18) will remind us of the Gospel writer John's big picture or the background against and out of which Jesus's earthly career unfolds.

The timeless, eternal, universal reality of God the Word, who creates all that exists, carries echoes of Genesis 1–3. This creation is very good. Life and light are its principal characteristics, but there is also darkness and a built-in tension/dualism between this light and this darkness, such that the light shines across this creation and the darkness does not overtake the light. The light prevails. This tension appears somehow to be a built-in characteristic of this good, healthy, God-centered/endowed creation.

But to make sure the light prevails over darkness and to bring about this prevalence of the light, the Word himself becomes human flesh and moves into the history of this creation, in order to facilitate knowledge and trust over ignorance and rebellion. This presence of the Word reveals grace and truth, the purpose and intention of the eternal God, so that all creation, especially human beings, have opportunity to choose light and love rather than darkness and evil.

John 3:16–22 is this Gospel writer's classic capsule summary of this cosmic scenario. Back to John 17:1–19. To paraphrase, "Dear Father, the time has arrived when you will glorify me here and now on earth. And this glorification means I shall soon be returning to you, taking leave of my earthly career here in the flesh, so that you and I together will resume the glorification we enjoyed before the foundation of the world.

"But I am concerned about my disciples whom you have called out of the world and given to me to cultivate, teach, and include within the processes of my glorification. You know them very well. They are not perfect, but they have struggled with your revelation in me, and this means you have brought them to eternal life, because they now know you and trust in your great love and creative purposes as you have revealed yourself in me and my works here among them.

"Of course, dear Father, your love and creative purposes are for the whole world, the whole creation. And I remember very well you are investing and spreading your love all across time and space, because your aim is to make all things new [Revelation 21:5]. Without in any way minimizing your love for the whole world, the creation as a whole, dear Father, right now I pray for your attention on behalf of those whom you have given to me. They of course belong to you, as well as to me, and they share my glorification. I have protected them, and we have lost only one, which happened in order that the scripture might be fulfilled. Now I ask you, dear Father, protect and guard them in your name that you have given me so that they may be one, united, as you and I are one.

"I ask these blessings upon them from you while I am still here in this world. But I will soon leave to return to your eternal presence, and I plead for them, that they may be joyful in their discipleship and obedience, as you and I are joyful together. I have given them your word, and the world has hated them because they do not belong to the world, just as I do not belong to the world. I am not asking you to take them out of the world, but I do ask you to protect them from the evil one. Make them strong through your Holy Spirit in your word, which is truth. As you have sent me into the world, so I am sending them into the world. As I dedicate myself to the work of your Holy Spirit, so make sure that my sanctification belongs to them as well."

Now we arrive at our lesson for this week, John 17:20. To continue to paraphrase, "I pray not only for my present disciples but also on behalf of those who will hear their words and believe in me through their labors of witness. As you, dear Father, are in me and I am in you, may these followers, these next generations of disciples, also be in us so that the world may hear and trust that you have sent me. The glory that you have given me I have given to them so that they may be one, that is, united in purpose and work, as we are one. I pray that as you and I are one, so they may become completely one so that the world may know that you have sent me and have loved them just as you have loved me.

"Gracious Father, the world does not know you, but I know you, and I have made sure that my dear disciples know you have sent me and thus know you as well. I have made your name known to them, and I shall continue to make your name known to them so that the love with which you have loved me shall indeed be in them as I am in them."

It is important to recognize that this intercessory prayer is not addressed to the disciples themselves but only and always directly to God the Father. This is Jesus's prayer about them and for them. However, they are not excluded from Jesus's presence during this lengthy prayer spoken for them and their successors who will follow them in future decades (and centuries).

This means that at this point, it is prudent to remember how this prayer reflects the new commandment Jesus gives to his disciples: "I give you a new commandment, that you love one another. Just as I have loved you, you also should love one another. By this, everyone will know you are my disciples, if you have love for one another" (John 13:34–35).

If Jesus's disciples are overhearing his intercessory prayer, they should hear loudly and clearly Jesus's recognition that their future behavior does not and can never depend upon their initiative, their dedication, or their fulfillment alone. Rather, they will always and everywhere be dependent upon the initiative and empowerment of God the Father, just as is the case with Jesus himself. This is why Jesus's words repeatedly plead with his Father God to continue to love the world and his chosen disciples with the same love that sent his Son to become flesh and complete his glorification now moving toward fulfillment. The next installment will be the continuation of this glorification in the lives and works of these disciples as well as those who follow them. Jesus in effect prays to God the Father to fulfill the promise Jesus makes in John 14:12, "Very truly I tell you, the one who believers in me will do the works I do and, in fact, will do greater works than these because I am going to the Father."

Jesus's disciples should trust this promise because Jesus trusts the God who listens and hears every word of his great High Priestly Prayer.

It is perhaps helpful at this point in our study of John 17:20–26 to recall the emblem, international symbol, of the World Council of Churches. This is a ship at sea under full sail, with no human rowers providing energy to propel the ship across the tumultuous waves, but with a bright, sunny sky above, filled with clouds, and winds blowing briskly through the extended sails so that with this heavenly wind (the presence and work of the Holy Spirit), this vessel never slows down, never deviates from its prescribed course, but always moves briskly forward across the seven seas.

CHAPTER FIVE

The Season of Pentecost

Lesson Twenty-Six: Day of Pentecost or Whitsunday; Read Acts 2:1–21, John 15:26–27 and 15:4b–15

There is one Pentecost Sunday in my life I shall never forget. On that Sunday morning, I was awakened by loud singing outside my hotel window. It was 4:30 a.m., still dark outside. From my hotel balcony, I gazed down upon fifty-five or so young men dancing arm in arm in a lively circle and singing, with vigor, in robust Hebrew. Turns out these were rabbinical students from a nearby *yeshiva* (theological seminary) celebrating the Festival of *Shavout* (Pentecost) of the fiftieth day after *Pesach*, or Passover. They were dancing their way through the streets of the Old City of Jerusalem, their goal being to reach the ancient site of the Temple Mount, or the Western/Wailing Wall.

What was originally an agricultural festival to celebrate spring fruits of labor, such as wheat and baby lambs, Shavout, grew over the passing years to celebrate the arrival of the former Israeli slaves following the exodus and their journey from Egypt to Mount Sinai and especially the gift of the Torah, the highlight of their storied sojourn on that legendary mountain. That journey consumed seven weeks, or forty-nine days, and so on the fiftieth day after Passover, their arrival at Mount Sinai turns attention from delivery out of slavery to the divine gift of the law, Torah, and especially all that the Ten Commandments came to symbolize in their movement from bondage to freedom as the people of God.

Needless to say, these young aspiring rabbis who disturbed my sleep with their unforgettable enthusiasm soon reached their goal, and all day long the streets of the Old City rang with the voices of many pilgrims who every year come to Jerusalem to celebrate the freedom, justice, and benevolence that the Torah embodies for all Jews, worldwide, especially after the destruction of the second temple by the Romans in 70 CE.

On the next Christian Sabbath, Sunday, I worshipped in an Anglican Charismatic Church, nearby in the Old City, a sanctuary with all inscriptions in Hebrew and no visible Christian symbols, such as a crucifix, etc. This congregation was a mission project from Western Anglican (Church of England) Christianity seeking to make the experience of the Holy Spirit the only language necessary to share the reality of the divine gift of salvation. During this unforgettable Christian version of Shavout, or Pentecost, my thoughts, while very positive, included such observations as "This certainly isn't Presbyterian!"

But I was stimulated to reread Luke 24:44–49, where Jesus instructs his disciples to remain in Jerusalem until God sends his Holy Spirit, as he has promised, so they may witness what God is up to, no longer stuck with the Torah alone but moving forward to new realities of salvation, which the Holy Spirit provides. That is to say, when God's Holy Spirit descends upon them, then they shall be empowered to proclaim this good news, repentance and forgiveness of sins, to all nations.

In other words, the Gospel writer Luke is already preparing his readers for the long-range goal of Jesus's career, that his ministry, his works propel him forward in and through his struggles with opposition and especially his crucifixion and resurrection, to extend the presence and saving love of God, his heavenly Father, not only to the natives of his homeland and to the nearby foreign soils of Galilee and Syria but also all the way to the ends of the earth (Acts 12:8).

And this is why the risen Jesus makes such a point of insisting that his disciples remain in Jerusalem until they are baptized with the Holy Spirit, clothed with power from on high, in order that repentance and forgiveness of sins shall be proclaimed in his name to all nations, beginning in Jerusalem (Luke 24:47–49 and Acts 1:4–5).

Notice his disciples are, understandably, still thinking of the people of Israel as the center of God's work in world history. They ask their own normal, predictable question, "Lord, is this the time when you will restore the kingdom to Israel?"

Jesus tries to let them down gently. "It is not for you to know the times or periods that the Father has set by his own authority." In other words, God the Father does not plan to follow their all too traditional agenda but, instead, has a much more ambitious plan in mind, and this vision means a much better prospectus runs this way: "You will receive power when the Holy Spirit has come upon you, and you will be my witnesses in Jerusalem, in all Judaea and Samaria, and to the ends of the earth" (Acts 1:6–8).

In other words, do not continue to think of Jerusalem as the center of the universe. God's work even now already begins here in Jerusalem but soon will be propelled outward from Jerusalem, not slowing down until this great, good news reaches all the way to the ends of the earth (symbolized by the apostle Paul's arrival in the capital city of Rome).

Content to wait, this disciple band, including others attracted to their promised mission settle down in their upper room, share prayers of anticipation, and tend to some necessary housekeeping chores (Acts 1:12–26). Soon their patient waiting ends. To paraphrase, "The promised blessing arrives on the Day of Pentecost. Suddenly, without warning, from heaven, the sound of violent winds rushes among them, shaking their house from floor to ceiling and rattling each one, head to toe. And they see tongues, divided as flames of fire, sitting on top of each other. The violent wind takes hold of them, and they begin to speak in other languages as the Spirit fills them to overflowing with ability to utter these new tongues. This rising chorus fills the rafters, shakes them all from top to bottom, and spills out the windows unto the streets.

"Now because of the obligations associated with these two festivals, Passover and Pentecost, Jerusalem is packed with pilgrims, devout Jews from every nation under heaven. As this house begins literally to 'shake, rattle, and roll,' street traffic gathers outside, gazing in amazement, bewildered because each person, from all across the known world, can hear these witnesses speaking each one in his or her native tongue.

"A cry rises out of this gathered crowd: 'Hey, what's going on here? All these guys and gals are Galileans, are they not?' Befuddled, confused, and intrigued all at once, they beg to know what in the world is happening. 'How is it that we can hear and understand what they are saying, each one of us in the language in which we were born?'"

They begin to take inventory, looking around to identify the home territory of everyone in this growing multitude assembled to gawk and gasp at this phenomenon, this miraculous cacophony sweeping through the city of Jerusalem. One by one, they call out their home territories: Parthian, Medes, Elamites, Mesopotamia, Judaea, Cappadocia, Pontus, Asia, Phrygia and Pamphylia, Egypt, parts of Libya belonging to Cyrene, visitors from Rome, both Jews and proselytes, Cretans and Arabs. An amazing assembly of so many foreign citizens drawn together to share these two festivals. They can agree, all together, that they are hearing these Galileans speak to them, each one, in his or her native language, telling or witnessing to the great and mighty acts of God. But in their amazement and perplexity, they discover they cannot answer this common question: "What can this possibly mean?"

This jolly, rollicking, ecstatic frolic, which mesmerizes all observers, of course, prompts one or two rascals to mock this whole scene, all too sure these overly wordy Galileans are simply full of new wine. Simon Peter to the rescue: "Citizens of Jerusalem, I hear some of you suspicious that new wine may be flowing. We remember how Jesus of Nazareth favored good new wine as a gift of God [John 2:1–11], but no wine is flowing here yet today because it is still early morning. Maybe later this afternoon."

Simon Peter continues, "Here is the truth! This cascading cacophony of languages from near and far is actually the fulfillment of the vision and promise given by God to the ancient prophet Joel. These are the last days, not chronologically, but the times of fulfillment, completion, when God's promises come true. In times past, our God gave laws. Now our God sends his Spirit, pours out his Spirit on all flesh. When your sons and daughters receive this Spirit, they shall prophesy. This does not mean they foretell the future, but it means they share this Spirit with everyone so that everyone knows the truth about our great God and hears of his great love and how he is fulfilling his promises not to the Jews only but to the whole world."

Simon has more to share. "Contrary to what is normal or expected, even young men lacking the wisdom of age shall see visions already in their youth and old men, jaded with age, shall not cease to dream but shall dream new dreams. Even upon slaves, both women and men, God shall freely pour his Spirit so they, too, shall share, shouting out loud the salvation our God brings in these last days.

"Even the heavens above, the earth below, the mountains and valleys, the sun and the moon, all creation shall trumpet the coming of the day of the Lord so that everyone, not the high and mighty, not the rich and powerful, not only the perfect and purified, but anyone and everyone who calls upon the name of the Lord shall be saved, shall receive the blessing of our Lord's eternal peace in the arrival of our Lord's promised new heavens and new earth" (Revelation 21:5).

This somewhat elaborate characterization of the Lukan Pentecostal event shows provincial Galileans suddenly empowered to speak languages readily heard and understood by a long, extended list of pilgrims from all across the known world. God's Holy Spirit does not ignore or eliminate cultural differences from his modus operandi but, on the contrary, moves in and inhabits cultural differences, co-ops them, in this case different languages, so that these cultural differences become working instruments, tools valuable and necessary in order to make witness real and true. It is worth remembering that the Hebrew *Torah* insists one time that "you shall love your neighbor as yourself" (Leviticus 19:16–18), while there are many, perhaps innumerable, examples throughout the Hebrew canon that insist upon love for the alien or the stranger whom you may encounter.

We discover here that the Gospel writer Luke uses the Jewish liturgical calendar to anchor the arrival and ministry of the Holy

Spirit, as promised, following Jesus's ascension. The book of the Acts of the Apostles, Luke's second volume, traces the new work of the Holy Spirit most profoundly in the expansion of covenant bonding far beyond Judaism and most notably to the Gentiles. One hears the apostle Paul's polemic in his letter to the Galatians running all the way through Luke's narrative, which reaches its climax with Paul's residency in Rome, "the ends of the earth." The Acts of the Apostles are really and truly the acts of the Holy Spirit, which Jesus promised before his ascension in order that his disciples can become witnesses to the salvation worked out in the life, teachings, suffering, death, resurrection, and ascension of Jesus, the fulfillment of the eternal vision and work of God the Father.

We turn now to the writer of the fourth Gospel (John 15:26–27 and 16:4b–51) who has less, if any, use for the Jewish Festival of Pentecost as a hermeneutical catalyst because when he writes, his contemporaries are being expelled from the synagogues and thus excluded from participation in the Festival of Shavout. The writer John is motivated to explore universal dimensions and perspectives, not denying Jesus's Judaism but looking forward to the Holy Spirit of God working to move outward from Judaism to encompass all creation.

The promised arrival of the Holy Spirit in John's Gospel, therefore, does not wait seven weeks for the arrival of Shavout but is concurrent with Jesus's initial resurrection meetings with his disciples (John 20:19–29), when Jesus breathes the Holy Spirit upon them, bestows his peace upon them, and commissions them to the work God sends them to do as his anointed apostles.

It is no accident that throughout his Farewell Discourses (John 13–17) Jesus is teaching his disciples all they need to know and understand in order to cope with his leaving them and indeed to prosper exactly because he will soon leave them. Ironically, it is exactly what they fear the most, his absence from them, that will make available the strongest and deepest blessing they can possibly receive.

Only if and when Jesus leaves them will the Advocate come to be with them. The Greek noun translated most often as *advocate* needs exposition. The word in Greek is *ho parakletos*, literally "the one called, sent, and assigned to operate exactly beside you, in close, intimate partnership, in tandem with you." Throughout his earthly ministry/presence in human flesh, Jesus is called and sent to them and serves them when and however they need him. They are never alone. Jesus is faithful and dependable. He makes possible their covenant bonding with him and through him with his Father God.

But now Jesus is called away from them, an important part of his glorification, and being normal human beings, these disciples have grown so dependent upon the status quo they are nervous and getting very anxious as they fear being left with only his absence, with fading memories, and cast upon their own resources and strategies to survive and to thrive as his commission calls them to do. Jesus counsels them, "Because I tell you I am going away, sorrow fills your heart. But listen to the truth. It is to your advantage that I go away, for if I do not go away, the Advocate will not come to you. But if I go, I will send him to you."

Jesus promises to send the Advocate, but who will call this Advocate to serve alongside them so that they may fulfill their commission? Perhaps Jesus is inviting, encouraging his disciples themselves to call this Advocate to come join them, to serve close beside them so that the Advocate's love, will, and work become identical with theirs. Perhaps Jesus is signaling his disciples that his absence is a huge opportunity for them to step up to the plate and welcome the Holy Spirit into themselves, to merge their hearts, minds, and souls with this new companion so that their Father God's commission will motivate and call them from deep within themselves, when their calling the Advocate and Jesus sending the Advocate become one united fellowship and working presence.

This is Jesus's vision, hope, and promise for them, which means when this new reality appears, his disciples experience a huge advantage and a great leap forward as they assume their potential roles as witnesses for their Father God. Their potentiality will become actuality when Jesus goes away, when Jesus sends and they call for this Advocate, whom they welcome and whom they internalize within themselves and with whom they serve with joy and love one for the other, just as Jesus's new commandment makes clear: "I give you a new commandment, that you love one another. Just as I have loved you, you also should love one another. By this, everyone will know that you are my disciples, if you have love one for another" (John 13:34–35). None of this will happen, of course, unless and until Jesus goes away.

"But when the Advocate does arrive," Jesus continues, "which means when you and this new companion are sharing together covenantal bonding and you are faithfully witnessing to God's love and expressing your divine commission altogether, you will discover the truth [1] about human sinfulness, [2] about divine righteousness, and [3] about divine judgment." These are three problematic dimensions of human spiritual experience that need clarity, and Jesus promises this new knowledge and experience exactly because his absence elevates his disciples into more responsible participation in the eternal, universal covenant. And this promise points to fulfillment not in Jesus's return on the clouds of heaven at some future date, but soon, very soon, as Jesus leaves and as his disciples call, receive, welcome, and work in sequence with his promised Advocate. Here, John, the Gospel writer, speaking through Jesus, argues for his vision of "realized eschatology" rather than "futuristic eschatology."

But wait a minute. Jesus may have much, much more up his sleeve as he surveys the universal dimensions involved in God his Father's pending new creation. And so Jesus delivers this caveat, "I still have many things to say to you, but you cannot bear them now" (John 16:12–15). Think modern science and the universe revealed both in the Holy Bible and in the theory of evolution, just for starters. And so we are left with our own questions and too few answers, but with Jesus's promise that patience is necessary, because "when the Spirit of truth comes, he will guide you into all the truth."

Jesus sees them/us as not quite ready, still unable, perhaps all too unprepared to deal with much Jesus has yet to share. And so not all truth is present reality after all. Not yet, even when his disciples call the Advocate to their sides. There is much more to come, exactly because Jesus leaves his disciples blessed with their new calling. Perhaps we are wise to remember this climactic promise, "Look, behold, I am making all things new!" (Revelation 21:5).

Lesson Twenty-Seven: Trinity Sunday; Read Matthew 28:16–20

The word *trinity* does not appear in the New Testament, although the ideas and issues connoted by this term certainly do. Since this term is postbiblical in origin, it alerts us to the reality of how Christian development, such as the designation of the biblical canon itself, the growing schools of Christian theology, and the development of standard Christian terminologies and liturgical rituals, while postbiblical, are very much based upon or dependent upon the contents of both the Old and New Testaments.

This observation makes the passage in Matthew 18:16–20 appropriate for study and proclamation on our long entrenched "Trinity Sunday," immediately following Pentecost Sunday. Our previous study of the background for Pentecost alerted us to how thoroughly Trinitarian issues and ideas are assumed and integral to the arrival of the long-promised, expected, and necessary Holy Spirit of God, to fulfill the earlier vision of the Festival of Weeks/Shavout, long practiced in Judaism. This rings loud and true in the versions of Pentecost in Acts 2 and in John 20. Both of these Gospel writers, Luke and John, as far as we know, were writing in about 90 CE, while both Matthew and Mark wrote earlier.

Mark, the first Gospel written, and followed in outline by both Matthew and Luke, focuses primarily upon the Passion Narrative, Mark 14–15, which ends in a hasty burial by Joseph of Arimathea, to avoid corrupting Sabbath observance, and observed carefully by the women who were also present at the crucifixion. In the original ending chapter of Mark 16:1–9, these women seek to minister to the dead body of Jesus, but the tomb is empty. The angel who seeks to comfort them issues a command, "But go tell his disciples and Peter that he is going before you to Galilee. There you will see him, just as he told you." And what do these women do? "So they went out and fled from the tomb, for terror and amazement had seized them. And they said nothing to anyone, for they were afraid."

This ends the original Gospel of Mark. There is no resurrection appearance of Jesus, only a report of his resurrection and a second-hand bit of instruction to the women witnesses to what is only, but certainly, an empty tomb. The later additions to this Gospel, a short one and a longer one, seek to cover up the abrasiveness of the original and certainly sever the connection between the resurrected Jesus and his promised meeting with Peter and them all in Galilee, the land associated more with Gentiles than with Jews but most certainly the area most associated with the beginning of Jesus's ministry. The writer Mark, in other words, deliberately ends his written Gospel with the first witnesses to the empty tomb and only by implication to the risen Jesus himself, with these women witnesses who do not follow the angel's instruction to "go and tell…" but who say nothing to anyone, because they are so afraid.

Now Mark has already assured his readers of Jesus's identity and the significance of his crucifixion with this report: "Now when the centurion, who stood facing him, saw that in this way he breathed his last, he said, 'Truly this man was God's son!'" (Mark 15:39). In other words, Mark does not leave the role and mission of Jesus in any kind of doubt. But Mark does raise the question of who, beyond these women, ever hear or come to know the reality and good news of Jesus's resurrection and how they hear or learn of this accomplishment or this fulfillment to the incarnation of God's Son. Mark, who is writing near to or soon after the destruction of the Jewish temple by Rome (70 CE), places directly into the hands of his readers the question of whether or how they have come to acknowledge and have faith in this Galilean prophet, if indeed these women's fear made them 100 percent speechless.

Matthew, most likely the second Gospel writer, picks up this challenge. Which brings us to this lesson for today. Matthew's version does not deny the women's fear, shows they are all too human, like the rest of us. But he has more or different tradition to work with than does Mark. In Matthew's development of this narrative, the same women not only have fear but also great joy and, instead of adopting speechlessness, are eager to tell this good news. Matthew's narrative says, "Suddenly, Jesus met them and said, 'Greetings!' And they came to him, took hold of his feet, and worshipped him. Then Jesus said to them, 'Do not be afraid. Go and tell my brothers to go to Galilee. There they will see me'" (Matthew 28:9–10). Notice Jesus is to meet with his "brothers," not his disciples, although these are the same persons. This promised anticipated meeting or reunion is possible only because of the witness of these few women.

The eleven persons, and probably others, hear and follow the instructions Jesus sends to them through these women witnesses, and they gather on a certain mountain that Jesus has chosen and designated for this renewal conference. Matthew refers to them as "disciples," although Jesus has called them his "brothers." The Greek language suggests Jesus has set aside a certain mountain for this meeting, as if this is a highly prized invitation or command/summons to attend a top-level press conference reserved only for the privileged but responsible few. After all, this is indeed a "home calling," a reunion of the commander in chief with his few but intimate first responders who have scattered since their first shared journeys, encounters, and activities together during their journey southward from their home territory to the alien districts of Judaea and indeed to the hostile capital Jerusalem itself.

This command meeting is, after all, the first appearance of the risen Jesus to his former disciples who, when he was arrested, all deserted him and fled (Matthew 25:56). Do they still carry within them some loyalty to him? When he refers to them as his "brothers" rather than disciples, this wording suggests he has not deserted them even if they deserted him. He now summons them and note vice versa. They belong to him even if they have deserted him. And if he sees them as brothers and not only disciples, this means they are no longer primarily learners but sharers of intimate family relationship with him and with one another.

This problematic but hopeful ambiguity is reflected in the simple wording that indicates it is only when they see Jesus this moment, which is Jesus's first resurrection appearance to them, only now can they respond to his new risen reality. And their response is described by two problematic words, *worship* and *doubt*. It is probably purposefully unclear whether this dichotomy is shared by all or only by some.

A good way to understand this tension is to recognize that some of them are probably now more "brothers" than "disciples," that is, family members prepared to bring full devotion and commitment to their Lord and Master, and some are more likely still "disciples" who are still learners, not yet fully mature in their knowledge and devotion but, as disciples, still struggling to factor out their apportioned relationships. But notice, while there is recognition and acknowledgment of this range of response throughout these disciples, there is no judgment or censorship upon those who may experience doubt. Nor does this commander in chief utter even the slightest reprimand, censorship, or judgment to remind them or to call them to account for their earlier desertion of him when he was arrested.

They all together share the blessing, joy, and overwhelming experience of meeting the risen Jesus face-to-face. And Jesus welcomes them all and begins to address them for the very first time as their risen Lord. And what does Jesus have to say? "All authority in heaven and on the earth has been given to me." He could just as well have included "and under the earth" to reflect the three-storied universe then held in common as a worldview. But he intends to express universal coverage. The Greek word translated *authority* is *exousia*, as in English, "to exercise power or control, possess energy, exorcize demons or other evil powers, and thus be wholly responsible for primal origins and ultimate directions or outcomes." Notice this is not power Jesus has conjured up on his own steam or wrestled intently with severe opposition to attain. Rather, this is power that has been given to him by the one who has sent him. He is the willing recipient because he has freely laid down his life for the sin and evil of the whole world and now has been raised from the dead by the same one who sent him to die.

But the divine work is not done yet. Jesus's ascension is imminent. He will soon return to his Father in heaven. Who will now receive and assume the responsibility Jesus has performed as his portion of the divine project aimed to bring salvation from sin and evil to the whole creation? Jesus answers this question this way, to paraphrase, "Since all authority everywhere and for all times now rests with me, this is how we shall continue this divine work our Creator has inaugurated and commits himself to bring to fulfillment. I now commission you, my dear brothers and disciples, to go forth from this meeting and witness to this good news to all nations so that through your witness these populations shall themselves become my disciples."

The role of disciple comes from the Greek word *manthano*, which describes one who is a student, a pupil, learning not only by formal pedagogy, as at the feet of a rabbi, but also learning by experience and trial-and-error struggle. This is a different concept than we hear in Mark 1:15 when Jesus expects and demands repentance and trust in the good news seemingly at once and in totality. The Greek word for *repentance*, *metanoeo*, implies a sudden, complete 360-degree reversal of mind or knowledge and behavior, whereas the word for *trust*, *pisteuo*, implies a commitment that realistically develops over extended experience, learning as a disciple. Matthew's Jesus calls for the more modest response, that of a disciple who, by definition, knows he or she has much to learn and commits to the discipline necessary to grow and move toward often distant goals. Perhaps Matthew's Jesus has learned more patience, modesty, and realism in what he expects from his listeners to his preaching than was evident in the Jesus whom Mark presents in his very first inaugural appearance in Galilee.

And where shall these spokespersons go to witness to this good news? Not to a portion of the human race but indeed unto all the nations. The Greek word *ethne* points to all social groups, usually designated by language, culture, not by race, region, or religion. These are the Gentiles, of course, not including the Jews, who have already heard and had their chance to respond. But this is a universal coverage since the divine work addresses the reality of sin and evil everywhere.

And how shall the work of God the Sender support and be involved in this process? These witnesses shall not only speak but also baptize, bringing the symbolism of water, essential for all life, to strengthen the movement of these Gentiles, these foreigners into the family of God, who is known by three names—the Father, the Son, and the Holy Spirit. In Hebrew thinking, to assume an intimate relationship with someone of a new/different name meant to place yourself under the protection and authority of the one so named.

It may be helpful to recall Matthew's version of the baptism of Jesus himself, Matthew 3:13–17. When John the Baptist tries to prevent Jesus's baptism, Jesus has his ready answer, "Let it be so now, for it is proper in this way to fulfill all righteousness." The descending Spirit of God from heaven and the voice of the Father assure John and all observers that this is the Son of God. Thus, Matthew anchors Jesus's ministry in the foundational reality (Trinity) he has Jesus point to in our lesson.

Baptism, of course, replaces or supersedes circumcision as the liturgical ritual of initiation into the new/continuous faith of Christians now growing and struggling to survive after the destruction of the Jerusalem Temple and the backlash of many traditional Jews against these beginning level believers who constitute Matthew's readers. What's more, with their baptizing, they are to be teachers, for new disciples must expect to be learners. And what is their official curriculum? "Teaching them to obey everything that I have commanded you." Wow, what a huge order, especially for beginners! But Matthew is sure his version of Jesus's ministry provides all the instruction needed because he presents Jesus as the new Moses who delivers the New Torah in the Sermon on the Mount (Matthew 5–7).

But notice well, new disciples are not expected to gain head knowledge or rational understanding of profound theological teachings as their first order of business. Instead, they will be called and equipped to obey. They obey with their trust and their behavior as they gradually seek to become intimate, responsible members of this new family into which they are called because their God, in his entirety, Father, Son, and Holy Spirit, loves them unconditionally, absolutely, and eternally as reflected in the three names that their baptism bestows upon them.

As these three persons of the Hebrew Godhead are clearly acknowledged and celebrated here in Matthew's version of Jesus's commissioning ceremony, Jesus has one more piece of good news of which to remind them: "Remember, no matter how tough it gets, when you seek to obey this commission, I am, now and forever, with you until the close of this age." He means he is with them, within and among them, in these three persons all at once, these three persons who together share equal membership in the one God of Israel.

The Franciscan scholar Richard Rohr makes this summary of what Trinitarian thinking means to him. In his daily meditation, he says, "Faith is trusting the big river of God's providential love, which is to trust the visible embodiment [the Son], the flow [the Holy Spirit], and the source itself [the Father]. This is a divine process that we don't have to change, coerce, or improve. We just need to allow and enjoy it. That takes immense confidence, especially when we're hurting" (Friday, May 26, 2017).

Lesson Twenty-Eight: Second Sunday after Pentecost; Read Luke 7:1–10

Having studied the celebration of Pentecost and the three dimensions of the Holy Trinity, we arrive at the season of Pentecost, also known as Ordinary Time. Our first exploration will focus upon Luke 7:1–10. As we review the context for this lesson, particularly Luke 4a:14–6:49, it is helpful to pick up on the major theme of Jesus's role as Messiah / Son of God, who both fulfills the divine promises made to the chosen people of Israel but who, in doing so, moves or leaps forward to extend and magnify those same promises to reach out to and include the Gentile world.

There is growing scholarly consensus that Luke-Acts was most likely written ca. 110 CE, making this the fourth Gospel to be written, after the Gospel of John, ca. 90–95 CE. Continuing to work with the hypothesis that Mark was written first (65–70 CE), then Matthew (ca. 85–90 CE), then John (90–95 CE) and that Luke follows the narrative of Mark, with no exposure to John, this sequence helps us to understand the unique role each Gospel writer plays in the portrait he presents of Jesus of Nazareth / eternal Son of God.

For example, Mark forges the first Gospel narrative, writing ca. 65–70 CE, to provide solid foundation for Jesus's career as Son of Man / Son of God in the face of the impending destruction of Jerusalem in 70 CE. Ironically, the historical anchor of Jerusalem still orients the promises of God for both the chosen people and the

Gentile world, whatever may be the imminent fate of this historical citadel. Mark 13, the so-called Little Apocalypse, reminds faithful readers of the Jewish apocalyptic worldview that both confirms and renders relatively all symbols and categories in deference to divine commitment to universal, including Gentile, components of the creation.

Matthew, the second Gospel writer, reconfirms this solid but not eternal role for Judaism and Jerusalem by presenting Jesus as the new Moses (Matthew 5–7, Sermon on the Mount), who both confirms the tradition of the Law and the Prophets and, at the same time, reinterprets these concepts to welcome spiritual freedom and inclusion of all human beings, notably Gentiles, within the potential/future arrival of the kingdom of God. For example, after the resurrection of Jesus, Judaism no longer pivots upon the city of Jerusalem, but rallying in Galilee is challenged to move forward to make disciples of all nations, made possible because Jesus now has authority over all, even until the end of the present age (Matthew 28).

According to this hypothetical development, John, the third Gospel writer, acknowledges the reality of the demise of Jerusalem historically and chronologically but elevates Jewish traditions from mundane physical components to divinely created spiritual and eternal components that fulfill the original vision and design of the Creator to incorporate the eternal, universal creation organically into the salvation, at least potentially inclusive of the whole world (*ho kosmos*), which the Creator loves so irrevocably (John 3:16–21).

Luke, writing ca. 110 CE, no longer makes the fate of Jerusalem and Judaism pivotal. He is convinced that Judaism and the Jewish people have run their course, have served the divine calling well, and now need, willingly and freely, to join the larger inclusive calling and reality of the entire human race, which is the Creator God's actual purpose and design originally and continually until final fulfillment.

One way to grasp this contrast between limited historical traditions and the necessary need for a new, universal, inclusive perspective on reality is to compare/contrast Matthew's presentation of Jesus as the new Moses in the Sermon on the Mount (Matthew 5–7) and Luke's adaptation of the same themes in the Sermon on the

Plain (Luke 6:17–49). Matthew's portrayal of the new Moses is solid, serious, deeply authoritative, formally rich with official symbolism, and full of reassurance that every nuance of the original divinely ordained and inspired covenant will inevitably and indubitably be fulfilled despite any and all doubts and evidence calling for contrary interpretations.

Basing his version upon the same literary resources Matthew uses, Luke, however, without omitting or rejecting any of the same serious issues and dimensions of human calling, conviction, and responsibility, weakens the formality and weightiness of the imperatives and decisions involved and breezes through the examples of human dilemmas with more calm and casual perusal. To be sure, the challenges to human care and concern are still vaunting, but the absolute Jewish context and insistence upon distinctive ghetto conformity are missing, and the horizon now includes every cultural context across the Gentile world. In other words, we still respect and learn from the rich legacy of Judaism. We would be foolish and sinful to do otherwise. But we now take this universal ethical calling seriously alongside of and as colleagues with all members of the human race.

We come now to Luke 7:1–10, adapted Gospel lesson for today, second Sunday after Pentecost. The context for this passage is Luke 6:12–19, mountaintop experience of prayer, calling/appointing his twelve disciples/apostles, and descent to a level-playing field where his own entourage is joined by a representative gathering of humans from all Judaea, Jerusalem, and the coastal regions of Tyre and Sidon.

This mixed/inclusive multitude seeks to hear him, to be healed of their diseases, and to be cured of their troubling, unclean spirits. Does he speak this Sermon on the Plain to his disciples alone or primarily or to this large gathering of suffering humanity as well? The ambiguity is purposeful. He speaks to both groups all at once, to include the human race whether or not they accept and interpret themselves to bear ordinary or extraordinary roles of responsibility.

As already discussed above, the evidence here shows that Luke's version of Jesus's sermon follows closely the same sources for this teaching episode that Matthew follows (Matthew 5–7, the Sermon on the Mount) yet deliberately loosens up or weakens the rigid formality and spreads the good news, both objective and subjective, outward to include distributed but no less serious and important constituencies with roles to play in this arrival of covenant promises being fulfilled here and now before our very eyes. The difference leaps out in the contrast between teaching delivered from the high and exalted mountaintop and teaching shared as colloquially as possible among the people of villages and streets more likely to be found on the lower levels of terrain, the plain easily accessible all across the countryside, to persons from all walks and venues of life.

Having completed this teaching episode out in the highways and byways of life, Jesus moves back to his favorite village setting, that of Capernaum. Earlier, Luke celebrated the inauguration of Jesus's messianic status symbolically in his invasion of his hometown of Nazareth (Luke 4:16–30). That purpose served, however, when Jesus gets himself ejected and exiled from Nazareth, Luke follows Mark who reports how Capernaum, hometown of Simon Peter and Andrew, now becomes Jesus's new working headquarters.

As far as we know, Luke does not know the Gospel of John, but Luke affirms, contrary to the disciple/apostle Nathaniel, that "something good indeed has come forth out of Nazareth!" (cf. John 1:46). Luke shows it is now time for this new leader to operate out of a new and different reference point, Capernaum, in order to reach out to include more of the human race in his ministry during the weeks, months, and years ahead. Jesus's spiritual family is expanding dramatically, as Mark has Jesus express, "Whoever does the will of God is my brother and sister and mother" (Mark 3:35). Luke agrees that covenant promises are moving rapidly from biological definition to universal theological and spiritual definition.

After Luke has Jesus wrap up for the time being his version of Jesus's Sermon on the Plain, Jesus returns to Capernaum to reassemble his associates and renew his relationships with colleagues in this his newly chosen hometown. Luke recognizes the cosmopolitan constituents' characteristic of this crossroads community when he introduces a new figure into his overall working cast. This is a Roman centurion and his cohort of colleagues who have established office and residency in Capernaum, not only a center of commerce and the fishing industry but also a toll station where busy roads crisscross, leading in and out of Galilee.

Let's give this new character in Luke's drama a personal name: Rolland, the Roman centurion. Now Rolland is no doubt a powerful Roman administrator and military commander who controls a legion of some one hundred soldiers. He most likely serves the tetrarch Herod Antipas, who rules Galilee directly for the emperor in Rome.

In his extended family, Rolland has a certain slave whom he esteems highly but who is very ill and close to death. When Rolland hears about Jesus, he calls together some Jewish elders and sends them off to find Jesus and ask him to come and heal his slave. When they find Jesus, they plead with earnest devotion, saying, "Our honored and esteemed neighbor Rolland deserves your care and attention, for he loves our people, and he is the one who built our synagogue for us."

Jesus stops what he is doing, turns, and goes with these elders to meet with Rolland. But before he gets there, he stops outside the house, for Rolland sends a delegation to speak with him. They bring this message from their commander, "Lord, do not go to this trouble, for I am not worthy to have you come under my roof. And I did not presume to bring my roof to you." (Actually, Rolland is sensitive and wants to protect this Jewish prophet from ritual contamination if he enters a Gentile-owned residence.) "But I beg you, only speak the word and let my servant be healed. For I know how authority works. I have many soldiers under my command. I say to one, 'Go,' and he goes. To another, 'Come,' and he comes. To my slave, I say, 'Do this,' and the slave does it."

Jesus listens, stopped dead in his tracks. Jesus is amazed at what he hears from Rolland the Centurion. At first speechless, soon turning to the crowd that follows him, he utters these few words, surprising to him, to hear them coming out of his own mouth, "I tell you this. Not even in all of Israel do I ever find such faith as this!" The messengers who meet him outside the house return there and find their master's slave in good health.

What is the big deal here that Jesus discovers to his great surprise, the presence of which leaves Jesus amazed and aghast? Jesus here recognizes and becomes aware of Rolland's discovery of, awareness of, and his expression of his own personal faith. Here, we find Luke's use of the normal Greek word for this concept, noun *he pistis* and verb *pisteou*. Translation usually stresses belief in the existence of certain fact, against all odds to the contrary. This distortion shifts the basic question from doubt and risk, which calls for trust, to knowledge of fact certain beyond any doubt. The basic meaning of this Greek concept, however, does not eliminate doubt or risk but recognizes the necessity for human doubt, risk, and especially for the two traits of loyalty and trust. This is a rare, delicate, precious, but highly valuable human discovery that Jesus hopes and expects to find somewhere, somehow, sometime in someone, surely in the now ancient and venerable covenant tradition of classical, if not popular, Judaism.

But where does Jesus actually find this rare commodity? Not in Israel, supposedly the womb of embryonic monotheism, where this miracle should be discovered, but instead here in the heart, mind, soul, and mouth of Rolland, the Roman centurion. This officer of the emperor, no doubt sworn to loyalty to the Roman doctrines of order, power, and control, here in his encounter with Jesus of Nazareth, expresses loyalty and trust not to this monolithic system that he officially serves, presumably with honor, devotion, and glory, but to the alien system, Judaism, which honors with reverence the traits of humility, patience, love, and humble servitude.

And what's more, Rolland the Centurion pleads for Jesus's mercy and healing not on behalf of one of his fellow officers, perhaps one of superior rank, but instead on behalf of a weak, powerless, insignificant slave, a human being (if such at all) with little or no freedom and one whose life is defined totally by someone else's order and control.

And now where does Jesus learn and expect to find such faith ever again? Hopefully, even if as now rare, within Israel, nevertheless not beyond all hope, vision, and reason. But more hopefully, Luke's Jesus envisions this faith, arising also from within other cultural milieus, even if peripheral to official Judaism, such as discovered here in the initiatives of Rolland, the Roman centurion.

Thus, we discover here early on Luke's vision of the future mutation, and maturation, the expansion of this same faith, as he fleshes out his writing project here in his Gospel and will continue to portray this good news in the second volume, the Acts of the Apostles.

As Luke begins his second volume, note his explanation of this strategy to his revered patron Theophilus (Acts 1), which prepares us, his present-day readers, to expect and look forward to the lectionary lessons that now continue to be chosen for our study during the portion of the liturgical calendar known as the season of, or after, Pentecost.

Lesson Twenty-Nine: Third Sunday after Pentecost; Read Luke 7:11–17

As context for this lesson, we should recall the content of Jesus's teaching in the Sermon on the Plain (Luke 6:17–49). We assume Luke has access to the same material that Matthew calls upon in producing his version of Jesus's Sermon on the Mount (Matthew 5–7). This is probably the hypothetical Q document, known only in parallel references in both Matthew and Luke. Both extant versions, first Matthew and then Luke, present Jesus as the new prophet of God who presses, warns, and entices his listeners to expect and to embody the new dimensions of the kingdom of God, which they need to hear and anticipate. As previously observed, Matthew's version presents Jesus as the new Moses whose wisdom continues but surpasses that of the Torah (Pentateuch, Genesis through Deuteronomy).

Luke's version streamlines Jesus's teaching into a more succinct, colloquial dialogue, perhaps with a central core that zeroes in on the special needs his listeners have to be sensitive not only to neighbors but especially to strangers and even to enemies (Luke 6:27–38). Jesus here stresses the surprising, unexpected, and normally repugnant opportunities that enemies present, including foreigners, no doubt, especially the Gentiles, in the mission he calls his disciples and the crowds to understand, accept, and express.

Thus, to reinforce this point, last week's lesson (Luke 7:1–10) revealed the eager approach of Rolland, the Roman centurion, to seek the blessing Jesus brings, in this case to his dying slave. Recall the teamwork between Rolland and his recruited Jewish elders who together respond with faith to the ministry Jesus introduces to their neighborhood of Capernaum. Their initiative, originating in the mind and heart of Rolland the Centurion, calls upon the love and compassion they trust is available and ready to work in the presence of this new prophet who has so recently explained himself and his mission to them, and invited their response, in his Sermon on the Plain.

This encounter reminds us of the earlier dramatic healing of the paralytic, also in Capernaum, when Jesus sees and honors the faith of his friends and companions (Mark 2:1–12, Matthew 9:2–9, and Luke 5:17–26), and based not upon the paralytic's faith but upon "their faith," both forgives sin and heals this suffering paralytic, thus restoring him to health and wholeness within his family and community. And it is surely no surprise when the Jewish officials excoriate Jesus both for blasphemy ("No one can forgive sin except God alone!") and for violating Sabbath law.

Likewise, in Capernaum, Jesus heals the Roman centurion's slave not because of the slave's faith but in response to Rolland the Centurion's vibrant faith and initiative, including the teamwork of the recruited Jewish elders. Jesus effusively overflows with excitement, as if unable to believe what he sees and realizes. "I tell you not even in Israel have I found such faith!" What more spontaneous exuberance could you expect to hear to confirm what Jesus teaches about the imperative to love your enemy?

When Jesus arrives in the city of Nain (Luke 7:11–17), with his disciples and a large crowd in tow, notice how the motivation for Jesus to respond to the presence of death arises not from the suffering constituencies, family, friends, and neighbors, external to Jesus, but from within Jesus himself.

To paraphrase, "Now as Jesus and his entourage approach the city of Nain, they are stopped dead in their tracks before the spectacle of a funeral procession leaving the city gates. A young man has died and is being carried outside the city for burial. His mother, a widow, is with this party, and he was her only son. Jesus intuitively grasps this situation and surveys the community solidarity, the crowd of mourners carefully avoiding ritual contamination in their expression of comfort and solidarity for this bereaved widow. She now has lost every male in her family and will likely suffer from alienation and severe poverty.

"Although Jesus looks over this scenario and knows this is a community event, not confined to the individuals, the dead young man and his mother, the widow. And so Jesus experiences his response and involvement with focus upon not the deceased person but his widowed mother." Notice Luke, the editor, chooses to say, "Having seen her, the Lord has deep compassion for her." The Greek verb here is *esplagxnisthe*, aorist tense, passive voice, from the root word *splagxnizomai*, which means "to experience intense emotional stress, arising from deeply within you bowels/entrails, complicated by a combination of anger, revulsion, fear, compassion, empathy, and desire for healing or reversal of suffering." Aorist tense makes the experience turn to action of heightened aggression, and the passive voice means Jesus is being acted upon by another source, not originating his feeling from within himself alone.

Who or what is acting upon Jesus? No doubt God his Father whose presence he embodies and carries within himself at all times. Why/how does Jesus's compassion arise from deeply within his viscera and not from his heart, soul, and mind? Because Jesus is deeply moved and motivated not only by his present relationship with this suffering widow but more fully by his cosmic awareness of the reality of death as such a real and necessary, inevitable component of human life individually and communally.

This awareness and sensitivity is Jesus's anointed insight into the fallen nature of human beings, created in the image and likeness of God their creator, and carrying within themselves, individually and communally, the reality of sin and evil. Jesus is angry, repulsed, and aflame with indignation at this truth, which characterizes the human race and indeed all creation.

And yet, more importantly, simultaneously Jesus responds with deep, indescribable compassion and love for those who suffer right here in his presence and who represent before his eyes and entrails the reality of the human race. Jesus has come into the world to bring life instead of death, health and prosperity instead of suffering, and this encounter calls upon and draws from within himself the deepest, fullest, most intense impulse to heal, reverse, and salvage this inevitable reality of the universal human condition.

Jesus therefore addresses this widow with these words, "Do not cry." How could she possibly not cry? Jesus knows this and indeed is crying himself, softly and quietly, within his bowels, his heart, and his soul. But with their tears, hers and his, Jesus knows and aims to heal her and this community, intends to release her and them from the grip, the prison of death.

"Consequently, while to cry is normal, something different and better than normal is arising from deep within him and will now emerge as his true motivation and reason for this encounter outside the city gates of Nain. Jesus defies convention, ritual laws, and approaches the funeral procession. He reaches out and touches the coffin, thus rendering himself ritually unclean. Everyone stops still in their tracks. Their role and responsibility, to sustain the reality of death, now ceases. Jesus speaks, 'Young man, to you I now speak. Rise up!' The dead man sits up and begins to speak."

Notice the difference between death and life is whether or not you can and do speak. Voice, words, ideas, connecting with whoever listens, and thus communication is the purpose and reality of human life.

"And what does Jesus now do? Jesus gives this young man back to his mother. His new life is not only a change in his personal physiology but, more importantly, a restoration of him to his relationship with his mother and, even more importantly, a restoration or recreation of the reality of the human community. And how does this community respond to this event, which is resurrection to new life? With both fear and praise. With fear because this sudden reversal of reality confounds their conscious awareness and understanding of the source of human life but, more importantly, with glorifying God and saying, 'A great prophet has been raised up / has been sent here among us' and 'Our God has visited his people.'"

The Greek verb for God's action here is *epeskepsato*, aorist tense, middle voice, from the root word *episkeptomai*, which means "to look at/upon, to visit and spend time with, or to recognize as worthy of divine attention and presence."

In other words, this sudden change from death to life, while a compassionate act of the prophet Jesus, who raises this young man from death to new life, more importantly is the saving work of God the Father, creator of all life, who, in this particular act, restores wholeness to the life of this entire community. It is this recognition of their God's special visitation and presence in and among them on this occasion that motivates and energizes this crowd, plus Jesus's disciples and the mourners from across the city of Nain, to spread this news abroad, across the countryside, and indeed throughout all Judaea.

"This news of course reaches the cousin of Jesus, John the Baptist, who excitedly sends his own disciples to ask Jesus, 'Are you the one who is to come, or should we wait for another?' Jesus answers, 'Go and tell John what you have seen and heard: the blind receive their sight, the lame walk, the lepers are cleansed, the deaf hear, the dead are raised, the poor have good news brought to them, and blessed is anyone who takes no offense at me'" (Luke 7:18–23).

According to the narrative, Rolland, the Roman centurion, after encounter with Jesus in Capernaum, generated within himself the faith that motivated and energized Jesus to save this centurion's slave from imminent death (Luke 7:1–10). Outside the city of Nain, the suffering of a broken family and community aroused compassion within Jesus that led him to restore life to a dead young man and his mother and to restore health to a fractured community (Luke 7:11–17).

As we study and seek to share in our life and worship these seemingly clear, positive, and poignant reports from long, long ago, how shall we derive and receive from these narratives inspiration, knowledge, vision, and energy through which the same Lord, Jesus the Christ, may bring healing and new life to us as individuals, as families, and as communities just as he promises to do?

Lesson Thirty: Fourth Sunday after Pentecost; Read Luke 7:36–8:3

Let us consider the context for this lesson (Luke 7:1–35). Following the so-called Sermon on the Plain (Luke 6:17–49), Luke presents episodes that show Jesus to be a new and great prophet among his people, perhaps greater than the ancient prophets who came before him.

Having already stressed the calling of God's people to reach out not only to neighbors but even, or especially, to their enemies (Luke 6:27–36), Jesus soon encounters an enemy officer in Capernaum (Luke 7:1–10), Rolland, the Roman centurion. Rolland seeks healing for his slave who is near death. He sends some Jewish elders to fetch Jesus, whom he trusts will bring life and health to his servant. Jesus honors their faith (Roland and his Jewish cohorts) and exclaims, "I tell you, not even in Israel have I found such faith!" They return home to find the slave in good health.

A large crowd follows Jesus, approaching the city of Nain. A funeral procession is leaving the city gates. A young man has died, and his mother, a widow, is with him. Jesus grasps her condition and the desperate destiny ahead for her. Jesus feels his bowels erupting with compassion, with anger and revulsion, with overwhelming desire for her to live and not be overcome by death. Jesus weeps within himself for the raw reality of the human condition, fallen into sin and suffering. Jesus remembers his words spoken both in his memory and in another Gospel, "I have come into this world so that you may have life, abundantly and overflowing" (John 10:10).

Jesus defies ritual law; he reaches out and touches the funeral bier. Jesus calls out, "Young man, rise up!" The dead man sits up and begins to speak. Jesus returns him to his mother and to their community. This time the energy of faith has arisen not from within an alien/enemy figure of authority (Luke 7:9–10) but from within the body of Jesus himself, upon whom God the Father is acting.

The crowds are filled with awe, apprehension, and fear and are motivated to observe. "A great prophet has arrived among us, because our God has looked with favor upon his people of Israel." At this point, Luke's narrative reflects upon the relationship between Jesus and John the Baptist (Luke 7:18–35). John prepares for and points ahead to Jesus's arrival with his baptism of repentance. Jesus is also a prophet, yet one who not only speaks but also whose works bring healing, health, and new life for the tax collectors and sinners who submit to John's baptism, though not for the Pharisees and lawyers who resist repentance and protect their self-imposed *status quo*.

Jesus gets quoted drawing upon street language of caricature and ridicule, for both John the Baptist and the Son of Man (Luke 7:31–35). Ironically, however, the wisdom of the ages, the Creator God's eternal wisdom, is vindicated by all his children. That is to say, by any and/or all sides of whatever persuasion, who inevitably play their chosen or determined roles in the historical drama of the human race. The conclusion Jesus draws is no doubt a strong expression of the writer Luke's philosophical overview of the Hellenistic world.

At this juncture, Jesus hobnobs with a certain Pharisee. We later learn his name is Simon. This colorful incident brings us into today's lesson (Luke 7:36–8:3). This Pharisee invites Jesus to dine at his home. Not every Jewish official rejects Jesus outright. Some were no doubt intrigued with both his words and deeds. Nothing to lose to check out this would-be prophet a bit more.

This particular Pharisee is not careful to check his guest list. Maybe he holds a kind of open house, with friends coming and going to enjoy his buffet (kosher, of course). But the atmosphere is proper enough so that guests recline around the central table, leaning on their left arm for support, using their right hand to serve themselves. Jesus barely settles in to take some nourishment when, among those coming and going, suddenly a woman tracks him down and approaches him from the rear. The writer Luke describes her as a woman of the city streets, a known sinner. He leaves to your imagination her lifestyle or just what qualifies her to be labeled "sinner." Commentators often label her a harlot or prostitute, but that is not specified. What is specific is that she is turned on, exuding emotion, panting, kneeling at Jesus's feet, desperate to show in some way her thanksgiving, her love, her devotion to this man Jesus, reclining in front of her.

Stooping, her tears begin to flow onto Jesus's bare feet. His feet become wet with her tears. She takes down her long hair and wipes her tears from and across his feet, kissing them as she weeps with intense sobbing. From the folds of her robe, she brings out an alabaster jar with perfume and anoints his feet. The air is filled with the fragrance. Across the table, mingling with other guests, the host cannot ignore the drama unfolding before everyone's eyes. But he speaks only to himself, thinking, *If this person Jesus of Nazareth were a true prophet, he would know what sort of woman this is who is touching him, because you can tell she is a sinner.*

Jesus, listening across the room, ironically because he is a true prophet, calls to his host, "Simon, may I have a word with you?"

"Surely," Simon replies.

Jesus has a parable ready. "A money lender has two clients. One owes five hundred denarii. The other owes fifty denarii." (A denarius was about one day's pay for a laborer.) "Neither of these debtors can possibly pay what he owes. Since they cannot pay their debts, the creditor decides, for whatever reason, to cancel them. Both clients are debt-free. Now what is the obvious lesson here?" Jesus asks. "Which client will love his creditor the most?"

Simon answers, "Why, I suppose, the one who got the largest debt cancelation."

Jesus replies, "Good judgment."

To paraphrase, Jesus turns to the woman from the street. To Simon, Jesus says, "Look at this woman. And look at yourself. I am a guest here in your house. You gave me no water for my feet, no kiss of greeting, nor did you anoint my head with oil. But from the time she arrived, she has bathed my feet with her tears and dried them with her hair. She has not stopped kissing my feet, and she has anointed my feet with precious ointment." Jesus continues, "Therefore, I tell you, her sins, which were many, have been forgiven. And this is why she has shown great love. But the one to whom little is forgiven loves little." What is Simon's response to this parable? Luke does not tell us. Why? No doubt because the parable is intended not only for Simon's ears but also for the ears of Luke's readers and for you and me.

But Jesus's purpose in telling the parable to whomever is listening is to call attention to the relation between human sinfulness and the need for divine forgiveness and the appropriate/necessary human response to divine forgiveness. Simon knows the correct response to Jesus's question. But his response is theoretical, rational, abstract, generic. Can Simon find himself authentically, honestly, realistically, personally, and privately within the options the parable opens up?

For example, does Simon as a proper Pharisee have little or no sins for which to be forgiven, in contrast with the street woman, for example, who is publicly known as a notorious sinner? If he is a nonsinner, then he has little or nothing for which to be forgiven and thus owes little or no love in return. His only expression of love for Jesus is his invitation to dine. Or could Jesus be implying that perhaps proper Pharisees, in their practice of perfection, could indeed have many sins of which they are unaware or deny? In which case, there may be an abundance of divine love and forgiveness waiting to be recognized and received. Forgiveness unclaimed! Reminds one of the state treasurer who every year advertises pages and pages of unclaimed assets waiting to be acknowledged, claimed, and taken to the bank. You cannot receive the money unless you identify yourself and ask for the benefit to be given to you.

The woman from off the street was awash with love and thanksgiving for Jesus, her connection with divine love and forgiveness. Her storehouse of sin was apparently confessed, including repentance, and for this outpouring of divine forgiveness, her response to Jesus reclining at the table was extravagant.

The prim and proper Pharisee, Simon, however, suffers from spiritual constipation. Skimpy hospitality because of insensitivity to the fallen human condition of which he is very much a member. Unable or unwilling to admit, confess, acknowledge his need for forgiveness, he receives little, if any, forgiveness, thus eschewing the purgation enjoyed by the improper street woman.

Curiously, Jesus's fellow tablemates, overhearing these exchanges, ask the right question, "Who is this who even forgives sins?"

And Jesus turns again to the street woman. "Your faith has saved you. Go in peace."

Lesson Thirty-One: Fifth Sunday after Pentecost; Read Mark 7:24–30 and 31–37

Jesus does some serious traveling, away from Galilee, northward into Phoenicia, and thus some distance from his native Judaism and into the territories of the Gentiles. Check your map. He aims at the area around the seaside city of Tyre, a prosperous city known for leisure and commerce. Apparently, Jesus seeks a "Myrtle Beach" kind of experience. He settles into a house and hopes for privacy and peace. How else can he and his disciples recover from their recent frantic days of tense encounters with the scribes and Pharisees?

But word of his arrival precedes him, and soon the neighborhood is abuzz with word that he is present. The first person to intrude upon his retreat is a woman who comes shouting at him. Since she is the focus of this episode, she deserves attention, analysis, and development of character and significance. Let's give her a name, Helen of Tyre. Furthermore, since Matthew's version develops this incident in greater detail, let's include his narrative details along with those of Mark's.

Matthew identifies this woman, Helen of Tyre, as a Canaanite, native to that region. Mark makes it clear she is a Gentile of Syrophoenician origin. So this is her home turf, and she is eager to welcome this outsider, this healer whose reputation has preceded him. She comes out shouting. She invades Jesus's privacy and accosts him with her demands. She gets right to her point. "Help me. Have mercy on me, for my little daughter is tormented by demons!" She is a mother whose maternal instincts know no bounds. She is desperate like any mother whose child is suffering with end-of-life agony, who finds herself helpless to save her child.

Furthermore, she is armed and prepared for this encounter. She claims to know just exactly who Jesus is. "Have mercy on me, Lord, Son of David," she utters in her despair. She knows Jesus is the promised Jewish Messiah. She no doubt recalls the reputation of this legendary, promised Savior. He comes to save his people from their oppressors. He comes to heal and save them from suffering and evil and to bring life instead of death. "Surely, this Son of God will have mercy on all innocent ones who suffer!" she reassures herself and shouts all the louder.

Jesus's first reaction is cold, stony silence. Who is this upstart female who dares violate his privacy and intrude upon his time of retreat, self-healing, and refurbishment with his stressed-out disciples? Has she first consulted the local healer in residence? Why has she found no comfort from the local healer?

No female, of course, should dare to make this kind of assertive appeal in public. Where is her husband or her father or her guardian, who should make this appeal on her behalf, approaching Jesus before she does? Despite her motivation, she behaves rudely, with arrogance and disrespect, disturbing the peace like this, not only the private peace of Jesus and his disciples but also the peace of this entire neighborhood.

Jesus's disciples are immediately aroused from their slumber. They leap to intervene to protect and honor their teacher and master. "Send her away, Lord, for she keeps on shouting at us," is their plea on behalf of Jesus's dignity and privacy. They are ready to call the local police to arrest and incarcerate her for inexcusable, aggressive, disrespectful, invasive disturbance of the peace.

Jesus himself finally, slowly ponders this confrontation, rises to his feet, looks all around at the gathered crowd, assumes a calm and dispassionate facial expression, and begins to respond to Helen's desperate pleas for help. "I was sent only to the lost sheep of the house of Israel."

Helen falls to her knees, sobbing with agony, and through her tears, crying out, "Lord, help me. Have mercy on me!"

Jesus listens to her pleas. Jesus stands straighter and looks all around him once again at the crowd that has gathered. He addresses everyone with a solemn tone of voice, "Let the children be fed first. It is not fair to take the children's food and throw it to the dogs!" A quiet gasp is heard from some in the crowd. A low murmur issues forth from some standing on the fringe. Some of Jesus's disciples relax to hear Jesus put this uppity female in her place. Helen herself is quiet for a moment, allowing Jesus's words to register and sink into her heart. Then she sinks lower, sobbing all the more with pain through her tears.

Gradually, Helen raises herself on her knees, looks upward into Jesus's face, and slowly, no longer with sobs, but gently directs these sober words to him and to his disciples, "Yes, Lord, you have come to save your people of Israel. Feed the children of Israel first. But even the dogs waiting down on the floor eat the crumbs that fall down from the children's plates on their master's table."

In both Jesus's and Helen's talk of dogs, the Greek word is *to kunarion*, noun with neuter gender, meaning "house pets," as opposed to dogs of the street or farm, thus living outside the house. The implication then is that these small lapdogs are actually full-fledged members of the household, not strangers or aliens. This suggests that Jesus is correct; it is all right for the householders of Israel to be fed first. But sooner or later, the lowest members of the family, including the pet dogs, should also be fed, and they normally receive the crumbs that fall from the table up above, during and after all the children of the family are being fed. Better crumbs beneath the table than nothing at all.

Jesus's disciples utter a collective gasp as they cannot believe their ears. This uppity woman dares to talk back to their rabbi, their teacher and master of healing. What rude behavior! What arrogance to refute him, to seek to correct him, to aim to teach him some truth she knows but he does not know! *Surely,* they think under their breaths, *our master will rebuke her and correct her and put her firmly in her rightful place where she most certainly belongs!*

Jesus, however, is quiet for a moment. Slowly, a gentle smile spreads across his face. He stoops to take Helen's hand and draws her up to stand before him. "Woman, your words share your faith, your strong trust in the love of Almighty God our heavenly Father. Go now in peace. The demon has left your daughter."

Helen can hardly constrain herself as she wishes to embrace this Jesus to express her thanksgiving for the mercy he has promised her. Instead, she turns and hurries back to her home, where she finds her little daughter sitting up, in her right mind, healed and demon-free.

Jesus decides it is time to move on from this city of Tyre beside the sea. As he leads his band of disciples across the hills, Jesus takes a moment to stop, turn around, and gaze thoughtfully, down from the mountaintop out across the city below and onto the sparkling Mediterranean Sea, which leads to the rest of humankind and, indeed, to all of creation. Jesus begins to chuckle to himself and reflect deeply upon his recent meeting, or confrontation, with Helen of Tyre. His smile grows into a broad grin as he gives thanks to God his Father for this learning experience, which has blessed him, coming as it has in a new and strange location and at the hands of this surprising woman, Helen of Tyre, an unexpected but ultimately welcome teacher. Jesus quietly thanks his Father God for another blessing of being human, and that is the necessity and responsibility to recognize and accept each and every opportunity to learn from sometimes surprising, unexpected encounters with other fellow human beings, also created in the very image and likeness of their Creator.

As an aside, in the interest of full disclosure, this exegesis and exposition is a condensation of a more lengthy essay I wrote earlier entitled "Helen of Tyre, the Woman Who Ministers unto Jesus."

Turning to Mark 7:31–37, we find Jesus on the road again. Either Jesus is a poor travel planner or Mark is confused about geography. To go toward Sidon, north of Tyre, is certainly not the shortest route back to Galilee and the Decapolis region east of the Sea of Galilee. Check your map again. But in this episode, a healing event does not depend upon location.

Reminds us of Mark 2:3–7, where four friends bring their paralytic buddy to Jesus, a person who needs healing and obviously cannot bring himself. When Jesus "sees their faith," he proceeds to heal this paralytic. In this new pericope, they bring a man who is deaf, with a speech impediment, and beg Jesus to lay hands upon him. This man may be mobile, but he lacks the two basic elements of human relationship—hearing and speaking. Notice, Jesus takes this man aside for a private encounter, as if to say not all of Jesus's saving or healing activity is open for public scrutiny or involvement. Jesus proceeds to heal this man, however, according to his own personal procedure and preferred engagement. Immediately his ears are opened, his tongue released, and he hears and speaks plainly, ready now for normal human social intercourse.

Time to celebrate, give thanks, shout with praise from the rooftops, right? Note the tension between this understandable exuberance and Jesus's concern to play down the popular acclaim and keep it more on the quiet side. This is an example of the so-called Messianic Secret, whereby Jesus worries about the popular expectations from the Son of Man and what he actually must expect and look forward to as he fulfills his calling in Jerusalem. This tension runs throughout the Gospels but especially in the Gospel of Mark, where the first person to actually recognize and identify Jesus as the Son of God is not one of Jesus's disciples, not even a Jew but the Roman centurion who oversees or supervises the crucifixion of Jesus (Mark 15:39).

Lesson Thirty-Two: Sixth Sunday after Pentecost; Read Luke 9:51–62

This lesson begins when Luke announces to his readers that the days draw near when Jesus will be "taken up," and this means he must turn his steps immediately toward Jerusalem. From this point all the way to Luke 9:28, Jesus and his disciples are on the way, in transition from Galilee to the capital city. Recall the preparation for this shift in direction recently discussed during the transfiguration event (Luke 9:28–36) when Jesus, along with Moses and Elijah, strategized about "his departure, which he was about to accomplish at Jerusalem."

The words translated in NRSV as *departure* are actually *ten exodon autou* in Greek and may be translated as *his exodus*. With Moses himself counseling Jesus, it is no surprise that what Jesus will encounter in Jerusalem (rejection, suffering, crucifixion, resurrection, ascension) may be anticipated along the lines of being a new exodus from slavery into freedom, this time aimed to save or release not only one nation, Israel, from sin and evil but also the entire human race.

If Jesus aims to reach Jerusalem soon, Samaria looms directly ahead when you leave Galilee. Luke is probably more interested in theology rather than geography, however, and this means Samaria is ripe and rich with potential exactly because of the centuries of alienation between Jews and Samaritans.

Jesus does not detour around Samaria, to play it safe and avoid hostilities, but he does send messengers ahead to reconnoiter the landscape and probably to give his disciples opportunity to practice his instruction recently presented and cataloged in Luke 9:1–6.

Spotting a village that looks promising, Jesus's advance team probably pulls out all the stops to make the entourage acceptable to these few households. No doubt they promote their master as a devout prophet of God on his anointed pilgrimage that will soon reach its destiny in Jerusalem.

Now let us remember that there is a centuries-old custom that travelers/strangers are always welcome to receive hospitality in remote, desert regions across the Middle East. This normal courtesy gets blackballed this time, however, as soon as these villagers hear that Jesus is headed to Jerusalem, no doubt for sacred exercises, and not to the Samaritan temple on Mount Gerizim. No hospitality available here. This advance team can only shake their heads in dismay when Jesus and company arrive.

Jesus understands. He was hoping to forge ahead with encounters leading to new dimensions of reconciliation (cf. John 4:1–42), but this resistance/hostility is the reality they meet here. Two of his disciples, James and John, however, do not understand. They are incensed at this snubbing of their master, this disloyalty to ancient custom in favor of rigid Samaritanism, and above all, this resistance to the new world they trust is in process of arrival, this cold shoulder turned against God's anointed prophet.

Now James and John were participants in the recent transfiguration event (Luke 9:28–36). If Jesus can invoke Moses's leadership to explain his upcoming "departure" or "exodus" events in Jerusalem, no doubt James and John can honor Elijah and invoke his prophetic leadership when he calls down fire from heaven to consume the captain and his fifty men not once but twice (cf. 2 Kings 1:11–12). Seeking to serve their Lord, they will learn from his example and from the transfiguration experience. They put their question directly to Jesus, "Lord, do you want that we should call fire to come down from heaven to consume them?"

Mark, in his Gospel at 3:13–19, gives us the first list of the twelve disciples whom Jesus calls and appoints because he wants them. "He names them apostles, to be with him and to be sent out to proclaim the message and to have authority to cast out demons." When Mark lists this twelve, as he comes to James and John, he indicates that Jesus himself gives a special nickname to these two brothers, "sons of thunder" (Mark 3:17). Does Jesus give them this title because he needs their brand of discipleship and prophetic leadership? Perhaps Jesus himself even thinks of the bombastic and fiery behavior of the ancient prophet Elijah. At any rate, Jesus does not, cannot accept their proposal as the appropriate response to this Samaritan village's rejection.

Luke simply says, "But he turned and rebuked them." Such a terse summary of what must have been a serious teaching moment for Jesus. Manuscript variations reflect how later readers sought to fill in the words missing from Jesus's mouth. For example, one manuscript quotes Jesus, "You do not know what spirit you are of, for the Son of Man has not come to destroy the lives of human beings but to save them."

It is appropriate to quote from one contemporary scholar, R. Alan Culpepper, who makes a strong contribution to this process of exegesis and exposition: "This episode allows us to study the temptation to use violence to achieve right. Does insult entitle one to do injury? Does being right or having a holy cause justify the use of force or violence? Elijah had called down fire on the Samaritans. Could not Jesus's followers do the same? Misunderstanding the identity of the one they followed, the disciples mistakenly thought they could achieve his ends by violence. How often have those who claimed to be following Christ repeated the mistake of these early disciples? They had yet to learn that violence begets violence and that Jesus had come to break the circle of violence by dying and forgiving rather than by killing and exacting violence" (*The New Interpreter's Bible*, vol. 9, p. 216).

Not long before, Jesus had counseled his disciples on how to behave when they are not welcome: "Whenever they do not welcome you, as you are leaving that town, shake the dust off your feet as a testimony against them" (Luke 9:5). Luke now says simply, "Then they went on to another village," leaving us to wonder if perhaps they fared better there.

What and whom will they encounter in all the many villages they will pass through on this journey to reach Jerusalem and the fulfillment of Jesus's mission on behalf of the human race? The rash commitment of James and John shows the continuing need Jesus's own disciples have for counsel concerning the roles, the behavior, the commitment necessary to share the destiny of this Lord and Master, as Jerusalem looms not too far ahead.

With the episode with James and John's enthusiasm, Luke takes from his own sources (hypothetical L). Luke's next two encounters both he and Matthew draw from their shared source (hypothetical Q). According to Luke, an anonymous man, meaning a typical, well-intentioned "average joe," initiates contact with Jesus and offers "to follow [him] wherever [he] goes." Wow! An unconditional commitment, if Jesus ever heard one. Jesus, of course, wants to welcome such devotion, but how to help this person realize what he's getting himself into? (Matthew, by the way, identifies this person as a scribe.) Jesus chooses to warn this devotee about the lifestyle he's risking taking up: "Foxes have holes, and birds of the air have nests, but the Son of Man has nowhere to lay his head." To paraphrase, "The weakest, most vulnerable creatures of nature find themselves provided for, while the most powerful figure in Jewish theology has to scramble to eat and sleep safely." Jesus no doubt has in mind the inhospitality of these Samaritan villages they are passing through. To paraphrase more, "Are you sure you want to adopt the lifestyle of the Son of Man, not only his day-by-day struggle to survive but especially if you understand what destiny awaits him and his disciples in Jerusalem?"

A second man seeks to probe the meaning of discipleship. Matthew says he is a disciple already but in need of patient counsel. Luke says Jesus seeks him out with the proposition, "Follow me." This potential disciple answers, "Lord, let me first go and bury my father." Now, according to law and custom, every devout Jew must help to bury the dead. On the surface, Jesus puts radical devotion to the arriving kingdom of God ahead of traditional devotion to this duty, the disposal of the dead. How can he force a pious Jew into this vice that strangles and distorts reality? Since Jesus poses this dilemma without a solution, Jesus must hope and trust this challenge will produce serious spiritual struggle within the individual that shall produce outcomes more positive than negative.

A third anonymous person, overhearing these discussions, responds to Jesus this way, "I will follow you, Lord, but let me first say farewell to those at my house." Built into the Jewish Torah (e.g., the Ten Commandments) is the necessity to honor your family, especially aged parents or in-laws. Now Jesus could have invoked here his teaching quoted in Luke 8:19–21, where he reinterprets the meaning of family relative to the importance and priority of the kingdom of God (cf. Mark 3:31–35 and Matthew 12:46–50).

But instead of addressing the concern this person raises directly, Jesus stretches metaphors and moves from the family hearth outward to the world of agriculture. "No one who puts his hand to the plow and looks back is fit for the kingdom of God." This is no doubt an aphorism with popular origin and support. You have to keep a sharp eye on which direction your plow takes. If you look aside or away, your plow will deviate and mess up your field for sowing. In other words, do not divide your loyalty. Instead, hone, refine, sharpen, focus your priorities.

Again, the words of scholar R. Alan Culpepper are helpful: "Because faithfulness would require Jesus to lay down his life, the call to discipleship to Jesus inevitably means unconditional commitment to the redemptive work of God for which Jesus gave his life. The disciple will be like the Lord. Therefore, one should not rush into discipleship with glib promises. On the contrary, the radical demands of discipleship require that every potential disciple consider the cost, give Jesus the highest priority in one's life, and having committed oneself to discipleship, move ahead without looking back" (*The New Interpreter's Bible*, vol. 9, p. 218).

Lesson Thirty-Three: Seventh Sunday after Pentecost; Read Luke 10:1–11 and 16–20

The previous lectionary lesson (Luke 9:51–62) provides the context for this lesson. Jesus sends messengers, beginning with his own disciples, to prepare the way for his mission now moving with purpose, strategy, and direction toward Jerusalem, beginning with the region of Samaria. James and John, the legendary "sons of thunder," serve to portray Jesus's advanced guard, full of energy and enthusiasm but sorely in need of patience, sensitivity, wisdom, and refinement of strategy and method.

The dilemmas of the three potential disciples portrayed in Luke 9:57–62 tempt us to question just who, if anyone, is suitable for the delicate, precarious minefield that lays ahead waiting to entrap anyone who dares to allow his trust and wisdom to risk commitment to Jesus's ambitious mission soon to reach fruition in Jerusalem. But Luke, of course, envisions Jerusalem as the necessary launchpad for extending Jesus's mission to the entire Gentile world, and this universal perspective seeks to open up discipleship to unlimited enrollments, suitable to negotiate the treacherous twists and turns that will carry the mission of Jesus to the ends of the earth (Acts 1:1–8).

Notice Jesus has already conducted a makeshift seminar on discipleship strategies (Luke 9:57–62). Time now to expand that teaching session into a full-blown workshop with hands-on experiences and open up enrollment from twelve regulars to a beefed-up squad robust enough to launch a movement to evangelize the known world. Time to appoint a larger contingent of messengers or evangelists to complement Jesus's initial band of twelve.

And so Jesus appoints seventy. The manuscripts differ on whether the number is seventy or seventy-two. If seventy-two is the correct number, then the rationale is that this event honors the seventy-two scholars who, legend says, translated the Hebrew Scriptures into Greek (285–246 BCE in Alexandria, Egypt), producing the *Septuagint* (LXX in Roman numerals). This number not only honors their labors but also points ahead to the Hellenistic world Luke's Jesus seeks to include up front in his mission strategy. In other words,

God has already worked a miracle in making the Hebrew Scriptures available for the Gentiles, and now this new appointment of seventy-two messengers anticipates the even greater miracle of the arrival of the full-blown message of salvation in Jesus himself among the Gentiles.

The number seventy-two does not stick in the surviving manuscripts. The number seventy appears here in Luke's and Matthew's source, the hypothetical Q document. But what is the significance of this number? It is a large round number denoting expansion far ahead of and beyond Jesus's original band of twelve disciples. And this number most likely derives from the list of nations given in Genesis 10, the descendants of Noah who spread abroad across the whole earth. The same number appears in the later Torah when Moses commissions seventy elders to help him (Exodus 24:1 and Numbers 22:16, 24). Scholars conclude that Genesis 10 is the earlier source and Moses repeats it to point to the universal significance of his leadership. Luke draws upon this momentum. (Mark and Matthew do not include this number at all in their versions of Jesus's mission.)

As Jesus appoints these seventy new messengers, he indicates they shall travel in pairs (two by two), probably for companionship and for mutual support in risky and dangerous neighborhoods. But also because it takes two witnesses to present and argue an important claim, much less one as presumptuous as Jesus intends to make. But more importantly, they do not go to fulfill their own agenda, nor do they choose their own itinerary. Rather, they are to aim explicitly for those cities and locations where Jesus himself is about to arrive. They are his advance crew. In other words, his opening act, warming up the audiences for their master's arrival. They promise ahead of time, pointing to the realization of the blessing they shall soon see for themselves. When Jesus arrives, full-blown among them, then they shall see him face-to-face.

To paraphrase, "God plants and grows crops that are overflowing with potential. No shortage of fruit or produce to reap and spread abroad among all the earth. But who will labor to gather this bountiful harvest ready for market and for human consumption? Overflowing bounty, but scarce labor to reap the harvest! Let us pray all together that our Lord who plants will also recruit and send and enable sufficient workers equipped to reap these blessings waiting to be harvested. 'And so it is you seventy whom I now send. And you must know I send you as lambs who will live and labor among wolves.' Study this symbolism. Who are you as lambs? Who are these wolves you shall encounter? Wolf DNA will be at work, for sure. What is your source for and expression of lambness?"

Matthew adds, "So be wise as serpents and innocent as doves. Jesus conjures up a menagerie. How do these creepy, crawly creatures help these seventy new messengers conceptualize their respective roles? And who will do the fundraising necessary to supply their needs for this ambitious journey? No problem, for no supplies or provisions are allowed. No purse, no beggar's bag, no sandal. No gold or silver or copper, only one tunic, no staff. And greet no stranger on the road, lest you be tempted to ask for assistance!

"Whenever you enter a town or village, perhaps someone will offer you hospitality. If so, salute this host with an invocation of peace. Receive this hospitality, eating and drinking what they provide, for you deserve this support. And do not seek better provisions in some other house, but remain there until you leave. Always eat what is set before you, and above all, preach to them, 'The kingdom of God is arriving and is now near.' Matthew now says, 'Heal the sick, raise the dead, cleanse lepers, and cast out demons.'"

Luke concludes Jesus's instructions with these summary words, "Whenever you enter a city and the citizens do not receive you, say to them, 'Even the dust that clings to our feet from your streets, we shake off as a judgment against you.' But above all, do not forget this, that the kingdom of God has now come near to all of us. And do not forget this. Anyone who hears you hears me and anyone who rejects you rejects me and anyone who rejects me rejects the one who is sending me."

As this episode reaches fulfillment, Luke continues, "The seventy returned to Jesus with expressions of joy on their lips, saying, 'Lord, even the demons submit to us in your name! This implies that if the most extreme enemies of your kingdom submit, then surely everyone and everything else has already or will also submit.'" (Note, we are privy neither to the length of time nor to the extent of geography included in this expedition but only to its significance.)

The Greek verb here translated as *submit* is *hupostassetai* and is in the middle-passive voice, which implies (1) passive voice (someone else is acting upon them, that is, their Lord and Master, which means Satan himself honors the coming of God's kingdom) or (2) middle voice (they themselves are in charge because these demons decide to behave the way that is in their own best interest, that is, recognition of the good news they are hearing, that the kingdom of God is so near it is advisable to behave accordingly). In either case, whether passive or middle voice, this reported and recorded reality brings great joy to the seventy because they experience tangible evidence for the arriving kingdom of God and thus evidence of their own witness to this universal event so close on the horizon.

Jesus, who commissions and sends out this advance entourage of seventy pioneers, has his own joyful report to share with them, "Behold, I saw Satan fall like lightning from heaven!" This response, delivered in true apocalyptic style, affirms that the Lord of this mission has been calmly but keenly observant of all that has transpired. And just why has the seventy been so effective in their witness, and why do they have reason to be so joyful?

Jesus reminds them of the source of their joyful experience, "Do not forget this truth. I have given you power to stomp on snakes and scorpions and power to smash your enemy. And nothing, absolutely nothing at all in all creation, shall ever be able to harm or injure you!" Interestingly, the Greek text here includes the memorable quirk of grammar we call in English the double negative. A double negative in English grammar logically eliminates the negative and renders the assertion the opposite, thus positive. Not so in Greek. Just the opposite from English, the double negative in Greek piles on more and more assertion of denial. Thus, mathematically speaking, this is denial to the twelfth power or, maybe we should say, to the seventieth power.

Now Jesus draws his congratulatory remarks to this close, "Do not rejoice because the spirits are subject to you but rejoice because your names are written in heaven." To paraphrase: "Do not take pride in the downfall of your enemies but rejoice with thanksgiving that God's servants, you yourselves, are blessed by God who welcomes and honors your hard and faithful work of witness to the arrival of God's kingdom."

What guidance, what information, and what inspiration do we discover here in our study of the role of this new body of disciples, the seventy, in Luke's delineation of their calling and commission by Jesus, in their report of their mission, and in Jesus's acknowledgment of and commendation for their work and witness? Luke, this Gospel writer, was highly motivated and equipped to provide this narrative for his original readers, and he provides the same narrative for those of us who are his readers today. What do we discover in our study of this lesson that may motivate us to enroll in some version of the seventy, which invites and supports us to share their witness and their joyful benefits?

Lesson Thirty-Four: Eighth Sunday after Pentecost; Read Luke 10:25–37

This lesson follows in the wake of the return of the seventy whom Jesus sent out two by two to prepare the villages and towns across the countryside for the good news that their master is now on his journey that will culminate in his "exodus" or "departure," which will fulfill his earthly ministry (Luke 10:17–20). Luke, from time to time, portrays Jesus turning aside to renew his communion with his Father God who sends him on this mission. Such a moment provides the transition from his engagement with the seventy to his engagement with the lawyer or scribe, which introduces the parable of the Good Samaritan.

In Luke 10:21–24, to paraphrase, "Having just now instructed the returning seventy, 'Rejoice because your names are recorded in heaven,' Jesus now finds himself sharing a moment of ecstasy with the Holy Spirit, who joins him in this eruption of exuberant expression. 'We praise you, dear Father, Lord of all heaven and all earth, because you have hidden these truths and realities from the so-called wise and supposedly intelligent leaders and instead have revealed them to little children. Yes, indeed, my dear Father, and you do this because we together discovering this development is turning out to be well-pleasing in your sight.'" The Greek verb *egeneto* (dynamic development) instead or the Greek verb *ane* (static being) reflects a universe (or creation) that is in the process of growing, developing, or evolving instead of a static universe established, already completed, once and for all time.

"Jesus pauses in their dialogue [Father, Son, and Holy Spirit] and takes stock of what all this means. As if looking at himself in a mirror, Jesus affirms his thoughts and reassures himself with these words: 'The Father has entrusted all things [all creation, past, present, and always] to me. And this means the Father is the only One who knows who is the Son and the Son is the only One who knows who is the Father, except all those to whom the Son wishes to reveal him'" (cf. John 14:6).

At this point, Jesus turns from this saturation of dialogue among himself, his Father, and the Holy Spirit and speaks to his twelve disciples privately, "How very blessed are all the eyes which see what you yourselves are seeing right now! For, indeed I tell you, many prophets, including those embedded in our holy traditions, and many kings, rulers of both Israel and the Gentiles, longed with all their heart and soul to see what you see but did not see it and to hear what you hear but did not hear it."

Thus, Jesus addresses his disciples and, by implication, the seventy also as the "little children" to whom God the Father chooses, through the work of Jesus himself, to reveal God's purposes and plans for his creation (Luke 10:21). This is a strong assertion to serve as a transition from the ministry Jesus has been nurturing as he pursues his journey toward his "exodus" or "departure," which awaits him and his disciples soon in Jerusalem. If Jesus's disciples and the seventy are the recipients of the truth withheld from the learned and the powerful, who now represents those who do not receive this truth?

Who else but a learned lawyer and scribe? Compare Luke's version of this encounter with Mark's version, which is probably Luke's source. Mark presents this episode after Jesus is already teaching in Jerusalem. Luke assumes this lawyer is lurking nearby, perhaps waiting for a lull in the action when he can "put Jesus to the test." In other words, he who is an expert in Jewish theology and law finds Jesus lacking and seeks to put Jesus on the spot and discredit him as a teacher who is worth or deserves all the attention and acclaim he attracts. Notice how Mark presents this encounter as a very positive exchange that enables and supports Jesus's teaching ministry (Mark 12:28–34). Luke, in contrast, discovers this adversary as a good way to introduce Jesus's parable of the Good Samaritan.

In Mark's version, this scribe asks a basic question concerning the big picture of legality within Judaism as a whole: "Which commandment is first of all?" Luke's version presents this lawyer as one who asks a very pressing personal question: "Teacher, what shall I do to inherit eternal life?" In Mark, as his answer, Jesus quotes the Shema prayer, which devout Jews recited twice daily (cf. Deuteronomy 6:4–9). Here, Jesus reduces the cumbersome and unnecessarily laborious 613 laws of Judaism to the essence of faith and piety.

In Luke's version, Jesus answers this lawyer's question by placing the responsibility back into his own hands. Jesus knows he is well educated and prepared to quote from Deuteronomy and Leviticus. The lawyer answers correctly, and Jesus commends his knowledge, "You have answered right. Do this, and you will live." The lawyer, however, is not really interested in correct knowledge but feels the strong need to justify himself. Notice he is confident he loves the one God correctly and adequately but finds it hard to be sure he loves his neighbor as he does himself. Can he be sure all other human beings are his neighbors, or may he pick and choose who qualifies and thus demands his love? And who does not qualify, and who can he thus ignore or treat unlovingly? Thus, his question to Jesus, "And just who exactly is my neighbor?"

Jesus, ever the inspired, carefully prepared strategist and teacher, does not launch into deep analysis and exposition of theology but simply tells a story. By this time in his career, his simple stories were given the descriptive name parable. This word derives from two Greek words, the preposition *para*, which means "beside, alongside of, or parallel to," and the verb *ballow*, which means "to cast, to throw, or to propel." (This word has a cognate in English, *ballistics*, which is the study of firearms and ammunition, a valuable component of forensics.)

In our current context, when Jesus tells this parable, he casts alongside the subject of discussion, in this case the quotations from Deuteronomy and Leviticus, the story of the Good Samaritan, with the expectation that this juxtaposition, this comparison will function as a metaphor and thus facilitate positive mental movement from the known (parable) to the unknown ("Who is my neighbor?").

As we listen to Jesus's parable, it may be helpful to recall the long, centuries-old history of hostility between the Jews and the Samaritans. During the two-century-long division between the northern (Samaritans) and southern (Judaeans) kingdoms, 922–722 BCE, the capital of the ten northern tribes was at Samaria, while the capital of the two tribes in the south remained Jerusalem. After the Assyrian conquest (722 BCE), the ten tribes of the north welcomed and intermarried with foreigners and never reestablished their former ten tribal identities (hence the expression the Ten Lost Tribes of Israel).

The two southern tribes, Judah and Benjamin, by way of contrast, considered themselves the legitimate heirs to the ancient covenant of God with the original patriarchs and the classical Torah. This rivalry intensified over time with no love lost between the two separate kingdoms, and the Jews especially were alienated from their northern kinsmen whom they condemned as betrayers and idolaters. (See the Gospel of John 4:1–41 for an interpretation of the rivalry between the two temples, Mount Gerizim in the north and Jerusalem in the south.)

And so Jesus, in answer to the lawyer's question, "Who is my neighbor?" begins to tell the story of the events that transpired on the dangerous twenty-four-mile journey from Jerusalem down to Jericho. In order to suggest how this same story, this very same parable, might be more effectively retold with slightly different characters, more suitable if this were twenty-first-century America, please permit some paraphrasing: "A black man was traveling south on the interstate highway from Jerusalem to Jericho. When he pulls over at the rest stop, a gang of guys hanging out there recognize him as a known gay regular back in town. They taunt him, beat him up, strip him, rob him, and leave him in the ditch, half dead. This gang makes a quick exit.

"About this time, two white Protestant evangelists, on a summertime crusade for Christ, pull into the rest stop. The black man in the ditch is barely able to whimper and cry out for help. They recognize him at once for who he is—a notorious gay pervert rumored to be drugging and pimping. 'Serves him right,' they agree and speed away as soon as they can.

"The man in the ditch is gradually struggling to pull himself up, but his bleeding wounds burn his eyes, and all he can do is moan and cry out weakly, 'Help me. Somebody help me.' Almost at once, a snazzy sports car pulls into the rest stop. The rear bumper sports this sticker in red letters, 'Allahu Akbar.' On the front seat lays a copy of *the holy Quran.* This young man, obviously of Middle Eastern descent, steps out of his vehicle and starts toward the pavilion. Suddenly, he hears cries for help and, turning around, sees this bleeding African American trying to raise his head up from the ditch."

"'Allahu Akbar!' utters this young Muslim. 'What's wrong, my brother? Allah be praised! You are still alive!' No more words, but with swift work, he lifts this bleeding black man into his arms and sweeps him into his front seat. He roars out of the parking area, working his cell phone to find where is the nearest emergency room. Once in the emergency room, the doctors begin to restore this suffering patient to some resemblance of survival. The sports car driver remains with his new friend, this victim newly rescued from the ditch, long enough to see him stabilized. He leaves his credit card and his contact information with the hospital agent and promises to return the next day to check out the patient's progress and to be of whatever support is appropriate." End of paraphrase.

Returning now to Luke's original version of this story, this parable. As Jesus completes his telling of this parable, he poses this question to the lawyer who is listening, "Which of these three do you think was a neighbor to the man who fell into hands of the robbers?" Notice this lawyer cannot bring himself to say "The Samaritan" because the very name, the recognition of the ethnicity of the person

Jesus calls upon him to identify is too offensive for him to speak in his own words.

This means, in the paraphrased version, a normal lawyer, officer of the court, in today's culture would be unable, unwilling to answer Jesus's question with the words "The Muslim." These two lawyers, then and now, prefer to live and work with the stereotypes, the caricatures, the clichés they have adopted and internalized rather than be open to a new and better solution to the question and all its ramifications, which Jesus puts to them so vividly in this parable.

Most important of all, notice how Jesus reorients the question that the lawyer puts to him. The lawyer seeks to justify himself because he hears and knows it is difficult to effectively love your neighbor as yourself, especially if and when the victim in need of love is an estranged, alien, hated enemy. Thus, if he can bring his own definition of "neighbor" to what is required of him, then he is able to be self-assured that he fulfills this law and thus earn eternal life. He wants to be in charge of his own destiny, of his own procedure for moving from this life to eternal life. He misses this opportunity to accept eternal life not as an earned reward but as a gracious gift bestowed upon sinful, underserving, but nonetheless sincere creatures such as himself.

In Jesus's skillful use of this parable as his answer to this lawyer's question, Jesus does not show him how to answer his question, "Who is my neighbor?" Instead, Jesus changes the question from "Who is my neighbor?" to "Who behaves as a neighbor? Who is willing to become a neighbor?" which leads to Jesus's command, "Go and do likewise." This means this lawyer's hearing and responding to Jesus's parable enables or requires him now to give this as the answer to his initial question, "What must I do to inherit eternal life?" Thus, more important than the question of who should receive my love is the question of how I can be the one who loves. Neighborliness is not a quality I should expect to find in someone else, but neighborliness should be a quality/trait I myself exhibit within myself and bring ready to give as love to someone (anyone? everyone?) whom I meet outside myself. When I do this as a response to Jesus's teaching, I do all that is required and what is sufficient to inherit eternal life.

Mark's version of this dialogue with the scribe leads this scribe to this astounding, perceptive conclusion: "You are right, Teacher. You have truly said that he is one and besides him there is no other, and to love him with all the heart and with all the understanding and with all the strength and to love one's neighbor as oneself—this is much more important than all whole burnt offerings and sacrifices" (Mark 12:32–33). This scribe is a member of the minority of learned leaders who do indeed recognize, perceive, and promote the good news Jesus brings into the world (cf. Luke 10:21–22).

Luke's more pessimistic version of the lawyer who seeks above all to justify himself verifies Jesus's words, which put more responsibility and hope into the hands of Jesus's disciples and the seventy than into the hands of the learned and powerful. It is perhaps appropriate at this juncture in the progress of Jesus's ministry to quote words from Luke's earlier initial introduction to or presentation of the promise now moving forward: "He has brought down the powerful from their thrones and lifted up the lowly. He has filled the hungry with good things and sent the rich away empty." These words are quoted from the lips of the Blessed Virgin Mary (Luke 1:51–53).

Lesson Thirty-Five: Ninth Sunday after Pentecost; Read Mark 12:28–34

Let's look carefully at the context that Mark has developed (Mark 10:46–12:27) to lead us to this very significant—should we say, pivotal—episode (Mark 12:28–34). Recall that the healing of blind Bartimaeus outside the city of Jericho shows how this blind beggar, symbolic of Israel, recognizes Jesus as Son of David, throws off his cloak, and leaps up to plea for healing, begging to be able to see again. Jesus responds, "Go, your faith has made you well." Immediately he regains his sight and joins Jesus's entourage. The people of Israel, when portrayed by Jesus's disciples, are quick to join his mission initially but slow to understand his destiny as the Son of Man and resistant to Jesus's expectation that they will share his destiny. They are like the blind man at Bethsaida, able to see partially but needing to see fully (Mark 8:22–26). But suddenly, Bartimaeus can see fully and leaps to join this teacher whom he recognizes and celebrates as the long-promised Son of David.

And so as he prepares to make his public entry into Jerusalem, Jesus knows he can expect to find more ambiguous/mixed reception, some enthusiasm or acceptance and no doubt reluctance or rejection, same as his own disciples have harbored. Two of Jesus's disciples pick up on this new momentum and arrange for Jesus's arrival and entry, as Jesus himself seems to orchestrate the details (Mark 11:1–7).

Preparations have already produced leafy branches, ready to be spread along with cloaks on the roadway, contributed by "many" who position themselves, some leading this procession, some following, altogether crying out a well-known Aramaic greeting, exhortation, and exclamation, beginning with the popular expression "Hosanna!" which may be translated as "Save us now, we pray!" This exuberance continues with these words: "The one coming in the name of the Lord has been greatly blessed! The arriving kingdom of our Father David has already been greatly blessed! Save us now as you pour out your highest blessing!"

According to Mark's itinerary, this is Jesus's one and only visit to the city of Jerusalem. Many scholars are very dubious about this limitation. For example, Luke has Jesus there at age twelve (Luke 2:41–51), with a reminder that it was customary to visit Jerusalem at least annually for the Feast of Passover. John's Gospel puts Jesus in Jerusalem several times before his final week there. A prominent New Testament scholar, Dr. Robert W. Funk, chair of the Jesus Seminar and thus a leader of "the new quest for the historical Jesus" movement, once shared with me that after a lifetime of New Testament research, he was quiet confident Jesus traveled to Jerusalem on several, if not many, occasions during his lifetime.

The writer Mark, of course, as far as we know, is working out of the oral tradition, with no written documents as sources, and this means his knowledge of many details in Jesus's career may be limited. At the same time, we should remember that Mark is not motivated by modern expectations of scientific accuracy. He does not attempt to produce an accurate literal biography of Jesus that would satisfy scientific research. Instead, Mark writes or paints a portrait of Jesus, limited in detail and focused in purpose, that presents a theological/spiritual message sharply focused upon Jesus's calling and mission as introduced in Mark 1:1–15 and as drawing to its dramatic conclusion when Jesus enters Jerusalem and proceeds to fulfill his calling (Mark 11:1–16:8).

And this is why this triumphal entry narrative (11:1–11) is briefly but succinctly focused upon who Jesus is and why he arrives here, takes stock of the temple, and retires to the suburb of Bethany for the night with his disciples, who appear to be fully on board with this positive, upbeat transition after their travels south from Galilee to their arrival, at last, in the capital city of Jerusalem.

On the way to Jerusalem, Jesus, on two successive days, has as a run-in with a fig tree. Like everyone else, Jesus must live in the same world with impotent, fruitless realities, whether trees or nations, when he is hungry and they bear him no nourishment. In this case, he turns his frustration or disappointment into an opportunity to counsel his disciples on proper procedures and expectations in their prayer life (Mark 11:12–14, 20–25).

But it is not only the fig tree that withers and is fruitless. More important is Jesus's public demonstration in the temple itself, driving out the money changers, overthrowing their stalls and tables, and denouncing this corrupt and blasphemous institution with quotations from the prophets Isaiah (56:7) and Jeremiah (7:11): "Is it not written 'My house shall be a house of prayer for all the nations'? But you have made it a den of robbers!" Thus, he inaugurates his arrival and activities in Jerusalem with recall and reminder of just how blind and spiritually dead the official Jewish leadership is, just as he discovers and continually experiences earlier in his mission (Mark 1–10). Also makes one wonder, How should this temple look if it were truly a house of prayer for all the nations? An invitation to keep tuned!

Of course, these officials seek to expel him and rid themselves of this nuisance, as they have plotted before (Mark 3:6), but this time, he grows even more in popularity, and they must wait until the next day, when their fully staffed delegation confronts him, not physically but with interrogation as to his authority to behave as he does (11:27–33). Jesus, of course, will not play their game on their terms.

Mark presents three episodes (12:1–27) in which Jesus teaches both to rebuff his opponents and to announce and proclaim to everyone, to the whole world, the good news of the arrival of the kingdom of God: (1) in 12:1–12, the parable of the vineyard and the wicked tenants; (2) in 12:13–17, taxes, when to pay Caesar and when to pay God; and (3) in 12:18–27, one bride for seven brothers. The heights and depths of Jesus's wisdom here amazes and delights his growing admirers and both perplexes and enrages his opponents all the more, cementing their commitment to engineer his demise.

Suddenly, Mark recognizes the complexity and rich ambiguity of the nation of Israel. Enter one of the scribes who does not carry a dagger aimed at Jesus's heart. And here we arrive at our lesson for this week. This scribe, overhearing these previous episodes, does not see Jesus and his opponents as primarily enemies. True, Jesus's adversaries are determined to eliminate him from their scene. But this scribe notes how Jesus does not respond accordingly. They hate and fear him, but he hates no one and responds to their initiatives with respect and honor for the kingdom of God, including these spiritually insensitive, if not already spiritually dead, officials. Jesus teaches the truth and lets the chips fall where they must.

This scribe puts a positive spin on this exchange because he recognizes how Jesus's wisdom far surpasses the dead ends his opponents insist upon. The Greek verb *suzateo* in use here suggests this scribe overhears an honest, open, free discussion, debate, or disputation going on, and although that may be what Jesus seeks, that does not appear to be what his opponents desire. And so this scribe allows and welcomes Jesus's attitude and demeanor to override and stimulate the exploration and search for wisdom instead of defensive, closed-minded despotism.

Hearing how well Jesus answers and asks questions of those who aim to defeat him, this scribe is turned on to ask his own pressing question, which for him is both theoretical and practical as well as personal, "Which commandment is most important among all of them?" According to one account, there were, by this time in the history of Israel, 613 commandments to be taken seriously. His is an honest and experience-driven inquiry.

Jesus does not have to research this question. He knows the scriptures and theology of Judaism very thoroughly. The Shema, Hebrew ("Hear"), is his quick reply, the very first word found in Deuteronomy 6:4. (At this point, read Deuteronomy 6:4–9 and Leviticus 19:17–18.) Notice the first commandment is actually a statement: "Hear, O Israel, the Lord our God, the Lord is one." This commandment is to hear and then to affirm this truth or fact. To hear, in this context, does not mean only with your ears but also to receive and accept or acknowledge this reality. The original wording calls for love "with all your heart, with all your soul, and with all your might," meaning with all the resources you have as an individual human being. Note well, Jesus adds a fourth element to this list, "your mind." And Jesus adds, "Love your neighbor as yourself" (Leviticus 19:8).

The first or most important commandment begins with hearing and agreeing with this affirmation: "The Lord our God, the Lord is one [and only] God." Only after affirmation of this foundational truth can you move to respond or to obey commandments that spring forth from this one God. What is your appropriate response? "You shall love." In Greek, *agapeseis*, second person, singular, future tense, from *agapao*, which, of course, precedes human response, and this human response should reflect and duplicate and express the same self-sacrificing love this one God gives so freely.

Because this word for the human lover is *you* (singular), Jesus speaks directly to the individual. This word for love is also in the indicative mood, not imperative, which you would expect for a command. Indicative mood suggests that once you affirm the Shema, reality of the one and only God, your appropriate response will follow as night follows day. The affirmation of God and the one reality that flows from this God means one who makes this affirmation expresses trust and commitment to the same God and does not need to be persuaded or coerced or prodded or motivated further, beyond this basic affirmation. Hence, imperative mood is unnecessary.

However, the verb *agapao* is in the future tense, which shifts the indicative mood somewhat into persuasive encouragement or a positive expectation or prediction that such love will surely, without doubt, follow the affirmation of this one God. This means optimism, confidence, vision, expectation, prediction, or even description of how you will behave.

The most common English translations of this greatest commandment (NRSV and NIV, for example) run like this: "You will love the Lord your God with all your heart and with all your soul and with all your mind and with all your strength." This popular translation can be improved upon. This common wording misreads the preposition before and the cases of the four kinds of love. "With all your heart, with all your soul, with all your mind, and with all your strength" is not a sensitive reading of the Greek text. The words in Greek for heart (*kardias*), soul (*psukes*), mind (*dianoias*), and strength (*isxuos*) are all in the genitive case, not the accusative case, which is what the common translation says. Accusative case means the limit, horizon, extent of your action. Go this far, to this goal, but no further.

Likewise, the preposition *with* is not what the Greek says. The preposition *ex holes* precedes each noun and means "out of all or arising from the whole, of heart, soul, mind, and strength." Since these four nouns, objects of the preposition, are in the genitive case, not accusative case, which means extent, a much better translation is "arising from out of all your heart, soul, mind, and strength." To use accusative case means love to the extent of the heart, soul, mind, and strength you have right now. The genitive case means to love arising from out of all the potential you have within your heart, soul, mind, and strength. Do not settle for who you are right now, or at any time, but love arising out of all your resources, those hopefully growing, multiplying, developing within your heart, soul, mind, and strength all the time and thus including all your potentiality, which should be increasing daily throughout your lifetime.

The common translations, in other words, are weak or inaccurate or distorted, narrow, and consequently limit the extent or inclusiveness or flexibility or growth potential for your love. This more literal translation opens up opportunities and visions for your love to increase and grow now and forever in your lifetime as your heart, soul, mind, and strength develop and increase, expand and stretch according to the love this one God has for you, which never slows down, never ceases, but always increases, may we say, evolves or unfolds, according to our God's promises "to make all things new!" (Revelation 21:5).

The second commandment, however, as commonly translated is right on the mark. The word for your neighbor in Greek, *ton plasion sou*, is in the accusative case, meaning love your neighbor as he or she (singular) is right now. Do not wait for change in your neighbor, as if he or she should first become more lovable. Love your neighbor, whoever this is, right now, as an end in him or herself, never as means to another end.

Mark, the Gospel writer, is careful to include this narrative episode to show that not every Jewish official is Jesus's enemy. This scribe listens, hears, and commends Jesus's wisdom, remarking that such love as Jesus commands here supersedes formal, ritual offerings and sacrifices. This may be a not so subtle attempt by Mark to make sure these words from the mouth of Jesus help to prepare his readers, Jewish and Gentile, for the approaching Roman destruction of Jerusalem (70–75 CE), when the formal sacrificial system practiced for so long in the Temple in Jerusalem will come to an end.

And Mark implies that this kingdom should be open to and expect to include wisdom both from Jewish sources and from Hellenistic cultural sources, which Jesus makes explicit when he adds the human mind to the Shema prayer's recognition of the human heart, soul, and strength. This expansion of the human personality to include mind, as well as heart, soul, and strength, places Jesus in the community of "wholistic thinkers" who are already prominent within the Hellenistic humanism spreading across the Roman Empire. The classical Greek philosophers, such as Aristotle (384–322 BCE), no doubt hear, smile, and approve.

Lesson Thirty-Six: Tenth Sunday after Pentecost; Read John 6:1–21

This lesson focuses first of all upon the fifth of the seven signs Jesus works or performs during the first twelve chapters of this fourth gospel. As usual, Jesus's sign is followed by extensive discourse in which Jesus teaches the deeper spiritual meaning to which the sign points. Jesus here continues the dialogue or argument he initiated with Nicodemus, who could not distinguish between the literal, physical level of Jesus' teaching, and the new, spiritual birth from above necessary to truly enter into and benefit from the good news of the arriving kingdom of God.

Scholars point out that this sign, feeding of the five thousand, is the only miracle of Jesus to appear in all four gospels, suggesting this episode carried strong weight in the oral and whatever written sources the Gospel writers drew upon. Furthermore, Matthew (14:13–21 and 15:32–39) and Mark (6:30–44 and 8:1–10) both appear to repeat the story. This version by John, however, is distinctive enough to suggest that this writer draws upon his own sources. Both Matthew and Luke appear to rely closely upon Mark as their source.

To begin to exegete John's treatment of this pericope, let's probe the context, extending back to John 5:1. Jesus has been teaching/healing in Galilee, specifically in Cana where earlier he had changed the water into wine. Note the traditional Jewish emphasis upon signs and wonders as proofs of divine presence (Cf. 1 Cor. 1:22), contrasting with Jesus's use of signs and wonders as opportunities to teach, to call believers to move from surface-level phenomena to deeper spiritual engagement with the grace and truth Jesus brings from God his Father (John 12:14). Review this emphasis Jesus has already presented in his discourse following his encounter with Nicodemus (John 3:1–21).

As if to say Jesus has done his duty in Galilee for now, the bigger picture beckons. One of the Jewish festivals calls Jesus to go to Jerusalem. (No distinction between the three annual pilgrimage festivals, Passover, Pentecost, or Tabernacles, is made here.) This is Jesus's second trip to Jerusalem, according to this Gospel. As already displayed in his first sojourn in Jerusalem (John 2:13–3:21), Jesus initiates contacts in the capital city seeking to teach, express, and demonstrate who he is, his true identity, not through surface-level proofs based upon the Law or traditions of Judaism, but growing out of his origin as the divine *LOGOS* (John 1:1–14) whose presence brings grace and truth from God the Father for the entire cosmos, the creation, or the universe, in modern parlance (John 3:16).

This sojourn in Jerusalem proceeds in three steps: healing (5:2–9), dialogue/interchange/outcomes (5:10–18), and discourse (5:19–47). Notice how the single question of the identity and/or presence of Jesus dominates this dialogue section (5:10–18). The sudden rise in sharp hostility toward Jesus is based upon surface-level, superficial questions of Jesus's identity and thus never involves the deeper levels of his origins and divine mission. The long and short of this episode is that Jesus confronts Jerusalem and thus Judaism with his presence, opportunity for God's people to recognize, receive, and accept this Son of God and the blessings of salvation he brings from God the Father. The Jewish leaders, however, are hung up on the Law and Jesus's blatant blasphemy because he identifies himself with God. Jesus goes over their heads and appeals to Moses, father of the Law, who deserves deeper and better understanding and treatment than these self-serving officials can express because they are unable or refuse to grapple with spiritual reality on the deeper levels to which Moses himself, and now Jesus himself invites them to pursue and engage. As a result of this impasse, Jesus here encounters the first persecution, rejection, and death threats found in this gospel. According to Mark, Jesus met this same response early on in Galilee (Mark 3:1–6). John, however, finds more pizzazz in this development by locating this united opposition to Jesus not in rural, remote Galilee but the capital city Jerusalem.

Segue now to this week's lesson (John 6:1-21). Apparently, having exhausted his frustrating teaching occasions in Jerusalem (John 5:1–46), Jesus seeks to return to Galilee apparently with his disciples. Notice how subtly John introduces the alternative name for the Sea of Galilee—Sea of Tiberius. This is the name, Tiberius, of the reigning Roman emperor—Tiberius Claudius Caesar Augustus (14 CE–37 CE). This is the Emperor whose coin prompted some Pharisees and Herodians to challenge Jesus on his tax-paying policies (Mark 12:13–17).

Historical background: Herod Antipas built the new city of Tiberias (18 CE) to replace Sepphoris as his capital of Galilee and named it for the reigning emperor. He wanted a site not too near the Decapolis region (East Bank of the Jordan River) and as far away as possible from Sepphoris. He chose the site of an ancient necropolis/cemetery, which made it ritually unclean for pious Jews, and thus out of bounds for them to visit. But this site was also on major trade/travel routes between Syria and Egypt. We have no record that Jesus ever set foot in Tiberius and this city is mentioned only once in scripture, near our present periscope (John 6:23). Apparently, Herod's push to change the name of the Sea of Galilee to the Sea of Tiberius was slow to catch on. But our present narrator, John, like Mark before him (e.g., Mark 6:17–29), finds it helpful to relate Jesus's ministry to certain not-so-peripheral elements of the broader Hellenistic world, a world in often unnerving transition then. Not at all unlike today's world, was it not?

Jesus crosses the Sea of Galilee from the East to the West. Geographically this is a long trip from Jerusalem for Jesus and his disciples, and a large crowd follows after them. Are they from Jerusalem, or do they pick up this following along the way? The Greek language suggests continual growth of this crowd, adding numbers every step along the way. No matter, the important point is this crowd congregates because its members are drawn to the signs Jesus does for the sick. Contrary to the Jewish and Roman officials back in Jerusalem, this crowd does not respond with hostility but with curiosity, expectation, and hope to Jesus's signs.

From his perch with his disciples up on the mountain, Jesus realizes they cannot escape for needed R & R (rest and recuperation). The crowd continues to grow down below. Jesus's mind moves from sensitivity to these people in need to remember that the Feast of Passover is near. This crowd draws Jesus's attention all the way back across the centuries to ancient Egypt and the very first Passover. God's very own people in need—slaves, as a matter of fact.

Lifting his eyes, Jesus finds himself overwhelmed with compassion for these spiritually hungry human beings, bringing whatever sickness or need they have to his attention. Passover calls to mind unleavened bread, the very finest of culinary preparation. Jesus turns to his disciple Philip. "Where is the marketplace, so we may buy bread for these dear ones to eat?" (He was testing Philip because he knew what he intended to do.)

"Two hundred denari (six month's wages) would not buy enough bread for each one to take even a little," Philip responds.

Overhearing, Andrew, brother of Simon Peter, is already on the ball, taking an inventory of food available across the crowd. "A young boy over here has five barley loaves and two fish [poor people's food!]. That's all. But what does this amount to with so many to feed?"

Jesus listens and begins to get the Passover Feast moving. "Tell these people to recline [assume the normal posture for a celebratory meal] and make themselves comfortable on this green grass."

The crowd gets ready, probably more than five thousand, altogether.

Everything being ready, Jesus takes the loaves of bread, gives thanks, and distributes to the ones reclining, and also as much of the fish as they want. (Question: Do the disciples help in distribution as in the synoptic versions?) Now when their stomachs get filled/satisfied, Jesus instructs his disciples, "Gather up all of the leftovers so that nothing may be lost." And they move through the crowd and gather up twelve baskets full of the barley bread, leftover by all of these people who have eaten.

And this large crowd of men, having witnessed this sign Jesus has worked, begins to reflect and to share this observation among themselves, "Surely this one is the prophet whom our God has promised to send into this world!" And Jesus knows in his heart, soul, and mind what's going on in this crowd that has been fed. He knows they see this Passover meal as an affirmation of their need to be assured of their hopes and expectations. He knows their next step will be to take him up on their shoulders and seek to make him their king who, no doubt the long-promised prophet leader/ruler, will continue to provide for their economical needs.

But this is not the kind of king Jesus has been sent into this world to become. He has become flesh (John 1:14) to share the grace and truth of his Father God with the whole cosmos (John 3:16). His signs are presented not to stamp approval upon the expectations these crowds already have. Likewise, his signs are not to stamp approval upon the negative roles the Jewish and Roman officials find in him

(John 5:16–18). In every instance, his signs are an opportunity for his constituencies, of whatever persuasion, to probe and grapple in depth with spiritual dimensions of the Jewish covenant they desperately need to become more engaged in, just as Jesus has already presented this case to Nicodemus (John 3:1–15). Not willing to allow this crowd to seek to enthrone him as the kind of king they envision and desire him to become, Jesus turns and slips away, grieving at their insensitivity, and manages to find a spot to be alone for a while.

As evening arrives, his disciples, waiting a while for Jesus, go ahead and embark on a boat to strike out for Capernaum. Darkness arrives, and still Jesus has not come to be with them. Suddenly, as happens on this body of water, a fierce wind arises and is churning up the water. Having rowed with stress for three or four miles, they see Jesus walking on the water, coming near their boat. They are terrified. Jesus quickly speaks to them, "Hey, guys, it's me. You don't need to be afraid." In the Greek language, Jesus says, "*Ego eimi*," meaning "I am who I am!" which may be interpreted as a claim to be divine. They calm down and beckon to him to get in the boat. But their boat is soon ready to land on the shore they are approaching.

True to the pattern John the gospel writer uses, Jesus first works these signs for the crowds and his disciples to experience and to learn from (John 6:1–21) and then Jesus engages in extensive dialogue, discussion, and discourse intended to stimulate more, deeper, and compelling exploration and hopefully understanding beyond surface-level, physical exposure/involvement. Read and study Jesus's teaching here in John 6:22–71 to allow yourself to be drawn deeper into Jesus's attempt to elucidate just what the experience of the signs hopefully will lead to.

Lesson Thirty-Seven: Eleventh Sunday after Pentecost; Read John 6:22–51

The context for this lesson is the feeding narrative and aftermath that follows. This miracle, feeding the five thousand, is one of the seven signs that Jesus performs in this gospel and the only miracle that appears in all four gospels. As previously, this gospel writer, John, has Jesus deliver lengthy periods of dialogue and/or discourse, since the seven signs are not ends in themselves, but Jesus's unique behavior or activities which point far beyond themselves to the deeper, true significance of the miracle which observers or participants are invited and urged/simulated, encouraged to grapple with to understand and accept. This challenge Jesus presents both to his disciples and to the growing numbers of citizens who are attracted to Jesus's teaching and behavior, such as the five thousand here on the banks of the Sea of Galilee.

This lesson grows sharply out of the feeding narrative. The picture in 6:15–24 is one of urgency. Jesus, riled up and turned off by the aggressive strategy of the crowd of five thousand whose stomachs have just been filled to overflowing, flees from them lest they hoist him on their shoulders and march on Jerusalem to crown him king. Such a grotesque yet all too real threat only magnifies how the powerful sign Jesus has just performed does not yet penetrate to the hearts and souls of these hungry, enthusiastic, but shallow-thinking revelers.

It looks like the crowd rallies itself for action, sends out scouting parties to track down Jesus and his disciples, lest they escape and thus evade their ambitious project. They round up their own boats and embark, determined to find Jesus and party, well-informed that he has most likely avoided them by escaping to Capernaum (6:22–24).

Some paraphrase here: "Sure enough! They track him down at Capernaum, and pounce upon him: "Rabbi, what are you doing here? Why did you leave us behind?" Jesus sighs, frustrated with their persistence; such energy for the wrong reasons! Jesus takes them aside, sits them down, and begins to explain, "Listen to me, dear friends. You are following me, but you are not seeking works our God is doing. You are happy because of the good food and you want more."

Literal translation: "Truly, truly, I say to you, you are seeking me not because you saw signs [Greek: *TA SEMEIA*] from our Lord but because you ate and were full. Do not rush to get more food that perishes, but focus yourself upon finding the food which does not perish, but food that remains with you and nourishes you all the way to eternal life. This is the food that the Son of Man will give to you. And this is the food which God the Father has certified with his stamp of approval."

The Greek verb translated "certified" is *ESFRAGISEN*, aorist tense, active voice, from the verb root *SFRAGIZO*, to stamp with a seal of approval or to certify as kosher. *Context*: The priests had to examine all animals brought to the temple for sacrifice to make sure they qualified (without blemish). There is no such seal on the five loaves and two fish, but this crowd neither looks for nor expects such a seal. They relish the food for their tummies. Jesus, however, affirms that this and all of his signs originate with God the Father and arrive on this scene to reveal who Jesus truly is and for what purpose he is here.

Word study: The Greek word for sign, *TO SEMEION*, carries two potential meanings. One meaning is to serve as an identification tag to satisfy your need to know this product is what you have ordered and paid for. So you bring to this search your prior definition of what you need/want and the sign, seal, or stamp removes your doubt and you are happy to take what is yours because you deserve it or you have already earned it and paid for it. The second meaning of TO SEMEION is an activity, an occasion, an event, or a deed which points far beyond itself and beckons you to follow to its source, and from there to where or with whom it seeks to draw you into a relationship and provide a new reality, a blessing, a benefit, or a new creation into which you are invited and which, if you accept, will bring you great change in yourself and all of your worldview. This second meaning, of course, is how Jesus understands his signs and this understanding motivates him to present his signs exactly because as *TO LOGOS TOU THEOU* (the Word of God) become flesh (John 1:1–14) he is full of grace and truth to express the love of God his Father (*HE AGAPE TOU THEOU*) which seeks to save, renew, and recreate this cosmos God the Father loves so very much (John 3:16–21).

This crowd, hearing some positive promise on the lips of Jesus, but not yet following where Jesus hopes his signs will lead them, opens up enough to ask what more works they may do, not waking up to what Jesus is trying to tell them—that their qualification is not the issue at all. They ask, "What then should we be doing so we may work the works of God?" (The redundancy on the concept of work here is surely intentional on the writer John's part.) The Greek word for "work" here is *ERGAZOMETHA,* first-person plural, present tense, subjunctive mood, middle voice. The Greek language has three voices—active, middle, and passive. This is the middle voice, which means to act upon yourself and to help yourself or so you are the beneficiary of your labors. Subjunctive mood means we ought to do something we are not already doing—that is, something new and novel. Present tense means to learn how to take up this new practice and do it continually so it becomes a matter of daily habit. In other words, they put themselves front and center and insist upon dealing with Jesus and his teaching upon their own terms. They either cannot or will not hear the alternative message Jesus tries to deliver to them and invites them to consider for themselves.

Jesus does not give up. Jesus is patient. Taking up their insistence upon the concept of work, Jesus replies, "This is the work our God wants from you, that you should believe in that one whom God has sent." *Word study*: the Greek word translated as "believe" here (*HE PISTIS*) has three basic possible meanings in English: "belief," "faith," and "trust." The problem with *believe* in English is it carries connotations of knowing or agreeing upon correct facts. *Faith* is better, but it also implies correct doctrine, etc. *Trust* is the best choice because it calls for the relationship of responsibility and commitment, arising from heart and soul, without demanding rational truth or accuracy. Thus, to redo these words of Jesus, "This is the work our God wants from you, that you should trust that one whom our God has sent, and thus commit yourselves to him and to the one who has sent him, and to the purpose of this entire project."

His listeners perk up. "Okay, rabbi, so what sign are you going to show us, so that we may see and believe in you?" (Show us? Huh? So his feeding them with five loaves and two fish was not a sign enough?) They grow impatient, twiddling their thumbs. "Here's a clue to help, rabbi. Our forefathers ate the manna in the wilderness, just as it is written, "He gave them bread from heaven to eat."

Jesus is willing to follow their lead. "Listen up now, as I tell you this truth. Moses did not give you this bread out of heaven, but

God my Father gives you the true bread from heaven. For the bread of God is the one coming down out of heaven and giving life to the world."

Jesus's listeners perk up again. "Lord, give us this same bread!" (Note, not "rabbi" this time.) Jesus says to them, "I am the bread of life. The one coming to me will never ever be hungry and the one who trusts in me will never thirst again, ever."

(Note: the Greek language loves double negatives, which do the opposite of what a double negative does in English.) Both verbs in this sentence, *hunger* and *thirst*, are preceded by OU ME, meaning in English, "not never." Jesus could not be more assertive in offering himself as the true bread of heaven whom his listeners should welcome and learn to devour, swallow, and assimilate as their expression of trust in his claim to the divine blessing, the nourishment God his Father sends freely and abundantly for the salvation of his creation.

Jesus labors now to stress his identification of himself as the bread of life and the contrast between himself and that bread which their ancestors ate (manna from heaven) in the wilderness and subsequently died. The difference is emphatic, "The one who comes to me will never ever be hungry again and will never ever be thirsty again." This affirmation and accompanying dialogue remind us of the lengthy dialogue in John 4:7–26 between Jesus and the Samaritan woman at the well. In that discourse, Jesus is strongly critical of the formal, institutional worship of both the Jews and the Samaritans, so much so that he labels their two temples, the one in Jerusalem and the one on Mt. Gerizim, as inferior or outdated or irrelevant and unnecessary, when contrasted with "worship in Spirit and in truth."

Paraphrase (John 6:36–40): Jesus, now obviously on a roll, continues, "The manna from heaven is but a memory from long ago. Today you see me and my works, before your very own eyes. You have eaten bread for your bodies, a present, physical sign which points to all our heavenly Father seeks to give to you. This sign seeks to draw you from the bread you ate on the mountainside to me, I who am also this present spiritual food/bread our Father God sends freely for your consumption so you will never be spiritually hungry or thirsty again. Our heavenly Father sent the manna in the wilderness. Now our heavenly Father sends me, heavenly food, the bread of life because our heavenly Father loves this creation, this cosmos so very much and wants to draw you and everyone else to himself."

Jesus continues, "And this is exactly what he wants, that I should give myself to you and this creation, so that through me, the bread of life, you will find nourishment for your souls, and through me, he will draw you and everyone else to himself. I give myself, the bread of life, to you so that no one will be lost, but so that all will be drawn to my Father. This indeed is what he wants, that all who see the Son of God and believe in him, trust themselves to him, will receive eternal life, beginning right now, and I will raise them on the last day."

Jesus now puts his capstone on this discourse, "Indeed, the bread which I will give on behalf of the life of the whole world is my very own flesh." Most references to Jesus as the bread of life seem to rest upon and grow out of his becoming flesh (John 1:1–14), the event known in formal theological circles as "the incarnation." The syntax here indicates, "Listen up," for here comes a new revelation. The verb "I will give" in Greek, *doso,* is clearly future tense, pointing to an event worth anticipating and looking forward to—that is, to Jesus's rapidly approaching passion (his suffering, rejection, crucifixion, and resurrection) which, of course, serves as his glorification, the dramatic climax of this the fourth gospel.

Lesson Thirty-Eight: Twelfth Sunday after Pentecost; Read John 6:52–71.

This lesson wraps up these lengthy and pithy discourses and dialogues Jesus has been leading and negotiating since his performance of his last miraculous sign, the feeding of the five thousand on the mountainside (John 6:1–15). The good news is how Jesus's signs (this is number five of his seven signs in this gospel) attract popular attention, enthusiasm, and approval and draw new or potential disciples who want more of what Jesus has to offer. The problematic reality, however, is the crowd's desire to have Jesus produce not something new but only more and more of what they already expect and demand.

It is Passover Season, and the crowds associate Jesus's blessings with their memory of Moses's leadership during the Exodus from Egypt and the stressful wilderness sojourn. Jesus struggles to show how nourishment such as the manna served its purpose then but that's all. Now Jesus aims to encourage these pilgrims to open up to something new, different, and far better that God is sending to them in the arrival of Jesus himself in their midst.

Their ancestors ate the manna from heaven in the wilderness and died. God now sends Jesus to them as heavenly food, not physical but spiritual, which to eat means to receive the new life of spiritual fulfillment and renewal and never to die but to live forever. The multiplication of the five loaves and two fish, they know not how, points to blessings from above Jesus offers to them. They are ready for more free food for their stomachs but slow or unable to accept and consume the Spirit Jesus brings because this Spirit beckons them to open up within themselves and receive stimulation or their movement from self-satisfaction to rebirth, new birth from above, to a new living relationship with the Jesus who is the divine *Logos* become human flesh, full of grace and truth (John1:1–14).

Their hesitation, reluctance to welcome and consume, digest, and assimilate this new definition of heavenly food illustrates the all too normal human condition the writer John identifies, portrays, and studies in each of the three contextual levels he has in mind and addresses in these narratives. They seek to take seriously

1. the original historical narrative record of the career of Jesus he has received and is passing on to his current generation;
2. he is especially motivated to speak directly to his fellow Christian believers under pressure from their Jewish friends and neighbors (ca. 90 CE–95 CE). These are the first readers of this written document to whom and for whom this writer struggles to speak as persuasively as he can since he himself shares their precarious existence and with whom he seeks to survive, not to mention thrive, as a faithful disciple; and

3. John looks far forward, ahead, outward, beyond, and abroad, with cosmopolitan and universal perspectives, to future culturally diverse generations of the human race whom the one Lord God seeks also to influence and bless (John 3:16–21).

Scholars are convinced that John is especially under pressure to present Jesus's discourses in a manner that speaks directly to his contemporaries in the second of these three contextual environments. If historians are correct that his friends and neighbors are threatened with or actually being expelled from their synagogues because of their profession of faith in Jesus as Messiah, then the repeated reluctance or inability of the crowds to think of Jesus's body and blood as bread and wine fits that context.

Jesus's verbal struggles to expound the symbolism of bread and wine as components of himself not only report his experience in the Capernaum synagogue but serve to instruct and counsel John's stressed companions in 90 CE–95 CE. At the same time, scholars note John includes no inauguration of the Eucharistic Celebration in the form of the traditional Passover meal during Jesus's farewell, discourses with his most intimate disciples (John 13–17), whereas the three synoptic gospels make that Passover ritual, especially the elevation and distribution of the bread (body) and wine (blood), a most prominent component or element of Jesus's final hours of intimate association with his twelve disciples.

This leads to the supposition that John's contemporaries need instruction and counsel when they are pressured either to exclude this ritual or observe it only as refugees from a war zone. In John 6:1–71, Jesus offers his extensive series of self-revelatory expositions of just who he is and just how he is the bread and wine of eternal life, not in the physical consumption of unleavened bread and processed fruit of the vineyard but the divinely inspired experience of new birth in the spirit freely given from above.

We should recall how Jesus's extensive dialogue with the Samaritan woman argued against continued reliance upon the traditional, habitual ritual as practiced in the Jewish temple in Jerusalem and/or in the Samaritan temple on Mt. Gerizim (John 4:19–26). If scholars are correct that John writs this narrative ca. 90 CE–95 CE, then Jesus was preparing his original listeners for the expected destruction of Jerusalem (ca. 65 CE–70 CE), which put an end to the priestly officiate, formal temple sacrifices once and for all and ushered in the development of what becomes known as "rabbinical Judaism."

Jesus addresses the Samaritan woman this way: *Paraphrase*: "It is indeed true that salvation comes from us Jews, but the time is drawing near when true worshippers will worship God the Father in Spirit and Truth. For we now know that our God is Spirit and calls, invites, and enables everyone to worship, always, anywhere, and all the time, in Spirit and Truth."

It is surely no accident that while Jesus does not point to himself as the bread of life broken for all, nor as the Cup of salvation poured out for all, during those intimate moments in that upper room, Jesus does take a towel and wash his disciples' soiled feet, presenting himself as a lowly servant, who even as a household slave, seeks to cleanse, counsel, and console his brothers and sisters who share the blessing of his most intimate presence in a time of stress and anguish (John 13:1–20).

In other words, thinking of the third contextual environment, for those who participate in the rebirth he offers as the sign and seal of God the Father's new creation, his nourishment is present and effective as the living presence and fulfillment of eternal life for all who trust, for all believers, all the time. This interpretation moves in the direction of the human experience of all creation (note John 1:1–14) as the locus of sacramental presence and the potential for the human experience of divine reality.

Perhaps it is appropriate to call attention here to the apostle Thomas, whose questioning and skepticism points to the Gentile, Hellenistic populations this gospel writer seeks ultimately to serve. After Thomas's profession of Jesus to be "my Lord and my God," Jesus confirms his affirmation when he says, "Have you believed because you have seen me? Blessed are those who have not seen and yet have come to believe!" (John 20:28–29) Jesus here points both to the first readers of this the fourth gospel and to all of the future disciples/believers who share Thomas's profession of faith, including those of us living today who seek to worship and serve Jesus as, using Thomas's words "my Lord and my God."

There is also scholarly suspicion that this gospel writer, John, is writing in a time (90 CE–95 CE) when some versions of gnostic-oriented Christologies may be circulating and tempting new Christians to experiment with docetic notions of spirituality to deflate Jewish opposition to the emphasis upon human flesh. Gnostics, let us remember, were fond of "docetism" because this Greek word/concept means that Jesus only "seems" or "appears" to have a physical body but was really only a spirit walking around deceiving everyone into thinking he was really human. This means, according to gnostic interpretation, Jesus did not die on the cross because he was wholly spiritual and spirits cannot die. Thus, the Gnostics insist, the whole crucifixion scene was deceptive and falsification of reality. John's corrective alternative to these Gnostics would be reflected in the strong emphasis upon the Logos of God becoming human flesh (John 1:1–14) and especially in 6:1–71 upon the importance of Jesus' very own flesh everywhere, every day, all the time, as the presence of the bread (body) and wine (blood) of salvation.

In today's lesson (John 6:56–65) Jesus runs his colors up the flag pole for all to see. Here is the gospel in a nutshell. Some of his "disciples" still cannot tolerate his strong language. Seeing they are offended, Jesus has one more card up his sleeve. *Paraphrase*: "What if you see the Son of man ascending to where he came from (death, resurrection, ascension)? The spirit brings life; the flesh is worthless. My words point you to both spirit and life, but some of you cannot bring yourself to trust what I say. Whatever I say, you will listen and trust me only if my father gives you new life, from above."

Hearing all this, many of his "disciples" turn away from following him. Simon Peter answers, "Lord, to whom shall we go?"(Greek: *APELEUSOMETHA*, first-person plural, future tense, middle voice, indicative mood, from root verb, *APERXOMAI*). Because this verb is middle voice, this question from Simon Peter should be translated thus, "Lord to whom shall we go to be good to ourselves?" In other words,

"What can we do to be true to ourselves other than stick with you, since you give to us the words of life. We have come to know and to trust that you are the Holy One of God." Jesus answers, "You are so correct, my good man. Did I not choose you, the twelve of you? "And even so one of you is a devil!" This is the first time Jesus uses the word *twelve*, which affirms his love for and inclusion of Judas Iscariot, who was going to betray him.

And so John concludes this long discourse with recognition of the distinction between Jesus's own chosen twelve disciples and the crowds, some of whom have tried to become his disciples, but for the wrong or shallow reasons, and who, the more they listened to Jesus, could not abide his language. After all these efforts, Jesus concludes, "After all of this, what I have told you is true. No one can possibly come to me unless this move has been given to him by the Father."

Lesson Thirty-Nine: Thirteenth Sunday after Pentecost; Read Luke 10:38–42

In this episode, Jesus and his entourage of disciples continue their journey toward Jerusalem. Entering a village, a local woman named Martha wastes no time but seeks them out and welcomes them all into her home. Scholars note how Luke deliberately reports this event following the parable of the good Samaritan (Luke 10:25–37) because both stories present unexpected, if not shocking, behavior. No one expects a despised Samaritan to show mercy and hospitality toward a suffering Jew when two fellow Jews have left him dying in the ditch. But this new exhibition of sacrificial neighborliness prompts Jesus to instruct the self-serving lawyer "to go and do likewise."

Who is this woman named Martha who takes it upon herself to welcome Jesus into her home? Women are not heads of households, keepers of the hearth! That is a man's role. Of course, we know nothing more of this family from Luke's narrative. Only elsewhere, in John's gospel (11:1–44), do we learn these two sisters, Mary and Martha, have as their brother Lazarus, assuming this is the same family and Bethany is the village of their residence. In John's narrative, the brother Lazarus's role is to take sick, die, and be raised from the tomb by Jesus. Both Martha and Mary express leadership, with perhaps Mary taking the lead role as liaison between Jesus and the neighbors who witness these encounters, which are very strong and powerful motifs, central to the fourth gospel's theology.

Back in Luke's narrative, the man of the family, Lazarus, is missing, and Martha initially steps up to serve as host and spokesperson for the household. RSV translation says Martha welcomes Jesus "into her home." The Greek text is not this explicit, but this is a reasonable conclusion about what is going on. That is to say, Martha is probably the older of the two sisters and naturally assumes the paternalistic duty of formally opening up this household to these weary travelers in need of some accommodation.

At the same time, however, Martha is, as host, also of necessity the hostess who must plan, do the shopping, and superintend the kitchen help who put together from scratch the necessary ingredients to provide a traditional meal that expresses suitable nourishment and cordial hospitality. This responsibility of course includes making sure the servants or slaves have bathed and dried their guests' dusty feet and made them comfortable on the cushions arranged appropriately on the floor.

Martha has her hands full and no doubt performs admirably and with true dedication to her duties, substituting as she is for the roles normally provided by the masculine or paternalistic persons presiding over this household. In the meantime, what is the younger sister Mary up to? Is she dutifully carrying her weight as a faithful, integral, organic component of Martha's team?

Jesus, of course, being suitably rested and made comfortable, proceeds to do what Jesus does best. He sits himself down, assuming his central, presiding position of teacher. His entourage, disciples both regular and probably newly acquired, or perhaps including members of the Seventy, settle in to hear and learn, each one finding a comfortable niche among the soft cushions. Nestled neatly among this circle of listeners, ears and eyes open and alert, is Mary, hanging on every word Jesus utters, mesmerized and enthralled as if hypnotized and transferred from her normal family into the heavenly family.

Not so Martha, who strains to catch a word or two from Jesus's lips, trying to make sure the food and drink preparation is shuffling along effectively. Martha realizes her sister has quietly deserted her usual position near the oven. Maybe she will hear enough soon and return to help her older sister with all these details of the culinary arts. But Mary is transfixed by her new teacher's compelling rhetoric and cannot take her eyes off his face.

Martha is soon at her wit's end. Her sister is abandoning her duty, her role as cohostess, and making like one of the disciple guests! Who is in charge here? Looks like Jesus is running this show. Martha slips over to his side and, with hesitation, nevertheless bends over to where Jesus can hear and, whispering in his ear, asks, "Lord, maybe you have not noticed but my sister has left me to do all this work by myself! Should you not remind her of her duty to help me?"

Now, why doesn't Martha call her sister on her own? Why does Martha look to Jesus to correct her sister's behavior? Because Jesus is a man. Because Jesus is in charge of the little synagogue family gathering which sits at his feet and draws orientation and direction from their Master's mind, heart, soul, and mouth. Because Martha knows Jesus values their hospitality and Martha's leadership and labor on behalf of this microversion of the kingdom of God. Jesus will surely affirm her roles and the necessity that her sister Mary is called not only to hear and learn but also to fulfill her role as Martha's coworker in the warm hospitality now being enjoyed. Martha gets specific, "Lord, can you urge my sister Mary to help me with these tasks which need to be done?"

And Martha is correct in her strategy and her recognition of her sister Mary's dual roles as a newly self-appointed disciple of Jesus and her continuing responsibility as cohostess in this her own family's residence. Jesus turns to Martha with affirmation and genuine warmth in his voice, "Martha, dear Martha, I know you are worried and troubled about many necessary details in this beautiful home, and I thank you so very much, from the bottom of my heart, for your loving care and devoted attention to our comfort and safety. We cannot make this our appointed journey without your initiative, your support, your encouragement, and your participation which contributes to the fulfillment of our goals."

Maintaining his teaching position, Jesus continues, "However, all of these details are important exactly because they arise from and lead to the fulfillment of the work we all seek to do as this journey we are on takes us before long all the way to Jerusalem. Mary has chosen to sit here as one of my disciples to learn and to focus upon the big picture of this process unfolding among us. All of the details you are devoted to are necessary and indispensable."

Sighing and taking a deep breath, Jesus continues, "But Mary, bless her heart, has stepped outside of her routine and joined this my disciple band because she has chosen a different, a new, a transformative involvement and role for herself, which is her choice to make. Take note, her choice is not the best, not absolutely perfect, but by comparison, the better choice for her than to remain in her previous roles. And now, let everyone listen up! Because this new role of listener, learner, and participant in my disciple band, is a better calling for her, let none of us, not you, her sister, or any other who may object to her, a woman, joining to share what has traditionally been a male-dominated domain, seek to discourage or hinder her faithful participation as a loyal and dedicated disciple and servant of the goals and objectives of this my calling, and what I describe as my departure or my exodus."

It is important at this point to recall why Luke brings the parable of the good Samaritan and this story of Mary and Martha together as he does. Both the Samaritan traveler and Mary are unlikely if not prohibited players in this overall drama bringing good news. But bring good news they both do. So that the lawyer comes to hear he should no longer search for whoever might be his neighbor and instead decide how he may become himself a good neighbor, as portrayed, unexpectedly, by the Samaritan citizen, normally an alien enemy to traditional Jews. He reluctantly gains the Good Samaritan as his new role model.

When Mary decides to move from the kitchen to the circle of cushions around Jesus the teacher, she no doubt prompts some sighs and groans among Jesus' traditionalist or orthodox disciples. Her sister Martha becomes the vocal resister to change and the voice who pressures Jesus to help her to hold on to the "good old-time religion!"

But Jesus insists Mary has chosen "the better part." Meaning while everyone has to eat sooner or later, Mary has chosen to listen and learn from the teacher who brings the good news of the great love of God the Father into the world and who learned very early in his ministry that "one does not live by bread alone, but by every word that comes from the mouth of God" (Matt. 4:1–4).

It may be prudent to recall that sometime after Jesus gave us the parable of the good Samaritan and this story of Martha and Mary, but some time before the gospels were written, the apostle Paul insisted that "there is no longer Jew or Greek, there is no longer slave or free, there is no longer male and female, for all of you are one in Christ Jesus" (Gal. 3:28). Anticipating the tensions he was inaugurating, Jesus foresaw the resistance of conservative Palestinian cultures and repeated his wisdom this way, "Mary has chosen the better part, which will not be taken away from her."

We see in both of these episodes, the good Samaritan parable and Martha-Mary drama, how Luke recalls and describes the techniques Jesus uses to move his disciples along with him on the road to his exodus or departure in Jerusalem. According to Jesus the Teacher, God his Father in heaven can and does include unexpected individuals, the alien Samaritan and a mere woman, Mary, as pioneers who are harbingers of how the kingdom of God will look as it moves from its strictly Jewish origins to impact the Hellenistic world. Perhaps Luke would be pleased if and when his faithful readers in the twenty-first century pay attention and learn from the example of the alien Samaritan and the woman Mary, who cannot resist exploring "the better parts."

Lesson Forty: Fourteenth Sunday after Pentecost; Read Luke 11:1–13

This lesson begins with the so-called Lord's Prayer, perennially popular down through the ages in western Christian liturgies. Interestingly this teaching of Jesus occurs only twice in the New

Testament, here and in Matthew's Sermon on the Mount (Matt. 6:9–13). Presumably, both gospel editors, Matthew and Luke, draw these words from the hypothetical document "Q." Luke's version is briefer than Matthew's version, and thus probably closer to Jesus's original words, assuming both versions reflect growing liturgical usage among young Christian communities. That is to say, each version reflects the editor's contextual presentation.

Matthew's version is more formal, stately, stylized to express the Jewish approval of prescribed, approved, probably memorized, and habitually used daily prayers. Notice Matthew's context. The problem in his circle is the public expression of piety. How to avoid false, improper, inappropriate almsgiving, prayer, and fasting? Here Jesus warns, "When you are praying, do not heap up empty phrases as the Gentiles do; for they think they will be heard because of their many words. Do not be like them, for your Father knows what you need before you ask him" (Matthew 6–8).

Paraphrase: "Instead of praying the wrong way, therefore, be sure that you pray this way: 'Father of us, the one in the heavens, let your name be revered, let your kingdom come to us, let your will be done, as in heaven, so also here on earth'"(Matt. 6:9–10) This address begins with the "Our Father," denoting this is a corporate prayer suitable for formal public participation. Scholars surmise that Jesus regularly used the Aramaic phrase *Abba*, which means "dear, precious Daddy" or "Papa," revealing spiritual intimacy and trust unique to this parent-child relationship. This Aramaic word appears only three times in the New Testament, each time in Greek transliteration "Abba" and translation "Father." (Mark 14:36, Rom. 8:15, Gal. 4:6).

This formal address, "Our Father," is followed by three acclamations, which are then followed by four petitions, all using the plural first-person pronoun, which strengthens the corporate role for this formal prayer, now become a document, perhaps not so suitable as a model for private, personal, individual usage.

Turning to Luke's version, note how Luke locates this prayer, not in a formal sermon, which Matthew provides to show Jesus is the new Moses who brings the new Law or *Torah* but more as spontaneous, occasional, casual teaching shared along the roadway on the journey to Jerusalem. Of course Luke continually shows Jesus often in prayer to his Father, and his disciples take notice. This particular disciple draws Jesus' attention to the practice of John (the Baptist) who taught his disciples how to pray. This reminder draws our attention to how closely interwoven Luke shows the roles of these two cousins in his introductory portrayals of their two families (Luke 1:5–80).

This same disciple becomes the motivator for Jesus's response, "When you pray, say this, 'Father' [Jesus probably originally said, "ABBA," since he spoke Aramaic and not Greek] followed by only two acclimations, not three, 'Let your name be held in reverence; let your kingdom arrive.'" Then Jesus speaks three petitions, not four. These three petitions are roughly the same in Matthew and Luke.

Paraphrase: (1) "Give us each day the food [bread] we need for that day;" (2) forgive us our sins against others since we forgive those who sin against us"; (3) "and may you not lead us into temptation." The verb in this third petition is in Greek, *ME EISENEGKES,* which is in the subjunctive mood. This means "we are not sure if you will do this or not, lead us into temptation, since the Holy Spirit certainly did this to you (Luke 4:1–13), and you seem to have learned much from that experience, and maybe you will teach us as we share such experiences. And so we are ambiguous as to how strongly to plead this petition, "but please be gentle with us!"

For the preacher, this dilemma may denote positive implications leading to investigations into just which temptation experiences may or may not be appropriate or relevant for consideration. One is reminded of the intercessory prayers Jesus raises on behalf of his disciples in John 17 when he asks the Father not to remove his disciples from this world, full of temptations, but to unite them in their corporate worship and witness and to protect or deliver them from the evil one.

At this point, Luke does not include petition no. four, as does Matthew, "But deliver us from evil." We may surmise that Luke's Jesus is preparing his disciples for the lengthy, perilous journey going forward to Jerusalem, which may indeed expose his disciples to several, if not many, encounters with evil along the way—demons, for example. Such exposure may serve positive purposes as Jesus teaches, supports, and prays for and with his disciples both during their journey toward and after they arrive in Jerusalem.

Next Luke introduces on the lips of Jesus a tangled parable (Luke 11:5–8) to bring some focus and order to just why and how Jesus's presentation of the Lord's Prayer is the appropriate answer to his disciples' request for Jesus to teach them how to pray. Let us remember that a parable is, in Jesus's teaching repertoire, a somewhat contrived, creative, often fictional, but compelling and thus artistic milieu that draws the listener into the dramatic narrative exactly because it may be abrasive, dysphoric, aggravating, problematic, worrisome, or downright alienating.

In other words, the parable has to be simple, down-home enough so our simplistic human minds can connect and be drawn directly out of our own needs into the dramatic problem or challenge set before us. In this case, call this the parable about three friends. *Paraphrase*: "You welcome your traveling friend to your home late at night but discover you have no bread [food] to make you hospitable and your surprise guest comfortable. You quickly rush next door and even though it is midnight, you bang on your neighbor's door, trusting your neighbors will share their bread with you. Embarrassed, you apologize, and beg for help. Your neighbor crawls out from under the bed covers, waking spouse, fussy children, and all the animals. Then what does he do? Gets his shotgun and cusses you out because you have intruded on his family and waked up the whole neighborhood? Middle of the night, pitch dark, wives crying, kids screaming, goats bleating, cattle mooing, dogs howling. Does the shotgun blast, or not? Call 911 or what?

Jesus now shares his understanding or his wisdom or his vision of the arriving kingdom of God, "I tell you this truth. He will not willingly rise and give food to his neighbor because he is a friend, but he will do this because his embarrassed neighbor is in such a desperate situation, because of his importunity, he will give him what he needs." In other words, this is not an "I'll scratch your back if you'll scratch my back, tit-for-tat, *quid-pro-quo* deal."

This friend who invades your privacy at midnight is honestly desperate to welcome his traveling friend. You will help him because that is what simple, human decency demands, whether he is your friend or not. But he is your friend. But you give to him not as one friend to another but because he has this specific need right now. His need draws from you whatever you have to share.

It's not the revitalization of friendship that opens the bolted door, but the realization of the petitioner's plight that moves the sleepy neighbor to give, to open up his resources, and pour out his own possessions to share with his neighbor whose need is powerfully compelling, indeed irresistible. This is Luke the artist's symbolic portrayal of the God of Abraham, Isaac, and Jacob whom Jesus seeks to teach to his disciples indirectly through this parable so that will be stimulated and turned on to work through these minefields and come to their own awareness, sensitivity, and strengthening of their faith as his disciples.

Luke, in this parable, both contrived and bluntly realistic, draws from Jesus's intuitive, comprehensive knowledge of and sensitivity to the comprehensive world of multiple faiths and diverse religions characteristic of the huge heterogeneous cultures that make up the Hellenistic world. Luke is eager to continue this portrayal of Jesus' outreach from Judaism to the broad Hellenistic World, a project which he will narrate as the Holy Spirit of God at work in the forthcoming document known in the New Testament canon as the *Acts of the Apostles*.

In the concluding verses of this lesson (Luke 11:9–13), Jesus seeks to bring these issues, spiritual dimensions, and enigmatic, even circumlocutionary puzzles to bear upon pragmatic, everyday conditions. The bedrock question is whether his disciples acknowledge, accept, endorse, and trust the covenant relationship he seeks to portray in this teaching episode, beginning with the Lord's Prayer and winding its way through the parable and now these pointed questions. If and when we trust God our Father, Jesus's argument runs. Then we trust him to welcome, receive, and answer all inquiries and requests we bring. How can we be so sure of God's answer? Because we trust him as Father God who will always answer our questions, our petitions, as he knows best; and this relationship affirms that whoever knocks with trust will find the open door and the divine answer, which the recipient will then continue to trust implicitly.

Jesus's colorful language brings this teaching episode to its dramatic climax, "Which father among you would give a snake to your child if the child asked for a fish? If a child asked for an egg what father would give the child a scorpion? If you who are evil know how to give good gifts to your children, how much more will the heavenly Father give the Holy Spirit to those who ask him?"

Lesson Forty-One: Fifteenth Sunday after Pentecost; Read Matthew 14:22–33

This lesson continues Matthew's fourth narrative section (ch. 14–17), which highlights the disciples' response, acknowledgment, and participation in Jesus's works, which are inaugurating the arrival of the Kingdom of Heaven. Let us glance back to Matthew 14:13–21 to check on the context for this lesson. Having been rejected by his hometown neighbors as a prophet sent from God (Matt. 13:54–58), and having received word of the execution of his cousin John the Baptist, Jesus then withdraws from his disciples and boarding a boat seeks to find a deserted place where he can be alone, no doubt for prayer and meditation.

At this point, the crowds gather in such numbers that Jesus is aroused, for he sees them as "sheep without a shepherd" and heals their sick. His disciples rejoin him and assist him when he breaks the five loaves and two fish and when they gathered twelve baskets full of leftovers. It is now time to dismiss the crowds. But first, Jesus corrals his disciples into a boat and launches them on a crossing to the other side of the Sea of Galilee, while he stays behind to dismiss the crowds; and now alone, he can resume his interrupted solitude and engage in the prayer he has had to postpone.

Paraphrase: Darkness takes control over this scene and Jesus is alone for hours in this precious, valuable, rare time of spiritual renewal while his disciples, following his directions, are a good distance out on the Sea in this their crossing to the other side. Jesus becomes aware a fierce wind is blowing against their boat's progress, agitating his disciples. He decides to join them, approaching walking on the surface of the sea. This happens during the fourth watch of the night (3:00 a.m.–6:00 a.m.). His disciples, seeing him walking on the waters, become terrified, and shaking all over, screeching, "A ghost!"

"Who or what is this we see?" they ask themselves, straining to make sense of this phenomenon in the misty darkness before dawn. They are intuitively very aware of the standard Hebrew suspicion that the waters of the earth are perennially enemies of God's good creation, and right here before their terrified eyes is an apparition who walks in safe harmony with this aquatic tirade which threatens their boat and their lives. Who is this? Is he for us or against us? At this moment they fearfully behold Jesus as ambiguous in identity and significance. Jesus is motivated to heal their fear. "Take heart," he calls out. "This is me. Do not be afraid."

More paraphrase: Simon Peter hears Jesus seeking to bond with his disciples, and wants himself to do what a disciple is supposed to do—that is, learn how to follow his Master's teaching. He blurts out, "Lord, if this is truly you, give me an order to come to you and walk with you on this water."

Jesus responds, "Come to me."

So Peter gets out of the boat and walks on the water to meet Jesus. But the fierce wind, thrashing all around them, puts fear into his heart. The text says, "When he sees the wind his is overcome with fear and begins to sink into the water."

In other words, as long as Peter looks to Jesus, he walks safely on the water; but when he looks away from Jesus at whatever force or enemy threatens them all, he can no longer walk on the water but begins to sink into the darkness below. Peter cries out, "Lord, save me." Jesus reaches out his hand and grabs hold of this sinking disciple and addresses Peter, "Dear one, trust me so that you will not question our relationship, and you will walk as I do." As the two of them get into the boat and Jesus is reunited with his twelve disciples, the fierce wind subsides, and the disciple band enjoys a time of increased devotion to their Lord and Master. Newly united in their admiration and trust, they join together to say, repeatedly, "Truly, you are the Son of God."

It is interesting to note Matthew's itinerary differs from his source, Mark, so that when this boat arrives onshore they are back on the West Bank of the Sea of Galilee, at the village of Gennesaret (Matt. 14:34). This means the celebratory meal of the loaves and fishes must have taken place on the East side of the Sea of Galilee. Not only does Mark omit the episode with Simon Peter, but he is much tougher on the disciples. According to Mark, when Jesus, alone, gets into the boat, the wind subsides; and the disciples are utterly astounded. Why? "Because they did not understand about the loaves and their hearts were hardened" (Mark 6:51–52).

In other words, Jesus's walking on the surface of the Sea of Galilee, for Mark, shows another example of just how the disciples, while participating in the sharing of the five loaves and two fish, lack adequate understanding of just what all is going on in Jesus's compassionate healing and feeding of the crowds, and this same lack of understanding repeats itself in their fear rather than trust when Jesus walks on the water. Mark, who writes near to the time of the destruction of Jerusalem by the Romans in 70 CE, is focused upon the Roman Empire and its brand of justice. Thus, the detailed narrative of the fate of John the Baptist (Mark 6:14–29).

Matthew, on the other hand, writing (ca. 90 CE) after the Roman destruction of Jerusalem, highlights Jesus's divine role and power as Lord not so much over questions of Roman justice, but over the huge questions of the natural world with its water opposition to the good creation and the potent forces operating in the world which may be demonic as well as angelic. No doubt Matthew's original readers had many questions about the ambiguity of Jesus's roles as they faced being thrown out of their synagogues, thrown to the lions in the Roman Colosseum, and had to argue in the marketplace with Gentile friends who were both drawn to the stories about and skeptical about just how this Jesus does and does not compare with the more traditional or popular gods with whom they are more familiar.

Today's lesson presents a striking and vivid portrayal of Jesus who is Lord over the natural universe as well as Lord over local synagogues and *Torah* study sessions. And the role of Simon Peter is one the average searcher can relate to because this disciple is both adventurous in his faith and yet still all too human, one who must plead to be saved when the going gets too tough. Sounds like a message at least some of Matthew's readers in today's twenty-first-century world should find relevant to their daily lives. Right?

Lesson Forty-Two: Sixteenth Sunday after Pentecost; Read Luke 17:5–10

Let us examine transitional teaching before we tackle this lesson. Beginning with Luke 17:1–2, we observe Jesus moving from his attention concentrated upon the scribes and Pharisees back to his disciples. Having addressed the reality of the influence that wealth has upon many supposedly righteous persons, the Pharisees being an obvious example, Jesus turns to address the daily experiences of more ordinary citizens, probably including the tax collectors and sinners earlier described. Since they, ordinary citizens, do not have great wealth as their source of temptation to sinful behavior, one might suppose they are less tempted, able to avoid, or even to become immune to serious temptations.

Jesus warns against such faulty thinking. What should he warn his hearers to be aware of? NRSV says, "Occasions for stumbling." NIV says, "Things that cause people to sin." The word in Greek, neuter plural, is *ta skandalan* and may be translated as "whatever causes sin or gives occasion for sin or that which causes stumbling, trouble or that which is an obstacle to faithful behavior." Note well we have a cognate in English, both noun, *scandal*, and verb, *scandalize*. We must likely think of the scandals which produce high ratings for television sitcoms.

Jesus takes these situations or events for granted as serious realities his disciples need to be well aware of. In fact, what he says is "It is impossible for the temptations to sin not to come." This is a double-negative construction in Greek, which works contrary to English grammar where a double negative becomes a positive. In Greek grammar, this construction highlights and emphasizes the negative all the more. In other words, Jesus recognizes that circumstances or situations which include temptations to sinful behavior are absolutely certain to occur; no doubt about this truth whatsoever.

This insistence implies there is always human participation in and responsibility for these inevitable events that present temptation to sinful behavior. This is a warning to his listeners to be especially careful, and sensitive as disciples to be on guard and to avoid any such participation in events that may tempt others to stumble into sinful behavior. Curiously, the inevitability of these events in no way reduces the guilt of whoever precipitates them. In fact, he says, "Woe to the one, or alas for the one through whom it comes!" How to drive this absolute truth home? "It would be better if this guilty person had a millstone hung around his neck and was thrown into the sea, than that he should cause one of these little ones to stumble into sin."

Who are these "little ones" for whom Jesus is so concerned? Presumably anyone vulnerable, naive, immature, and innocently gullible for whom his disciples have responsibility integral to their appointment to his original band of twelve. In keeping with his vision for the future mission of Jesus's disciples reaching into and across the Hellenistic world, Luke most likely pushes Jesus's words to include the Gentiles who are "little ones" precisely because they do not inherit the rich legacy of status as God's chosen nation. That is to say the Law and prophets are not an ingrained, inherent component of their cultural heritage.

In Luke 17:3–4, now Jesus turns his attention away from others/outsiders and back to focus upon his disciples themselves. *Paraphrase*: "Pay attention to what goes on among yourselves. If anyone who is your brother should sin, you must rebuke him with a strong warning." The verbs here are in the aorist tense, subjunctive mood. This means "you may not expect this to happen, but if and when it does, you should take this event very seriously and call your brother to the task. And if your brother repents, be quick to forgive him."

But what if your brother sins against you over and over again? "Now if your brother sins against you seven times in one day, and he repents, you should immediately forgive him, every time." Interestingly, the gospel writer Matthew heightens the drama in this exchange with his version, "Then Peter came up and said to him, 'Lord, how often shall my brother sin against me and I forgive him? As many as seven times?' Jesus said to him, 'I do not say to you seven times, but seventy times seven'" (Matt. 18:21–22).

With these contextual reports in mind, we turn to the lesson for this Sunday, Luke 17:5–10. By this time, Jesus has laid a huge, heavy load of inevitable, necessary, cautious, demanding thinking and responsibility upon his disciples. Perhaps this is why the narrator Luke now refers to his target audience, or his listeners, as "the apostles"—that is, those appointed both to learn (discipleship) and, having learned, sent out to announce or to proclaim. Jesus has both intimidated them and challenged them with the advanced kingdom-of-God responsibilities, such as both to rebuke and to forgive without limits or boundaries. Mind-blowing!

Feeling at once both overwhelmed and pumped up, these apostles, even as they're both befuddled and empowered, come to Jesus and plead, "Lord, give us more faith. Fill us up with greater faith!" The verb here in Greek is *PROSTHES,* from *PROSTITHEMI,* aorist tense, imperative mood, which means "almost an order or an insistence that given all you have said, you must now do this. You have set us up and committed yourself to the next step. So do it!" What must he do? "Increase, add to, multiply our faith." Their expectation does not seek new or better or higher quality faith, but an increase in the basic substance of the substantial faith they already have. "We want more quantity, bigger punch in our faith." They beg or demand more of the gift God and his Son, Jesus, have to offer to equip themselves to perform the tasks, the labor they are beckoned and inspired to deliver.

Jesus, ever seeking to draw his disciples, these apostles, closer and deeper into his communion with God his Father, now responds with the often-used comparison of faith with a grain of mustard seed, the smallest of all seeds. They expect growth, increase, expansion of their faith. But faith does not have bulk or size but is basically trust, which calls upon both the origin and goal of faith, to continue to grant the love that saves them, indwells them, and blesses them with the behavior, obedience, service they seek to express in this their response of hope and commitment.

For an earlier demonstration of this delicate relationship between human faith and divine blessing, turn back in this gospel to Luke 5:17–25. In this pericope, some men bring a paralyzed companion to Jesus and must work their way down through the roof to get this suffering victim near to Jesus.

> When he saw their faith, he said, "Friend, your sins are forgiven you… I say to you, stand up and take your bed and go home." Immediately he stood up before them, took what he had been lying on, and went to his home, glorifying God.

Notice the key phrase "when he saw their faith." Their faith is their trust in the works Jesus is doing. Jesus recognizes and honors their faith, but it is Jesus who does the healing and not their faith. They express their faith, their trust, in their work, the labor it takes to bring their paralyzed friend to this crowded home, all of which provide evidence and visibility for Jesus to become aware of. But the size of this faith, their trust, maybe the size of a mustard seed or larger; but the quantity is not an issue. Their trust in the promises of God they see being fulfilled in the career of Jesus trigger God to act in this manner "so that you may know that the Son of Man has authority on earth to forgive sins."

Forward to Luke 17:7–10. Jesus launches a parable, a short story with characters his hearers can understand and identify with. A solitary homeowner or master has one servant or slave. (The Greek word *HO DOULOS* is ambiguous and can mean any version of servant or slave.) Apparently, this is a modest household for there is only one staff person who, having plowed fields and shepherd sheep all day long, is expected to cook dinner and do other housekeeping chores while his boss rests with his feet up on a cushion.

This role is a rather hokey, crude metaphor for a Christian disciple of whatever culture in whatever time frame. But it serves to bring to attention a couple of examples of what Jesus and Luke consider to be true and necessary relationships and roles that Jesus's disciples/

apostles need to ponder and explore as they journey from Galilee south to the approaching "exodus" of Jesus in Jerusalem.

The two roles described here express and reflect stability, loyalty, and confidence, faith or, better, trust in each other and the structure of the household. The master of the house expects and receives a regular, competent, loyal, and faithful performance of duties from his servant. He treats him with common decency, respect, and justice. The servant understands his roles and neither expects nor receives extra attention or reward when a long day's work is complete. As simplistic, domestic, and mundane as this scenario appears, it invites Jesus hearers to ponder the meaning of human faith, belief, or trust and the blessings that accompany the inevitable and necessary obligations and opportunities that call for human understanding and responsible, faithful involvement, and fulfillment.

Scholars are quick to point out that the institution of slavery assumed in this parable is neither addressed nor evaluated as a social institution. Rather, it is recognized and accepted in passing as a part of the landscape. For modern readers, this begs huge questions about justice and the meaning of human life. But in this contrived parable only modestly serves as a framework to stimulate questions and learning.

Perhaps the punch line in this parable should be rephrased this way, "When we disciples/apostles do everything our lord invites and expects us to do, we deserve no extra praise or compensation, but we try to outdo each other to bring overflowing praise, thanksgiving, and love to our Lord and Master who blesses us with life and discipleship" (Luke 17:10).

Lesson Forty-Three: Seventeenth Sunday after Pentecost; Read Luke 17:11–19

This pericope/episode continues to explore the serious questions or problems that are involved in human perception or seeing and understanding what you see. For example, in the earlier parable (Luke 16:19–31), the rich man did not see Lazarus who conspicuously occupied space at his front door, even with all his coming and going. When he died and found himself suffering in the afterlife, the same rich man could see Lazarus, for the very first time, resting in the bosom of Abraham, all too well. This belated sighting could bring him no good, however, contrasted with the earlier sightlessness when he could have done Lazarus (and himself) some good, but was blind to Lazarus's presence.

In Luke 17:1–10, Jesus teaches his disciples how to think of their faith qualitatively rather than quantitatively. They ask him to increase their faith. He explains that faith as minuscule as a mustard seed is sufficient because to believe means to trust in the power of God to heal as a response to and recognition of their faith. Their faith, that is to say however large or small, does not do the healing but shows their trust in God to heal and thus to provide for their needs. This scenario portrays the disciples and their Lord as involved and committed to each other in a personal relationship based upon, growing out of trust, not as a *quid-pro-quo* business contract structured on impersonal, factual obligations.

As we study this lesson (Luke 17:11–19), we find Jesus teaching his disciples as they move between Galilee in the north and Samaria to the south, the territory being crossed as this expedition continues to move toward the goal of arriving in Jerusalem. As Jesus enters an unnamed village he observes a band of ten leprous men approaching. They stop, keeping their distance to obey the Law, and first cry out, "Unclean! Unclean!" Jesus and his entourage also stop and ask themselves if they should perhaps toss some left-over food for these outcasts to retrieve.

These ten wretched men, however, raise their voices in a plaintive, desperate cry, "Jesus, Master, have mercy upon us." Jesus hears and takes in this painful reality of human suffering, ten lepers, weak, but still able to utter a hopeful plea for healing, for restoration to a normal family, village community life.

Jesus lifts his voice to overcome the distance between them, and speaks, "Turn around, go show yourselves to the priests." The ten, shunned by their families, stumble away to follow Jesus's directions. As they move away, obeying their realization that Jesus sees them, hears them, and sends them to fulfill the Law, they discover themselves being cleansed, healed step-by-step, their sliver of hope, their longing, their trust becoming true and real.

Before very long, Jesus notices that one of this group of ten, having discovered himself being cleansed of his disease, comes running back. No longer having to ostracize himself and eager to rejoin the human race, he falls on his face at the feet of Jesus, thanking him with words and sounds altogether inadequate to express his thanksgiving. Several of Jesus's disciples take note that this cleaned-up man is a Samaritan.

Jesus takes in this scene with a smile and reaches out to give this man a huge hug. But his smile soon turns to a sober look. Jesus strains, looking down the road, but sees no one else. He asks, "Were there not ten leprous men in this group, all of whom have been cleansed? Where are the missing nine? Why do they not return to give praise and thanksgiving, like this man, who, after all, is a foreigner?"

Jesus turns to this man of Samaria, saying, "Rise and go your way, return to your family. Your faith has saved you, delivered you from your disease and your suffering." The Greek verb here is *SODZO,* which carries the concept of salvation or divine deliverance from sin and evil.

Why does Luke, in recalling this episode in Jesus' journey southward toward Jerusalem, highlight how the only cleansed leper who returns to thank Jesus and praise God for his new salvation is not a Jew, but a Samaritan? Probably for the same reason that in Luke 43:25–30, Jesus points not to his hometown Jewish brethren but to foreigners, specifically the leper Naaman the Syrian, as exemplars of what his career is all about. God sends his Son, Jesus, into the world not only to fulfill covenant promises for the chosen people of Israel but to point also to the promise of Isaiah the Prophet that the chosen people are called and sent out to be God's light to all the other nations of the world (Isaiah 42:6 and 49:6).

Why is it so visibly true that this one leper out of ten excitedly returns to thank Jesus and to praise God for his cleansing? Could it be, asks Luke, that some Jews who have the Law and the prophets see and understand less about their Father God's original covenant than do some foreigners, like this Samaritan, who do not officially inherit this treasure but who for whatever reason respond with more sensitivity, insight, thanksgiving, praise, and trust?

Luke, of course, shows how Jesus raises this same question even more pointedly in the parable of the good Samaritan (Luke 10:9–37). In that parable, as we remember, the two Jewish officials, a priest and a Levite, see but do not see the victim lying beside the road. A foreigner, however, a Samaritan, both sees and understands, grasps the big picture of the victim's desperate needs. His insight or empathy or rapport with the victim enables him to risk his own safety to trust his impulse to extend mercy and healing to this suffering one.

Luke seems to be pointing to the basic theology and worldview he espouses in the book of Acts that the will and purpose of God their Creator are no longer, if it ever has been, confined to the originally chosen nation of Israel but moves forward to include all of the Gentiles who populate Hellenistic world and indeed to reach all the way to the ends of the earth.

Now reach two verses beyond this lectionary lesson and listen to the words of Jesus in Luke 17:20–21. Here the Pharisees once again challenge Jesus on his interpretations, his knowledge his understanding, his vision of the coming of the kingdom of God. These Pharisees are the keepers of the *status quo ante* who protect their enshrined self-calling and assumed an appointment to enforce orthodoxy, much like the hometown heroes in Luke 4:14–30 who prompt Jesus's remark that "a prophet is not without honor, except in his own hometown."

The Pharisees, here and in most other occasions when Jesus analyzes and accesses their worldview, interpret their role to be keepers of the treasurers of the covenant heritage granted to the chosen nation of Israel and assured by God of this unquestioned authority. Actually, the Pharisees are not as fossilized in their attitudes and behavior as are the Sadducees. The Sadducees reject the oral Torah, the continuing discovery of new dimensions to the original *Torah* and the inclusion of these developments within growing and expanding versions of the original *Torah.* Examples are the resurrection of the dead to eternal life and such visions as the apocalyptic worldview provide, including the work of the promised Son of man, arriving on the clouds of heaven.

This tension between major factions of leadership within orthodox Judaism does reveal this covenant people to include living, moving, ambiguous, developing dimensions which offer hope for growth and change. But not yet enough growth and change to satisfy the vision of Jesus and Jesus's apostolic mission as represented for one example here in the work of this gospel writer, Luke.

Note how Jesus answers the Pharisees in this passage: Luke 17:20–21. These questioners, reflecting their Jewish culture's worldview, centered in linear, horizontal, forward-looking calendar time, want Jesus to reveal to them, be specific, and tell them exactly, precisely the date and time when the kingdom of God is scheduled to actually literally arrive in full-blown fulfillment. After all, this rabbi keeps pointing to and promising this future event over and over again in his daily teachings and acts of healing and mercy. These Pharisees are confident they are not only reflecting their own preconceived worldview but also honoring this prophet's claim to such spiritual knowledge. They pat themselves on their backs because they are so much more open and receptive to new knowledge than their rivals the Sadducees.

So the least Jesus can do, they insist, if indeed he has all this knowledge he claims to possess, is to satisfy their curiosity and their spiritual need for reassurance, and give them the precise calendar date and time when this promised kingdom of God will materialize for everyone to see. Notice Jesus respects and honors their presence and their request. But he must correct their presumption that this arrival will meet their expectations and demand for empirical verification.

And so Jesus answers according to his worldview and his terms, seeking to re-orient their thinking and thus enable them to accept and work within the dimensions that his calling and mission express. He says (paraphrasing), "I cannot give you the times, dates, and places you demand to know. But I shall answer your question in a much better way as I myself understand the true meaning of the concept of the Kingdom of God."

Continuing the paraphrase, "The kingdom of God is not coming bringing events or developments that can be observed, measured, or identified according to what we already know and expect. Nor will observers be able to say, 'Look, here it is!' or 'There it is!' Why is this not possible? Because in fact, the kingdom of God is already here, right here within and among you, within and among all of us!"

And so does Jesus seek to drive home this his teaching on the reality of the kingdom of God, which in truth is not primarily a future happening but instead a present reality. Now, this does not deny that there shall be anticipated, future events, dimensions, and developments that also compose elements of this same Kingdom. And this affirmation includes most certainly his upcoming arrival in Jerusalem, his mission and activities there, and all the events which will comprise his new exodus. The anticipation of his Jerusalem itinerary, however, as important as that will be, does not minimize the truth that this same kingdom is already present within and among them, as indeed also among everyone here and now.

But why do these Pharisees yearn to be able to observe, identify, and empirically verify this kingdom as events not currently present but, being now absent, are for them events whose reality can only be longed-for as future, anticipated turn of events? The answer must be that they have allowed themselves to be indoctrinated with an epistemology (theory of human knowledge) that insists upon empirical verification to establish the truth and minimizes, denies, or overlooks the role of trust, hope, and anticipation of the promises of God their creator. They anticipate the kingdom of God's arrival but do not, cannot, see the kingdom's presence already within and among them, however unverifiable this kingdom's presence and reality may be.

Luke the redactor (editor) highlights the appearance and role of foreigners, in these cases Samaritans, to point to the new and unexpected, surprising, perhaps shocking, truth that their God's kingdom may indeed be closer to them, right here and now in their midst, than they can fathom due to their lack of practice in exercising their capacity to trust in preference for/insistence upon verification. Verification, according to their epistemology, removes all risk, such as guaranteed by the terms of an airtight contract, whereas trust is open to, even welcomes, risk as integral to living within relationships based upon, flowing out of free and loving initiatives and responses.

Earlier, in the twentieth century, the Jewish philosopher and theologian Martin Buber (1868–1965) articulated these alternative interpretations of his inherited religious tradition, Judaism, in the title of his well-known book, *I-Thou, and I-It*. His title points to his elucidation of the crucial contrast between life-giving kingdom relationships based upon trust and mundane, popular, but life-denying relationships dependent upon verification. May we who have ears to hear, hear, and we who have eyes to see, see!

Lesson Forty-Four: Eighteenth Sunday after Pentecost; Read Mark 9:38–50

This lesson begins with attention to the disciple John, one of the inner cores of three special disciples (Peter, James, and John) whom Jesus took with him up on the mountain top for the transfiguration experience and the teaching event following (Mark 9:2–13). John approaches Jesus with a rather burning problem on his mind. This initiative follows the second prediction of the Passion (Mark 9:30–32) and Jesus' concerned attempt to counsel or rebuke his disciples' mindset which insists upon exaltation and rejects humiliation in any form as a role model for both Jesus himself (Messiah and Son of man) and his followers. Jesus counsels them, indeed urges them, to adopt the image of the lowly child, innocent, weak, and helpless to stimulate their continuing need for self-examination and serious repentance (Mark 9:33–37).

Jesus's very own disciples are so very far off the Mark here, they become good examples of what need for a change of lifestyle Jesus calls for in the inauguration of his mission (read Mark 12:14–15). *Paraphrase*: after John the Baptist's work was completed, Jesus comes into Galilee, proclaiming the great good news God his Father has for the human race. "The time has come and is now here, and the kingdom of God's arrival is very close, so everyone is invited and should shape up your thinking and behavior accordingly and trust this good news and the promise of this new reality to make our lives altogether new and fulfilled according to our Father God's purposes for us all."

The Greek verb *METANOEO,* normally translated as "repent," means "to do a radical, one-hundred-degree reversal of your mindset, your worldview, your value, your hopes and dreams, your lifestyle, and your behavior. "The time has been fulfilled" means God has been at work forever since creation to bring this about, and everything is now ready for God's blessings to take over and remake all of human reality. "The kingdom of God has come near" means this new kingdom is in process of arriving, breaking into history, not fully here yet, but imminent and beginning to appear all around us.

The implication for Mark's readers is "get with this new agenda, all you wavering folks." And how do you do this your new responsibility, which is actually a necessary part of all the movement from old to new? Two changes, please: "You repent, and you believe (trust) in this good news." The Greek verb *PISTEUO,* normally translated as "believe in this good news," is better translated as "trust in all of this good news." These changes already going on and drawing us into a new reality and above all, trust in this promised beginning and the process, although not yet complete or final just yet. "Trust" is a better translation than "believe" because belief implies correct or factual knowledge of indisputable evidence, whereas this good news is not indisputable but promised and thus invites trust from out of your heart and soul, not infallible knowledge of facts that your mind/brain and reason can control. To reflect contemporary psychological sensitivity to the human brain's anatomy, this message appeals to right-brain behavior more than, or in preference, to left-brain orientation.

With this background context that recognizes the dynamics, Jesus is operating with as he delivers these three predictions of his passion (Mark 8:31, 9:31, 10:32); and as he seeks to counsel his disciples on the implications of these dynamics for their life and mission together, it is understandable that this special disciple, John, approaches Jesus with his burning question (paraphrased), "John says, 'Good teacher, we saw someone in your name casting out demons, and we tried to stop him from doing this because he is not part of us.'" Ironically, this reported encounter comes on the heels of Mark

9:14–29, the episode when these same disciples are unable to cast demons out of the possessed child, but Jesus can do this requested healing. Is John jealous and protective of himself when he spots an unknown outsider who can cast out demons in Jesus's name when he and his comrades cannot?

John's gripe appears to be that this stranger is intruding upon his/their private disciple-Master relationship to Jesus. This unknown stranger is actually calling upon God to honor Jesus' name when he has no connection to Jesus. Yet apparently, this unknown stranger is successful and does indeed cast out demons even though he is an interloper intruding upon their territory which is not his and not available to him. John expects Jesus to approve of his interpretation and to praise him and his comrades for their negative behavior.

But how does Jesus react? *Paraphrase*: "Jesus responds, 'Do not try to stop him. For no one who does a mighty work in my name can then speak evil of me.'" Put this into positive words and Jesus means "everyone who does the same works I do belongs to me and my mission." As Jesus also puts it, "Whoever is not against us, is for us." Discipleship as a closed, exclusive enclave misses the good news of Jesus's mission, which is inclusive, open-ended, and growing or expanding.

Put all this in the context of Jesus's mission to the Jews in Galilee and beyond and this episode shows how Jesus's disciples have increasing discomfort and anxiety about their own understanding of and solidarity with their teacher. For example, Jesus has revealed/exposed the narrow mentalities of the Jewish authorities (scribes, Pharisees, and Herodians) who conspire to eliminate him because he challenges their legalism and also their authority. Are Jesus's own disciples now feeling more in tune with these Jewish authorities' negativism and less in synch with the positive, open freedom Jesus calls for?

In contrast to the Jewish authorities' legalism and intransigence, Jesus continues to offer his own mission, including his disciples, who defy such orthodox, rigid legalism and seek to bring new freedom and healing to all of the least and the lost. Apparently, Jesus's disciples were originally turned on and receptive and participated positively in this mission.

As Jesus presents the three predictions of his Jerusalem destiny, however, and as it becomes clearer that his disciples/followers must sooner or later "take up their cross and follow him accordingly," they appear to slow or reverse their endorsement of his destiny and move noticeably toward the same protective and restrictive mindset portrayed by the Jewish officials.

Jesus has this teaching moment for them. *Paraphrase*: "Remember, anyone who gives you a cup of water to drink in my name, that is to say, because you belong to me and serve me, trust me now when I tell you, this person will inherit the kingdom of God which is coming to him (or her)." In other words, Jesus's mission is to show forth the great love of God his Father which shares, opens up, and freely gives new life and freedom to everyone who accepts this gift. The walls and fences around the good news have excluded and rejected far too many whom Jesus' coming destiny seeks to liberate. Here, Jesus has in mind his recent aphorism, "Whoever welcomes one such child in my name welcomes me, and whoever welcomes me welcomes not me but the one who sends me here"(Mark 9:37).

Is this promised, arriving kingdom of God to be open, inclusive, and welcoming of everyone who needs salvation; or is this new kingdom to repeat and remain an exclusive enclave restricted to the few clean and perfect, privileged officers whose self-perceived roles are to protect themselves at all cost? Put more colloquially, is this new kingdom of God to behave/function as a playground for saints or as a hospital for sinners? Who can/will trust these promises Jesus seeks to teach is the question Jesus leaves on the mind and heart of his disciple John in this episode.

Now, as if Jesus is following upon his teaching or co-teaching with the little child (Mark 9:33–37), Jesus is concerned that such innocent, unsophisticated, naive, childlike persons whom he describes may fall victim to insensitive, bungling, or crafty manipulators who will take advantage of their gullibility. Mark has Jesus compose and deliver a very stern collection of aphorisms that caricature self-mutilation as measures necessary to prevent mistreatment of childlike persons.

The key concept here is repeated in the Greek verb *SKANDALIDZO*, "to cause someone to stumble in their faith." This is the source, of course, of our English words "scandal and scandalize," which carry a variety of colorful nuances. *Paraphrase*: "Now whoever may offend one of the little ones, one of those who trust me, it would be much better for him to hang the millstone of a donkey around his own neck and get someone to throw him into the middle of the lake." Better than what? We must follow Jesus's assertive train of thought here.

> And if your own hand causes you to stumble, amputate your hand. It is far better for you to go through life crippled than to keep your hand, and with two hands have to go away into Gehenna, into the indistinguishable fire.

Gehenna—originally a notorious location outside Jerusalem where nefarious religious practices (such as human sacrifices) called for continuous fires burning. By the intertestamental and New Testament times, this word points to the state of the final punishment of the wicked. It is variously described as a fiery furnace, an unquenchable fire or an eternal fire prepared for the devil and his angels.

Jesus continues, "And if your foot causes you to stumble, amputate your foot; it is better for you to go through life lame than to keep your two feet and have to be cast into Gehenna. And if your eye causes you to stumble, take it out, for it is better to enter the Kingdom of God with one eye, than to keep your eye and with two eyes to have to be cast into Gehenna, where your worm never dies and the fire is never extinguished."

Aside: I remember seeing the movie *Glory*, starring Jimmy Stewart, who plays a Pentecostal minister in West Virginia. This minister has a glass/artificial eye. Once when he is preaching to a group of released convicts, he quotes this warning, reaches up and removes his glass eye, and holds it up for everyone to witness how seriously he takes Jesus's words. A few startled, maybe freighted, gasps and groans followed from his listeners; and as I recall this episode, there were several serious conversions that day.

The fire of Gehenna is a powerful metaphor in Jesus's mind, denoting alienation from God, irreversible judgment, and hopelessness vis-à-vis the approaching kingdom of God. Perhaps fire carries a positive meaning in addition to the negative symbolism in Gehenna. Better still, why not combine the traditional symbolism of salt with fire? Salt is a reference to the common element necessary for human life and indispensable for processes of purification and preservation. Jesus has issued stern warnings to his disciples and Mark's readers, and now Jesus turns to powerful metaphors to counter the negative with the positive promises of his mission and message.

Paraphrase: "The good news is this: Everyone should expect to be salted with fire. This is coming to us all." The verb in Greek here is *ALISTHASETAI*, future tense, passive voice, indicative mood, from *ALIDZO*, to salt or I salt. Passive voice means this is a process that is coming upon you, the work of someone outside of you—in this case, God the Father. You thus are the recipient rather than the initiator of this event or series of events. But what if this salt is old, not protected, impure, and thus has lost its taste and its power to serve our human needs? Make sure your salt is fresh, strong, or pure and useful and ready for our God to use with his fire to keep us all at peace with one another!" In other words, each person has some very important responsibility to participate in this process on his/her own behalf, as well as to be passively receptive to this cleansing/healing process. Thus, does the good news of Jesus' mission out-weigh the opposition the Jewish authorities hold on to and supersedes whatever second thoughts Jesus's disciples may be harboring.

I call your attention to the scholarly work of our colleague in ministry, Dr. Boyd C. Purcell, honorably retired member of the Presbytery of West Virginia, whose treatment of Mark 9:49 forms the powerful backbone for his two books, *Spiritual Terrorism: Spiritual Abuse from the Womb to the Tomb* and *Christianity Without Insanity: For Optimal Mental/Emotional/Physical Health*. This author very persuasively shows how Jesus's skillful use of these powerful symbols: child, scandal, amputation, Gehenna, fire, and salt points to the positive good news of the gospel Mark seeks to share, and offers Jesus's corrective to the negative worldview so prevalent among his Jewish contemporaries including, regrettably, to some extent, his own disciples. Perhaps most importantly, Dr. Purcell, who is both a biblical scholar and professional counselor and psychologist, argues persuasively for the positive interpretations and use of these symbols within and among all of our constituencies of all ages in the work of education and ministry and therapy within all pastoral and healing contexts in today's world.

Lesson Forty-Five: Nineteenth Sunday after Pentecost; Read Mark 10:1–16

This lesson consists of two periscopes (first, Mark 10:2–22 on the permanence of marriage question and then 10:13–16 on the role of little children in Jesus's ministry). Jesus leaves Capernaum and heads toward Jerusalem. Mark apparently is not too familiar with the map, but likely he wants to keep Jesus in earshot of the tetrarchy of Galilee (Herod Antipas's territory) and along the Jordan River where the career and fate of John the Baptist are still warm in human memory.

Paraphrase: Everywhere Jesus goes, crowds flock around him and he relishes every moment as an opportunity to teach these hungry souls. His old adversaries, some Pharisees, are lurking nearby; and they seize this opportunity to put him on the spot in front of everyone to bolster their case against him (Cf. Mark 3:6). Most likely Jesus was bombarded with questions on and on from the crowd, and so the Pharisees know how to fit right into this milieu.

They interject this question in front of this audience of eager learners, "Is it lawful for a man to divorce his wife?" Jesus of course knows their intentions. They do not seek information. They are not ignorant. Jesus knows they are putting him on the spot in front of his audience, hoping that whatever he says, they can trap him in his talk. And Jesus, ever the skillful teacher, will not play their game according to their roles but will turn this encounter into a teaching moment that will serve his own mission.

They have asked a question about the Law. Jesus, as he often does, turns their question back upon them and directs them to their own sources for answering their own question. And so his answer is his question for them, "What does the Law of Moses command?" In other words, "You know the Law of Moses as well as I do, so go ahead and answer your own question." 'And so they report what is written in the Law of Moses, "Moses permitted a man to write a certificate of divorce, hand it to his wife and say, 'Here, with this document, I divorce you. Get out of this, my house'" (Cf. Deut. 24:1–4).

Jesus nods his head, to acknowledge these Pharisees know, remember, and can quote the Law of Moses. They are confident they have caught him now in a trap. They know Jesus does not conform to the letter of the Law. But this Law they quote is very simple and clear. Just how does he plan to wiggle out of this vice they have clamped upon him?

Jesus pauses a moment or two, stands up, and begins to speak, "You quote the Law correctly, but I must tell you Moses writes this directive not for the best of reasons, but strictly as an accommodation to deal with your hardness of heart." (Greek preposition *PROS* followed by the object of the preposition in the accusative case, *TEN SKLEROKARDIAN*, means that your hardheartedness drives this decision.) "Moses makes this allowance to recognize and honor your self-serving demands and limits. You insist upon your power, privilege, and right to divorce your wife as the necessary procedure to remove your wife from your household for whatever motivations and outcomes that may serve your pleasure."

Jesus continues, "Moses is the great lawgiver and this law derives directly from his decision to recognize, honor, and facilitate the desire of the male or the husband in any marriage. However, I must point out to you that this command from Moses forgets, overlooks, or rejects the original intents, purposes, goals, and objectives of the Creator himself, Almighty God, our Father."

Jesus's voice grows more intense. "From the beginning of all Creation, God our Father makes them male and female, exactly so that they shall not live alone, but live together. For this very reason, a man leaves his birth house, leaves his father and his mother, and will be joined to the woman they choose to become his wife (a reference to an arranged marriage, a custom common in most ancient cultures). And whereas they were two fleshly human beings, now they will no longer be two but will become one flesh.

Jesus has presented his argument or rationale for the sanctity of human marriage (Cf. Gen. 1:27–28, 2:24). And if the psalmist is correct that human beings are cocreators with God the Father (Ps. 100), then Jesus is certain that Moses's certificate of divorce must rank far down the line of appropriate or necessary concessions to the changing, evolving cultural variables through which the covenant people of God inevitably find themselves in transition with resulting various expectations and demands.

Jesus reaches for an appropriate conclusion for his reply to these Pharisees, "Whatever human relationship is formed in covenant initiative by God among his people, surely the rest of us human beings should seek always to honor and sustain. But never, ever do anything to bring separation or alienation."

The Pharisees, listening with dislike but also with amazement, recognize that they have been bested in this dialogue because Jesus has affirmed the reality of Moses's certificate of divorce but also argued decisively and convincingly for *an apriori*, deeper, stronger rationale for stable, permanent, faithful human marriage as the better alternative to divorce. And Jesus does this with dignity and respect that communicates how and why Jesus seeks to move away from legalism and focus upon the Spirit behind, before, and after all Laws, whether in the Torah as this one comes from Moses himself or in the growing body of oral laws such as the Pharisees cultivate but the Sadducees and Herodians reject. Jesus clearly prefers the Spirit as a teacher instead of written laws, whether written in stone or on parchment. The Spirit, after all, is more likely to write upon the human heart and soul.

Mark prefers to present Jesus as a teacher first and foremost out in the open, in public meetings, whether with the crowds who are positive/supportive, as well as with scribes, Pharisees, and Herodians who oppose him. As frequently happens, however, Jesus also has a more intimate relationship with his disciple band. In this case, a nearby house is ready to receive Jesus and his disciples for a more private consultation.

Jesus's disciples have questions about what they have already heard when Jesus encountered the Pharisees on the question of Moses's Law. Jesus develops his answer to the Pharisees to say, "Yes, there is this law from Moses that allows a man to serve his wife with a 'certificate of divorce.'" However, this law serves a very shallow, weak, selfish, purpose, that is, to approve, accommodate, and support the husband's personal desires, whatever those choices may be.

This law overlooks, forgets, rejects, and thus circumvents the much more basic, original, design, and necessary relationship instilled in human beings created in the very image and likeness of their creator himself. This covenant of marriage between a man and a woman includes the participation of their creator and thus just as his covenant comes into being initiated by God and is sustained by God likewise this covenant cannot or should not be broken by one party or the other, but only by God himself. Thus in popular language, this is a covenant blessed always "until death do us part."

With this background discussion ringing in their ears, Jesus' disciples are still confused about how this law from Moses can be acknowledged and in effect. Jesus does not deny the existence and practice or enforcement of this law. But just as the Sabbath law was not as basic as the human need for healing and wholeness of being (Cf. Mark 2:23–3:6), so this Law of Moses on divorce pales when superseded by the original claim of the covenant the creator has upon all of his creation.

And so when Jesus's disciples press him for an explanation, Jesus admits this law does exist and is in effect. However, Jesus interprets, "Whoever divorces his wife and marries another practices adultery with her." In other words, the Law permits this process; thus, as man is free to proceed this way, gut legality does not ignore nor negate the reality of covenant responsibility built into human nature by the Creator.

We should remember that across the Old Testament world the meaning of "adultery" was basically to steal another man's wife. Adultery had little to do with sexuality or fleshly pleasures but much to do with power and control. In Jewish culture, polygamy was not rare, and a rich man could and usually did have as many wives as he could afford. King David, for example, as far as we know, had many women at his disposal. His affair with Bathsheba, although he lusted for her, did not get him into trouble because of the sexuality involved but because she was the wife of Uriah the Hittite. The prophet Nathan came on the scene not to condemn carnal indulgence, although that was probably involved, but to deliver the judgment of Almighty God upon the injustice in David's theft, not to mention David's arranged death of Uriah the Hittite (check out 2 Sam. 11:12–12:15).

And so when Jesus connects divorce and adultery he is once again calling attention away from Law, which is supposed to teach, protect, and enforce original covenant principles and toward primary human responsibility for the quality of human relationships, few of which could be more important than human conjugality and domestic commitments, leading to the extended family, the tribe, and the kingdom of God that should grow out of faithful and loyal commitments.

Not to leave this picture incomplete, Jesus adds, "And if she divorces her husband and marries another, she commits adultery." Now, as far as we know, women did not (could not?) divorce their husbands across the Jewish world. Mark, of course, is writing for the Hellenistic world, the Roman Empire, which did permit women to initiate divorce from their husbands. Jesus was probably aware of Hellenistic influences spreading even across Galilee and adjacent territories. For example, the fate of John the Baptist grew out of divorce proceedings, not only of Herod Antipas from his spouse but of Herod's sister-in-law so that she could marry her brother-in-law. Somewhat like Nathan long before, John the Baptist was sent by God to question (condemn?) such quasi-incestuous relationships.

John, of course, lost his head when said female took offense at his calling her and Herod's concord into question. Perhaps Jesus has this recent sad story in mind when he refers to a woman divorcing her husband. And/or perhaps Mark makes sure Jesus extends his wisdom to include the Hellenistic world among which Mark's readers already and increasingly will find themselves embedded following the imminent destruction of Jerusalem by the Romans (ca. 70 CE).

The second periscope in this lesson unfolds apparently in the same house or nearby when some of the crowd bring their children to Jesus for him to touch them, seeking his blessing. This goes on longer than it should. Jesus's disciples rebuke these parents, apparently protective of this time they claim with Jesus, but also to shield Jesus from this unwanted and unnecessary intrusion upon their master's precious schedule. Above all, Jesus's disciples seek to shield him from invasion by these worthless creatures, children, whose parents should know they make absolutely no claim upon this rabbi's time and energies.

Paraphrase: Jesus sees his disciples rejecting these children and it turns his stomach. Indignation surges up from his bowels. Anger turns his face red. "Let these children come to me. "Do not hinder them. For out of such as these is the Kingdom of God arriving among us." In other words, Jesus seeks to make clear just exactly who constitutes the source, the beginnings, the impulse and energy whose presence and participation make possible the arrival of the kingdom of God. It is not the high and the mighty but the weak and the lowly. How soon Jesus's disciples have forgotten Jesus's lesson for them in Mark 9:33–39, in which the genderless child becomes the model, the indispensable element for understanding the arrival of the kingdom of God. Jesus now has this new opportunity to remind his disciples of what he said then, "Whoever welcomes one such child in my name welcomes me, and whoever welcomes me welcomes not me but the one who sent me here."

Jesus sighs, disappointed he and his disciples can be so far apart in understanding and sensitivity. He quickly takes the children one by one up in his arms and laying his hands on them, blesses them, each one. For his disciples, comes this warning, "Truly I say to you, whoever does not receive the kingdom of God as a little child, will most certainly never, ever enter into this kingdom."

Lesson Forty-Six: Twentieth Sunday after Pentecost; Read Luke 18:1–8

This lesson delivers a parable found only here in the four gospels. This parable seeks to offer insight and comfort as well as direction and encouragement in an age of confusion and disparagement when hope and commitment appear to be severely challenged by insensitivity and lack of justice, which the promises and visions of the coming Son of Man are supposed to alleviate.

A quick review of Luke's preparation for this parable: In Luke 17:20–21, Jesus hears the Pharisees' puzzlement about when the promised kingdom of God will arrive with the spectacular appearance of the Son of man, anointed to bring justice and peace upon the earth. Notice how Jesus carefully, cautiously, but directly seeks to draw their attention away from future spectacular events as the primary elements which compose the coming kingdom of God, and assure them that the kingdom of God is already here and now or "in the midst of you."

Continuing his counsel (Luke 17:22–24), Jesus cautions that many false sightings of the Son of man are likely to happen, as expectations increase. But his hearers should not be distracted and follow this excitement. Now Jesus introduces his own, personal role he is destined to play in the coming of the Son of man (Luke 17:25), "But first he must suffer many things and be rejected by this generation." Here Jesus points ahead to the goal and climax of this journey from Galilee to Jerusalem. And Luke knows very well that Jesus's contemporaries as well as his own readers are no doubt confused and consternated about how the events of Jesus's Jerusalem sojourn fit into the promised coming of the kingdom of God.

And so Luke begins to quote Jesus with warnings (Luke 17:26–37), "As it was in the days of Noah, so will it be in the days of the Son of man." Recall the human strife, stress, and suffering in Noah's story. Likewise in the story of the family of Lot. All of which may be summarized this way, "Whoever seeks to gain his life will lose it, and whoever loses his life will preserve it.

Having reminded both hearers and readers of biblical precedent for struggle and persistence to grapple with the reality and the meaning of the coming of the Kingdom of God, including the works of the Son of Man, Jesus now offers a parable to assist their process of understanding and commitment Here begins this week's lesson, Luke 18:1–8. Note well just exactly why Jesus tells this parable, "And he told them a parable to the effect that they ought always to pray and not lose heart." In other words, Jesus has a specific outcome he hopes to achieve by telling this parable. No matter what the forces or temptations to cease or eliminate prayer, his listeners should not be discouraged and weaken their motivation, lose heart, but sustain or increase their inspiration and maintain their regularity in their practice of prayer, as well as the other disciplines which prayer includes.

Jesus knows well and has already warned and prepared his listeners for the difficulties ahead for them if and when they honestly and prayerfully seek to discover a deeper level of insight, understanding, and strategy for themselves in their daily spiritual walk and communication with God concerning this important question of this their God's promised kingdom.

And here (Luke 18:2) Jesus begins this narrative which, while true, locally serves to provide a general context for everyone's individual human experience. The laws and customs of Judaism (*the Torah*) call especially for sensitive care and treatment of widows, orphans, and strangers. If you fall into one of these categories you can quickly identify with the frustration of this widow in Jesus's parable. But if you are not one of these three, you are nevertheless expected readily to identify with or to share compassion for this person's predicament.

The judge described is a caricature for the least possible qualified and faithful kind of leader or public servant in the kingdom of God. He cares neither for God nor for human beings. With such ignorance and apathy for Jewish Law, one wonders how did he get his job! Actually, his appointment for the wrong reasons is not rare then or at any age. But he brags and flaunts his absolute independence and his aggressive apathy as well as disdain. How can he keep his position without facing impeachment!? Jesus' point is that, all too regrettably, this judge is not so much an exception as he is typical of the problematic leadership with which God's people have to wrestle and put up with every age. He makes necessary and possible the struggle for righteousness that human faith must accept and assimilate.

And he meets his match. A poor widow in that city keeps arguing her case in this judge's court. Being a widow, she has several claims on her heart/her agenda, for she has lost the care and protection of her late husband. Jewish Law, of course, provides for the nearest male kin to inherit both assets and responsibilities for the family obligations. But this widow, against most interpretations of the Law, feels in her heart and soul that she has a case she must pursue, and she has an adversary who opposes her claims and argues against her. This court is plastered and ablaze with the public dramas of these two oratorical adversaries demanding justice.

Because the judge delays or denies a verdict, the adversary to the widow assumes he is winning the case and withdraws his appearance. But this widow persists. And she persists! Now the judge goes into recess, into his own council chamber, his mental assets. After all, since he fears or respects neither God nor man, the only collaborator or sounding board he has is he himself. He argues his case before himself.

And we shall not be surprised how the argument of his own case turns out, "Because this widow is so unbearably persistent, if I keep hearing her case, she will literally wear me out, and I shall become incapacitated and incompetent. Then I shall have to leave the bench and lose my appointment. The only way I can get her to shut up is to grant what she demands. I shall vindicate her so she will go away and I can have some peace." Thus ends this session of consultation within himself!

As Jesus brings this parable to its close, how shall he draw its teaching to a focused conclusion? Jesus says, "Listen to what this unrighteous judge says. He may be unrighteous, or he may proceed with self-centered, poorly motivated reasoning. But by whatever route, this poor widow receives her vindication." This may be a famous case of justice being granted for all the wrong reasons. But if and when justice is granted for whatever reasons, righteousness is the goal and the kingdom of God seems to draw closer.

Jesus continues, "Will not God vindicate his chosen ones, his elected people, who cry out to him day and night, even more persistently than this widow did? Will he make them put up with long delays?" In formal logic, this is known as moving from the lesser or weaker model to the greater or stronger model for purposes of argumentation. That is to say if this unjust judge eventually delivers justice, however slow, then how very much more should we expect and trust that the most just judge of all will accordingly do even a much more faithful and just vindication of his very own chosen/elected people?

This last identification is what makes all the difference. We are talking about "God's eternal promises to his chosen people Israel, meaning God has an irrevocable attachment and commitment to the nation of Israel, and through them, since they are God's promised light to all of the nations of the world, to all of humankind, and indeed to all of creation."

It is because of this, God's promise of eternal righteousness, that makes a comparison with the unjust judge so effective. And this strong logical and rhetorical persuasion leads Jesus to ask, "Will he delay long over them? I tell you he will vindicate them speedily." But Jesus promotes this dialogue and this parable in particular exactly because he knows how problematic it is to the Pharisees and most believers and disciples that they routinely live day by day with the persistent struggle to strive for yet find elusive justice in so many different areas of their lives. And so, with his assurance of God's justice so strongly affirmed and assured, Jesus asks this last question, "Nevertheless, when the Son of man comes will he find faith upon the earth?"

Back to the beginning of this Lesson. Jesus tells this parable "to the effect that they ought always to pray and not lose heart. No playing down of the obstacles that hinder prayer. Much encouragement and affirmation of the need for and blessing of faithful, persistent, regular, honest prayer.

A huge, honest, and aggravating predicament for the people of Judaism, the chosen people blessed with the eternal covenant: "Will the coming Son of Man find faith on earth?" The primary word here is *faith*, HE PISTIS in the original KOINE Greek language, which may more appropriately be translated as "trust in God." The word *faith* or *believe* in English has come to mean ideas of correct factuality rather than trust and thus puts too much emphasis upon human mental exercise rather than upon active, living, trusting behavior in communion with the living God.

If we may wrap up Jesus's teaching in these passages concerning the arrival of the kingdom of God, we may recognize that he seems to say that this concept, kingdom of God, is both a present and a future reality. The aggravations of the present time should not dissuade us from citizenship in this kingdom, but we should exercise our trust with persistent prayer and hopeful, righteous behavior, as well as trustful anticipation of the future blessings that the fulfillment of this promise will bring upon us.

"Hallelujah! Amen."

Lesson Forty-Seven: Twenty-First Sunday after Pentecost; Read Matthew 21:33–46

The context for this lesson is Jesus's continued teaching in the temple, where he is confronted by the Jewish authorities, who are threatened by his aggressive affirmations concerning the imminent arrival of the kingdom of the heavens, especially as his knowledge, visions, and insights appear to promise blessings to which they do not/cannot lay claim.

The episode of John the Baptist leads these authorities stooping to hypocrisy, denying what they know all too well to be true, with egg on their face, and Jesus holding all the cards (Matt. 21:23–27). Jesus has more pithy parables up his sleeve, this time showing how the outsiders, tax collectors, and prostitutes inherit the kingdom of God before the insiders, chief priests, and Pharisees. The honest sinners receive the kingdom as a gift of righteousness, whereas the ruling authorities demand to rule and control the kingdom not as a gift but as false righteousness they earn and control.

Paraphrase: The Jewish covenant in miniature—Jewish ethnicity, of course, includes, then as always, a wide variety of cultural expressions and thus serves as an appropriate symbol for the entire human race created by and answerable to one source of authority, protection, and ultimate salvation. How to recognize, balance, and take seriously such huge discrepancies/discordances, etc., with the ultimate vision the Creator promises to fulfill?

When we study human history, most cultural entities answer this question by appealing to polytheism, the assumption that a great pantheon of some sort of several, if not many, gods is working helter-skelter, seeking to bring order out of chaos. With the arrival of the prophet Moses, however, we observe one God and one only saving his chosen people from whatever distorts their lives (in this case, Egyptian slavery) and assuring them that the newly given *Torah* (Mt. Sinai) will be the answer to their needs for guidance and protection; and most significantly, this same "High God of Israel" promises his judgments, mercies, and blessings will serve not only the new people known as Israel but eventually and most assuredly all people and indeed all creation anytime, everywhere, and forever.

This is a tall order, however, you chew on it, and here as Jesus continues to honor the Jerusalem temple as his primary location for teaching, Matthew has portrayed Jesus digging deeply into recent history to include his cousin, John the Baptist, as a prophet who was then and still is teaching how the chosen people of God should understand themselves as caretakers of the holy treasurers of Judaism, centered right here in the holy temple itself.

Having drawn his listeners into the parable (Matt. 21:28–32), the story of the two sons whose father seeks to involve them in the process of cultivating the family vineyard, Jesus points to the blessing/responsibilities/tasks the people of Israel are called to bear so the Creator may indeed be enabled to fulfill his own promises to his creation. In other words, this Creator promises to see the process through all the way to the end and guarantee it a success. But he much prefers to include his chosen people as colleagues who join him in doing the work necessary.

And when the initial, preferred order of participants gets reversed (God presumably prefers chief priests and Pharisees, not tax collectors and prostitutes), this new order does not minimize in the least their Creator's commitment to getting the job done. Once again, Jesus is repeating his all too truthful platitude, "Those who are first now will be last then while those who are last now with be first then."

But on to today's lesson (Matt. 21:32–46), where Jesus has a new parable ripe to deliver, most scholars conclude this story is better treated as an allegory, which Matthew has distilled from Jesus's teachings to counsel/teach his readers in Antioch of Syria how to negotiate/cope with their Jewish-Christian tensions (ca. 85 CE–90 CE). More paraphrase: This landowner is especially skillful and flamboyant in his entrepreneurial output. He overextends himself in the design and elaborate provisions for a vineyard no doubt intended to overwhelm the agricultural neighborhoods of the entire Middle East. And this outlay is not for his own daily involvement, since he turns the whole enterprise over to tenants, whom he intends to benefit and be blessed by his long-range vision; he now leaves the scene to involve himself elsewhere.

Harvest time arrives! This landowner sends his personal delegation to receive reports and income from his investments. But his tenants are not on the same page of contractual understanding, to say the least. His tenants seize his collection agents, beat one, kill another, and stone one. The landowner sends a second delegation, and his tenants treat them the same way. Finally, the landowner decides different tactics are necessary, and so he sends his Son, trusting that his tenants will welcome and honor a member of his own family.

But his tenants have other goals in mind. They form a huddle. What play to run? "Come now," they conspire together, "this is the heir. Let us kill him and take his inheritance for ourselves!" So they seize him, throw him out of the vineyard, and kill him. Finishing up this parable, Jesus now turns directly to his listeners and focuses upon the chief priests and elders/Pharisees, asking, "Now when the owner of the vineyard comes, what will he do to those tenants?"

The Jewish authorities are quick to answer, "He will give those wretches a miserable death and lease the vineyard to other tenants who will give him the produce at harvest time." Settling up, judgment time has arrived!

But as an allegory, what else or what different reality does Jesus ask his listeners to hear and understand? The absentee landlord, all-powerful, trusts his tenants will behave legally, honorably, and with devotion to duty. Such is the portrait of *JAWHEH* the Jewish tradition portends. Likewise, Moses the prophet delivers the *TORAH* (first at Mt. Sinai then a second time in Matt. 5–7). The wisdom and revelation God's chosen people need and expect, God eagerly and faithfully delivers through his prophets to Israel, following Moses, as well as through both the former prophets and the latter prophets. The canon of the *TANAK*, the collection Christians call the Old Testament, let us remember, is closed in three steps—Law or *TORAH* (400 BCE), *NAVIN* or prophets (200 BCE), and *KETHUBIM* or WRITINGS in ca. 90 CE. Notice that this canon was still open, and in process of closing, most probably during the time of Matthew's ministry in Antioch of Syria.

If the absentee landowner of Israel was ever faithful to his visions and promises, so also was he expecting his tenants, Israel, to be faithful to their calling, and if indeed they sometimes were and sometimes were not, *JAHWEH* never abandons his promises and struggles to discover/negotiate/deliver a posture of faithful labor and never-ending/always-persistent commitment to getting the job done.

To wit, when Jesus's listeners recommend a quick solution to how the wicked tenants have treated the Son, the Heir to the vineyard (i.e. "Smash them to smithereens!"). Matthew is just as quick to have Jesus show a much better way, "Surely you must have read in the scriptures this pivotal piece of a profound revelation: 'The stone that the builders rejected has become the cornerstone; this was the Lord's work, and it is amazing to behold!'" This is a quote from Psalm 118:22–23 (Cf. Acts 4:11, 1 Pet. 2:7).

This means that the Heir, Son of the absentee landowner, whom the wicked tenants kill and cast away from their presence, strangely, surprisingly, and ironically soon becomes the cornerstone for the entire establishment which the landowner is in process of building. Jesus continues to address all of his listeners but especially the Jewish authorities, knowing full well their plans are soon to treat him the same way the Son is treated in the parable. What will be the outcome of this development? Through the process of elimination of Jesus from their midst (trials, suffering, death, etc.) the stone that is rejected will become the cornerstone for the new establishment now under construction (resurrection, ascension, Pentecost, etc.).

"And what will be the outcome of this process?" Jesus asks his listeners. "Not only will the new building of the kingdom of God proceed to fulfillment before our very eyes, but therefore I tell you, the kingdom of God will be taken away from you and given to a people who will produce the fruits of the kingdom." Jesus's words continue to echo through the halls of the great temple, "Anyone who falls on this stone will be broken in pieces, and this stone will crush anyone on whom it falls" (Cf. Jesus's words here with his earlier observation and pronouncement in Matt. 7:24–27). This central, pivotal role for this figure of Jesus of Nazareth, reminds one of the late Drew University Theologian, Dr. Carl Michaelson, who coined the phrase "the hinge of history."

This episode ends with Jesus's ordinary common listeners coming forward, they having been eclipsed so thoroughly by the authorities. They are astonished because Jesus teaches them as one having authority and not as the scribes. This is Matthew; the editor's way of prodding his readers to examine and to discern just what this difference is all about and to encourage them in their day-to-day struggles to become faithful disciples who model themselves along the lines of the tax collectors and prostitutes and not following the Jewish authorities.

But look at the provocative issues and questions this raises for Matthew's readers. The chief priests and Pharisees shall be replaced by leaders who welcome and receive their salvation/righteousness as a gracious gift from the Creator/Redeemer God himself and never from some alternative source such as themselves. But this does not mean Matthew's version of the future pushes some kind of supersession version of a new Israel or a new Jerusalem. The apostle Paul argues very persuasively against such sectarianism and for stronger collegiality in Romans 9:11.

Likewise, the emancipated, freedom-loving followers or companions of the tax collectors and prostitutes should avoid egoistic libertarianism of the various sorts and kinds probably seeking popular approval and practice across the Hellenistic cultures in which the diaspora Jews find themselves struggling to discover how to grow in their faithful/Christian disciples.

The apostle Paul, lest we should forget, offers profound models for wrestling with these same issues—for example, in 1 Corinthians 11–13 and perhaps above all in Philippians 2:12–13.

> Therefore, my beloved, just as you have always obeyed me, not only in my presence, but much more now in my absence, *work out your own salvation with fear and trembling*, for it is God who is at work in you, enabling you both to will and to work for his good pleasure. (emphasis mine)

Lesson Forty-Eight: Twenty-Second Sunday after Pentecost; Read Mark 12:28–44

The context for this lesson reaches back to include the previous two periscopes. When we look again at Mark 12:28–34 we see the scribe who is not hostile to Jesus but who genuinely expresses his open curiosity and who is eager to learn from and with this teacher who moves beyond the dead letter of the Law to encourage exploration and anticipation of new dimensions of theological understanding and vision. We see this reflected in the different words for "mind," which Jesus uses and this Scribe uses.

When Jesus urges love for the one God arising from out of all your mind, the noun in Greek is *TES DIANOIAS*. When the scribe repeats this phrase, he uses *TES SUNESEOS*. You can detect the difference in the prefix to each noun. In Jesus's case, *DIA* asks for dialogue as opposed to monologue, whereas the prefix the scribe uses, *SUN*, seeks logical connection or necessary conformity. What is the difference? Monologue means there is only one word or idea being explored even if two or more persons are involved. Their communication asks no in-depth question but simply amounts to the clarification of basic ideas they already agree upon. Dialogue, however, means an encounter between two or more persons who may come from diametrically opposite starting points and who thus meet as strangers needing to get acquainted and to explore whether or not they share any mutuality that will make communication at all possible.

Monologue, therefore, is necessary and desirable when you are settling simple, quantitative, or business matters of information where no life or death issues are at stake. Dialogue, however, means you are dealing with opposite starting points, such as Almighty God and human nature, sacred and profane, spirit and matter, angels and demons, grace and judgment, life and death. This gospel writer Mark, of course, presents Jesus as seeking to rise above common-sense, non-controversial information and welcome the deepest questions about the meaning of human life within the worldview of the one God who is both the source of all creation and the faithful, benevolent Lord who graciously rules over and within all his creation from beginning to end.

Mark identifies his questioner as one of the scribes (Greek: *EIS TON GRAMMATEON*), leaving open any further characterization of his ideological or theological preferences. Mark thus recognizes once again, that although opposition to Jesus among the Jewish officialdom is strong, it is not unanimous; and in fact, there are probably some of them who are more mature, not so uniform in their spiritual struggles with the realities of their Jewish faith when threatened as they are by impending Roman invasion of Jerusalem. Although this scribe is used to a different word for "mind" than Jesus uses, he responds positively to Jesus's choice of words.

Interestingly, both Matthew and Luke, in their versions of this episode, identify this scribe as a lawyer, Greek *NOMIKOS*, from the

Greek word for *LAW*, *HO NOMOS*. And both, contrary to Mark, explain that his purpose is to test or challenge, or discover to what extent Jesus is legitimate. Thus, when Mark has his scribe use the different word for "mind," *TES SUNESEOS*, than Jesus uses, *TES DIANOIAS*, Mark acknowledges that this scribe represents the jurisprudence mindset. All the more reason to expect that this questioner, if he is indeed a lawyer, which Mark leaves open, expects Jesus to insist upon legalism.

When Jesus does not point to specific laws, however, but first and foremost to divine love and then to human love in response, it is all the more remarkable that here Jesus encounters a Jewish official who is open to the good news Jesus seeks to offer. And as if agreement on the priority of this love is not strong enough evidence for this scribe's maturity in faith, he puts the icing on the cake, "This love you describe, good teacher, is greater than/far surpasses all whole burnt offerings and sacrifices." Thus, does Mark once again counsel his readers to expand their vision of liturgical realities far beyond those who have dominated Jewish thinking and practice for so many centuries and are now threatened with elimination from the scene of human history due to the imminent threat of Roman invasion?

This periscope (Mark 12:28–34) is arguably the most significant moment in this first-to-be written gospel, Mark. This is why the narrator concludes this encounter with these words, "Seeing how wisely [Greek: *NOUNEXWS*, thoughtfully, sensibly, with careful balance of all intellectual options] this Scribe answers, Jesus says to him, "You are not far from the Kingdom of God.'" *Paraphrase*: "You are indeed surely suitable for citizenship in the kingdom of God." And now, Mark ends this episode with this capstone, "At this point, no one was brave enough to ask him any more questions."

This brings us to the short periscope before today's lesson (Mark 12:35–37). *Paraphrase*: Having finished his dialogue with this Scribe, Jesus continues to teach in the Temple, using his favorite method of asking leading questions. Although his identity as Son of David has been affirmed earlier (Mark 10:46–52 and 11:1–11) Jesus is concerned lest his own destiny will be interpreted too much along the lines of the militarism of the kingdom of his ancestor, King David. After all, King David established Jerusalem as the capital of United

Israel through militarism, and in tradition David serves as Messiah, anointed one, whose throne or household/kingdom shall never come to an end (2 Samuel).

Jesus seeks to stimulate his listeners to open up to the same kinds of opportunities for spiritual growth that his version of the kingdom of God offers. As the previous scribe discovers and affirms (Mark 12:28–34), the divine love of God and love returned as the appropriate human response should temper if not eliminate and replace the militarism associated with the traditions of King David as well as that of the Son of man, understood according to the Jewish apocalyptic worldview.

How to stir up questions, doubts, excitement, new visions, among his listeners prompts Jesus to quote from a favorite "Coronation" or "Royal Psalm" (Psalm 110) in which militarism is reaffirmed as divine promise and action leading to victory over all enemies, and this is accomplished by the close association between the new king of Israel and the Messiah. Here David acknowledges the Messiah as his Lord, so how can this Messiah also be David's son? Simple conundrum logically, but the profound mystery that Jesus speaks to provoke his listeners and Mark his readers stimulate them to expect less militarism and more spirituality in the events which lie soon ahead for Jesus and his disciples.

Mark concludes this brief report by concluding that now as Jesus teaches off-the-cuff but with profound motivation in the temple precincts, the Jewish officials have strategically cooled their challenges to his teaching and his authority, "And the huge crowd was listening to him gladly."

At this point, when Jesus the teacher appears to enjoy popular, benign tolerance, acceptance, and even encouragement, no doubt from his own disciples as well as from the crowds who are filling Jerusalem in anticipation of the Feast of the Passover, Jesus feels motivated to portray and interpret what goes on within certain circles of the Jewish establishment.

Without ceasing his teaching on the coming of the kingdom of God, Jesus must share his sensitivity to the peculiar or unique characteristics of some, if not many or most, of the Jewish officials.

Paraphrase: "Take notice, do not fail to take into account how among all of the scribes, there are some who love to parade about in pompous costumes, expect you to bow and scrape before them in the market places, demand the front-row seats of prestige and privilege when they enter the synagogues, and demand to sit at the table of honor during every formal banquet. These are some of the same ones who steal widow's houses and property under false pretenses [Cf. Mark 7:9–13]. Whenever they are called on to pray, they try to outdo one another in putting on a show in making their prayers much, much too long and superverbose, with extravagant and pretentious, flowery words. How very far these Scribes miss the mark in receiving and sharing true spirituality! When all is said and done, the ever-faithful and steadfast love of Almighty God will take the form of judgment upon this behavior!"

Having weathered the storms of living, teaching, healing, and seeking to express the imminent arrival of the kingdom of God in his home territory of Galilee, Jesus finds new and arousing opportunities to observe his fellow human beings in this urban environment of the capital city of Jerusalem. Jesus finds a place to sit where he can observe the traffic going on as pilgrims transact their necessary duties at the nearby treasury. How predictable it is to observe the pomp and ceremony that the rich people put on as they draw attention to themselves. They make sure people are watching and make as much noise as they can when they empty their bags of gold coins into the receptacles of the treasury.

When the crowd in line gets thinner, a poor widow approaches and can put in only two small copper coins, which are worth next to nothing, maybe a penny. Ever seeking to make what is real around him into a teaching opportunity Jesus calls to some of his disciples who are nearby. Jesus begins to say to them, "Do not miss what this poor widow has to teach us about the coming of the kingdom of God. Truth is, she has put more into the treasury than all these others who have emptied fat bags into these receptacles. Why do I say this? Because they give from out of their abundance, and they still have much more they do not give. But she, this destitute woman, lives in poverty, and yet she has given all she has. She has no more, even to live on. But more importantly, she gives not only all of her possessions, tiny though this is. She gives herself, all she is herself, and this gift is huge! One hundred percent. This much do the wealthy give. This much does she give!"

Lesson Forty-Nine: Twenty-Third Sunday after Pentecost; Read Luke 20:27–38 and Mark 11:1–19

Jesus has wrestled verbally and spiritually with the scribes, the Pharisees, and the Herodians, and in this lesson, he has a serious encounter with another self-confident leadership sect in Judaism, the Sadducees. This small, exclusive, aristocratic, wealthy enclave dominated the Jewish priesthood, as well as the Sanhedrin council and rebuked the scribes and Pharisees who openly accepted and welcomed the so-called oral Torah, such as belief in the resurrection from the dead and eternal life. The Sadducees insisted upon strict adherence to the written Torah of Moses, rejecting the new-fangled, adventurous teachings which appear in the Jewish apocalyptic worldview in the book of Daniel and afterward.

In other words, whereas the scribes and Pharisees advanced the world of Torah as the best and necessary spiritual system for themselves and the Gentiles as well, the Sadducees closed the door upon any possibility of Gentiles ever being acceptable whatsoever within the parameters of the kingdom of God. Within this context of lively spiritual discussions within the ranks of Jewish leadership, let us examine where Jesus comes from in this discussion and alternative vision for understanding the concept of the arriving kingdom of God.

For example, Jesus first appears on the scene in Jerusalem in the writings of Mark, specifically in Mark 11:1–19. Let us remember that, according to Mark, this is Jesus's very first visit to Jerusalem, his earlier years of ministry having been expressed northward, mostly in Galilee. After the so-called triumphant arrival or entry into Jerusalem, Jesus makes an uneventful, initial survey of the temple area and retires for the night.

The very next day, however (paraphrase), his first order of business is to revisit the temple. And without any delay, Jesus begins to cast out, to expel from the temple all those who are buying and selling there. And he overturns the tables and chairs of the money-changers, sending their coins rattling across the marble floors. He blocks the doors, so no one can bring new merchandise or supplies into the temple. To put it mildly, he deliberately and successfully engineers "a disturbance of the peace," guilty and ready to be arrested for this illegal behavior. Everyone is aghast and speechless. And so, he begins to teach, to explain, to defend his actions.

Here is the truth direct from his mouth, "Has it not been written in the Holy Scriptures that MY HOUSE SHALL BE CALLED A HOUSE OF PRAYER, ESPECIALLY FOR ALL OF THE NATIONS?" He does not quote from the TORAH but from the PROPHETS (Isa. 49:6 and 56:7), "BUT YOU HAVE MADE THIS HOUSE INTO A DEN [cave, refuge] FOR BANDITS OR ROBBERS."

It is interesting that in their quotations from their source, Mark, both Matthew and Luke include Jesus's words "IT IS WRITTEN MY HOUSE SHALL BE CALLED A HOUSE OF PRAYER" but omit the words "FOR ALL THE NATIONS." For Matthew and Luke, it is alright for the Jewish temple to be cultivated as a HOUSE OF PRAYER, as long as this promotes communion and worship for God's chosen people, but this HOUSE OF PRAYER should not be open to Gentiles unless and until they convert and become authentic Jews. The Greek phrase *PASIN TOIS ETHESIN* denotes Gentile cultures, language, arts and letters, religion, economics, politics, etc. In other words, acceptance of worship and communion with Gentiles, anathema to orthodox Jews, is exactly and foremost what Jesus has come into this world to teach and proclaim and now presents first and foremost as the good news they need to hear, Jerusalem and his fellow Jews.

This brief lesson, Luke 20:27-38, reminds me of the broadway play *Seven Brides for Seven Brothers*, which entertained audiences by calling attention to, making fun of contemporary human family life, both lighthearted and impossibly complicated. The Sadducees honor Jesus both as a rustic prophet from Nazareth and as an impossibly idealistic teacher who believes in grandiose, ridiculous ideas such as resurrection from the dead and eternal life with the angels in heaven. They present him with a humorous story or narrative we call SEVEN HUSBANDS FOR

ONE WIFE. Jesus reads for them the story of Moses and the burning bush, where God affirms that Abraham, Isaac, and Jacob are not dead, but alive. This truth may present more questions than answers, but the Sadducees must agree this is taught in the orthodox *TORAH* and thus presents good news for everyone to chew on. Perhaps this is a good example of a teaching of Jesus that Gentiles may come to understand when they shall be included more and more in the blessings the Jewish Temple presents as a HOUSE OF PRAYER FOR ALL THE NATIONS.

Lesson Fifty: Twenty-Fourth Sunday after Pentecost; Read Luke 21:5–19

In the previous short lesson, we heard Jesus describe the role and purpose of the Jerusalem temple, "Just as it is written in the prophets, MY HOUSE SHALL BECOME AND BE DESCRIBED AS A HOUSE OF PRAYER FOR ALL THE NATIONS [GENTILES TOO]." Here some folks are impressed with the temple as a magnificent structure designed and built by King Herod the Great. Jesus is quick to explain this temple is not an end in itself and, in fact, is soon to be destroyed. Here, Luke has Jesus refer to the imminent destruction of Jerusalem in 70 CE–75 CE.

But Luke is writing this his gospel some twenty years later, after the destruction of Jerusalem by the Romans, and now he has Jesus predict and describe the upheavals and turmoils that lie ahead, "Look at the long list: False prophets will appear, wars and insurrections; nation will rise against nation, kingdom against kingdom; earthquakes, famines, plagues, dreadful portents and signs from heaven. But before all this, they will arrest you and persecute you, hand you over to synagogues and prisons, and you will be brought before kings and governors, because of my name.

"You will have many opportunities to testify, but do not prepare your defense in advance, ahead of time. Why not? Because I myself will give you words and a degree of wisdom that none of your opponents will be able to withstand or contradict." Remember, this is the Holy Spirit of Almighty God speaking through Jesus Christ, the Son of God. He continues, "You will be betrayed by parents and brothers, by relatives and friends; and they will put some of you to death. You will be hated by all because of my name. But not a hair of your head will perish. By your endurance, you will gain your soul."

This is the gospel writer Luke's presentation of Jesus's long-range overview and introspective description of human history given the reality of the great good news the Christian gospel provides and at the same time the gruesome realities of the Roman Empire and many other empires reaching all the way into the twenty-first century and until the climax of all of this created history.

As the gospel writer Matthew puts it in his version of the resurrection narrative, "Now the eleven disciples went to Galilee, to the mountain where Jesus told them to go. When they saw him, they worshipped him, but some doubted. Jesus came near and spoke to them, 'I have received all authority on heaven and on earth. Therefore, go and make disciples of all nations, baptizing them in the name of the Father, and of the Son, and of the Holy Spirit, teaching them to obey everything that I've commanded you. And look, I myself will be with you every day, until the end of this present age.'"

Be sure to move forward now to study Lesson Fifty-One, the final lesson in this series, "Christ the King/The Reign of Christ," where we have the gospel writer Luke's version of just how Jesus Christ becomes the King, the Ruler of all creation, through his willing sacrifice of himself on the cross as the expression of the love of Almighty God that rescues/saves us all from death and destruction and blesses us all with eternal life.

In Lesson Fifty, we studied Luke's version of how Jesus the Christ portrays the threats to human life expected soon to hit the world of the Roman Empire and how Jesus himself will provide the words of defense or proclamation of victory for Christians; so his listeners, individual Christians themselves, should not rush to prepare their own defenses. Rather, they should all wait, patiently for the Holy Spirit to show/tell them how to understand and participate in their salvation of their own souls.

Here are three examples of just how this promise has been presented and honored in the modern world of which we are part today. In other words, here are occasions when our predecessors and contemporaries have and still do hear, receive, welcome, and expedite Jesus' wisdom freely shared in times of threatened annihilation.

Example One

American slavery was a horrendous example of evil when homo sapiens from Africa were dehumanized, forced into the slave trade, denied spiritual freedom, and persecuted when they claimed it anyway. Many Africans brought their native spirituality with them, and here is one example of how they blended their original faith with those of their captors, and the voice of Jesus could be heard bringing promised freedom and salvation. This is a popular, well-known, and loved spiritual:

> I got a robe, you've got a robe, all of God's children got a robe.
> When I get to heaven goin' to put on my robe,
> Goin' to shout all over God's heaven.
> Everybody talking 'bout heaven ain't going there,
> Heaven, heaven,
> Goin' to shout all over God's heaven…goin' to shout all over God's heaven.

Example Two

Modern civilization brought many changes—modern science, European colonization, the Industrial Revolution, just for starters. In 1883, American poet Emma Lazarus wrote this poem, which was inscribed on the Statue of Liberty in New York Harbor:

> Give me your tired, your poor, your huddled masses yearning to breathe free, the wretched refuse of your teeming shores, send these, the homeless tempest-tossed to me. I lift my lamp beside the golden door!

Example Three

The American experiment in democracy claims many spectacular victories and likewise leaves many individuals panting with disappointment in terms of freedom for faith or spiritual experience.

Hymn: "For Everyone Born"

For everyone born, a place at the table, for everyone born, clean water and bread.
A shelter, a space, a safe place for growing, for everyone born, a star over head.

And God will delight when we are creators of justice and joy, compassion and peace,
Yes, God will delight when we are creators of justice, justice, and joy.

For woman and man, a place at the table, revising the roles, deciding to share,
With wisdom and grace, dividing the power, for woman and man, a system that's fair.

For young and for old, a place at the table, a voice to be heard, a part in the song,
The hands of a child in hands that are wrinkled, for young and for old, the right to belong.

For just and unjust, a place at the table. abuser, abused, with need to forgive,
In anger, in hurt, a mindset of mercy, for just and unjust, a new way to live.

For gay and for straight, a place at the table, a covenant shared, a welcoming space,
A rainbow of race and gender and color, for gay and for straight, the chance of grace.

Refrain:

For everyone born, a place at the table, to give without fear, and simply to be,

To work, to speak out, to witness and worship, for everyone born, the right to be free. (text and music by Shirley Erena Murray, 1998)

Lesson Fifty-One: Christ the King/Reign of Christ Sunday

The church calendar concludes. Read Luke 23:33–43.

On this Sunday, the year-long church worship calendar arrives at its conclusion or climax; and on the next Sunday, the Season of Advent once again ushers in the beginning of the worship calendar for a brand-new year. The Advent Season once again introduces Jesus as an infant, the weakest moment in his career, but this fragility and innocence anticipate his role as Messiah when he reaches his peak of power or rule on this final day or week of worship when he is recognized as King who reigns over his Father God's creation.

Advent Season celebrates the arrival of this male child who joins the human race, taking his natural place as the first-born son within a working-class family in the rather remote region of Galilee. This gospel writer Luke drops a strong clue of this boy-child's destiny when in his adolescence he both shares his family's Passover pilgrimage to Jerusalem and confounds them with his prodigious behavior, already taking his rightful place in the Jerusalem temple, his Father's house (Luke 2:41–51).

Luke shows Jesus as an adult baptized by his cousin John the Baptist as a routine member of the surging crowds who receive this blessing. But only this young man receives anointing by the Holy Spirit and empowerment to withstand the three temptations at the hands of the devil (Luke 2:41–51).

This same Holy Spirit schedules a teaching session for Jesus in his hometown synagogue, where he announces his anointed career responsibilities, which are "to bring good news to the poor, to proclaim release to the captives, to let the oppressed go free, and to proclaim the year of the Lord's favor" (Luke 4:10–14). Sounds like he intends to do a whole lot of talking! As a matter of fact, his hometown neighbors find him to be a good bit too uppity and putting on airs. In his response, Jesus exclaims, "No prophet is accepted in his own hometown."

Notice this is the first time Luke gives Jesus a working title, an identity for his career. Jesus claims the role of prophet and expects the resistance or rejection prophets often, or normally, receive from their listeners. Indeed, in this same incident, Jesus becomes so effective in his prophecy, his analysis of what God his Father is up to in dealing with two foreigners, the widow at Zarephath of Sidon and Naaman the Syrian leper, his hometown neighbors try to tar and feather him (Luke 4:25–30).

As Luke reports and describes the development of Jesus's career, leading him from Galilee all the way to Jerusalem, Jesus gets very busy in the roles of teacher, rabbi, counselor, comforter, and challenger. But he never seeks to exercise supervisory or administrative or ruling powers. He is not an executive, but very much a prophet. Although he and his disciples do stage a so-called triumphant entry to the city of Jerusalem (Luke 19:29–43) and he does disturb the peace when he drives out the money changers from the temple, which must have included some physical as well as verbal violence and disruption of the peace (Luke 19:45–46).

As long as Jesus speaks, teaches, argues, and interprets Jewish Law and tradition he annoys and disturbs some if not many or even most of the officials of Judaism, including scribes and Pharisees, priests, Herodians, Sadducees, and the Sanhedrin. They soon come to fear his popularity and suspect he harbors an ambitious vision for inspiring, promoting, leading, and even supervising new and sharply different directions for the spiritual, social, political fulfillment of ancient and perennial goals and objectives for the covenant people of God.

And indeed he does offer new insights, heights, and depths of alternative human understandings and patterns of behavior, as was earlier made clear in Luke 4:16–30. Understandably, some Jewish leaders fear his proximity to the Roman military presence may prove dangerous. When the question of military violence arises, however, Jesus is quick to squelch any such pretensions to political rule (Luke 22:49–53).

On the night of Jesus's betrayal some men holding him mock him as a prophet. As if playing a game, they blindfold him and urge him, "Prophesy! Who was it that struck you?" This title serves no serious purpose for them. But only one of ridicule (Luke 22:63–65). When daylight comes and they drag Jesus before their council, the titles "Messiah," "Son of Man," and "Son of God" fill the air although no one, neither Jesus nor his accusers, uses even one title with Jesus's own understanding of himself as a prophet (Luke 22:66–71).

When they arraign Jesus before Pontius Pilate, Jesus's accusers are certain they have strong evidence against him as a messianic or royal pretender. They accuse him of conspiracy and treason in his self-appointed role of king. Pilate, of course, sees all this commotion as an intramural squabble among rival Jewish parties and asks Jesus dismissively, "Are you the king of the Jews?" Jesus, in effect, replies, "This title, 'king,' provokes your concern. But I make no such claim as my accusers insist I do" (Luke 23:1–5).

Hearing Jesus hails from Galilee, Pilate sends him to Herod Antipas, tetrarch of Galilee, since Jesus is one of Herod's subjects. Herod of course has been aware of Jesus for some time and gives him more than just the time of day, but mocking and dismissive derision provides no evidence for the record that Jesus has any messianic pretensions. Luke alone among the synoptic gospels provides this episode in his narrative with the touching finale that whereas Pilate and Herod had been enemies previously, as a result of this set of circumstances, they become friends. This means the prophetic role of Jesus serves to reconcile enemies and promote peace and harmony that overcomes geographical and cultural barriers, portrayed in this episode by the détente experienced by the scion of the Herodian dynasty and the ruling Roman proconsul (Luke 23:6–12).

Now Pontius Pilate becomes the aggressive defender of Jesus's innocence of any culpability. Three times he concludes, argues, and acclaims that Jesus is guilty of no behavior that deserves or warrants the death penalty. The narrator Luke is motivated to portray Pilate here as the representative of Roman jurisprudence, efficient, perceptive, and cutting through all the false and amplified accusations to get to the bottom of this dilemma. Pilate above all wants to promote peace and prosperity among his Judean constituencies and he is aware of Jesus' popularity with some of his less militant citizenries. But the present mob shouts the loudest and longest and to keep the peace here and now he gives in to their demand to release Barabbas and to crucify Jesus (Luke 23:13–25).

We arrive now at the explicit lesson for today (Luke 23:33–43). How does this lesson show us, Luke's readers, just exactly how Jesus' behavior here shows forth his identity as Christ the King or his Reign as Christ? We remember that the Greek word *HO KRISTOS* means the anointed one in Hebrew or the "Messiah."

Luke's transition (Luke 23:26–32) notes that this process of Roman execution is daylight, prime-time public event followed by numbers of people, including women. The routine process of crucifixion was probably expedited when several candidates were rounded up to share the same event. In this case, two other "criminals" were led away to be put to death with Jesus, one on his left side, the other on his right side.

When this formal, routine procession reaches a prominent location for this shared execution, Luke omits the Aramaic word *GOLGOTHA*, which Mark and Matthew include, and simply says this is the place called "the Skull," descriptive of an outcropping of rock, outside the city walls of Jerusalem. Notice Luke, following his source Mark, reports no details of the routine procedures involved in the process of crucifixion—a wooden cross, nails, chains, naked or not, etc. Likewise, as painful and excruciating as the victim's agony must be, Luke focuses first of all upon the exchange between Jesus and his heavenly Father. As Luke shows throughout this gospel, Jesus frequently initiates direct communication or dialogue with his source of life and destiny when the most pivotal events are imminent. Jesus prays, "Father, forgive them, for they do not know what they are doing."

Who are "they" for whom Jesus prays? His accusers, all those who seek his elimination from the Jerusalem scene, but especially the array of Jewish officials, Pontius Pilate too, and right now the soldiers and their cohorts who carry out this official Roman sentence to death. But how could they not know just exactly what they are doing? Luke is interested in the concept of knowledge in the formal, Hellenistic Philosophical sense of the Greek concept of Truth, *HE ALETHIA*, which means "mathematical, logical reality," which arrives only within the mind, purpose, and revelation that can only come forth from the Creator God himself.

Of course, altogether, Jesus's accusers assume that they know what they are doing. But their actions express their values and "truth" as they trust themselves and their present ethnic loyalties. They are totally ignorant of their need to know and trust the God of Israel from whom all blessings flow. Jesus pleads with his Father God to forgive this ignorance, this lack of knowledge which they have. And Jesus asks for this forgiveness so their Creator shall patiently extend to them his grace and blessing which will enable them to learn and to gain the knowledge they need, indeed make progress toward this goal growing out of their present guilt and experience of this their acts of judgment and execution. This, Jesus's very own prayer of intercession on their behalf is how Jesus both serves them and reigns over them as their King, as their Messiah, anointed to bring restorative judgment and life eternal on their behalf.

The soldiers cast lots to divide Jesus' garments among themselves, thereby completing their duties to dispose of his last possessions. The crowds seem transfixed at all of this spectacle, and "the rulers scoff at him," this being their customary duty, saying, "He saved others, now let us see if he can save himself, if indeed he is the 'Christ of God.'" Yes, he has saved others, and it is exactly because he seeks to save more, including those now making fun of him, that he will not save himself. He gives himself up as an offering to his Father God. He will not save himself because he seeks God's grace and forgiveness so that salvation may be given, offered, and made available to these and so many more within Israel and because of this salvific event, be extended to so many more all across the Hellenistic world. This is how and why Jesus reigns over them and all creation as Christ their King.

The soldiers also mock him as a group, seeking to justify their actions. Making fun of the champagne toast due to honor a reigning monarch, they offer him vinegar and nail a sign over his head that says, "This man is the king of the Jews." Laughing and sneering, they raise their voices in chorus, "If you are the king of the Jews, save yourself." Ironically, because he is the anointed King of the Jews. He chooses not to save himself because his purpose in life, the mission he now fulfills, is to save all of the Jews from sin and evil. And not only the Jews, but by extending their purpose bring the same good news all the way to the ends of the earth. This is how and why Jesus reigns over all of them as Christ their King.

Jesus's death draws near. But Luke reports a poignant, touching dialogue between Jesus and the two criminals hung up with him. One of them rails at Jesus, "If you are truly the Christ, save yourself and us!" The other criminal rebukes his companion, "You'd better wake up and fear God! For both of us are condemned just like he is, but we are guilty, and he is not. We are getting what we deserve; he has done nothing wrong. He is innocent." Turning, he says, "Jesus, remember me when you come into your kingly power." He knows Jesus by name and he recognizes Jesus is a King, but a King without or not yet in militant control of his own Kingdom. But Jesus is indeed in spiritual control of his own Kingdom, and exercising this authority, Jesus responds, "Truly, I say to you, today you shall join me in paradise." And this is also how and why Jesus reigns as their King. He will not save himself, exactly because he intends to save his two criminal companions.

The word *paradise* comes from a Persian word which means "a walled garden, symbol of ideal living conditions, with water and flowering plants, peace, and tranquility, perhaps soft music, goals for travelers to find at the end of a long day in a land of harsh, dry deserts." Along with the image of the garden of Eden, this vision summarizes the promised healing and restoration of human beings to the fulfillment of human potential and reconciliation with Almighty God. Notice Jesus promises this ideal future to one criminal, but the narrative does not preclude that the other criminal may also arrive at the same goal. After all, his companion's rebuke includes the truth that Jesus is innocent. This reality opens up new knowledge of who Jesus is and the extent of his love as he shares the fate these two companions undergo justly, they being guilty while he being innocent aims to steer both of them to paradise.

Notice how in Mark 15:47, this the first gospel writer highlights how the Roman centurion, observing Jesus's crucifixion makes the first human confession of true faith when he affirms, "Truly this man was the Son of God." Luke changes Mark's wording to "Certainly this man was innocent." The formal title shows Mark's choice of meaning, Jesus's filial relationship with God the Father, whereas Luke, as we have discovered, is primarily preoccupied with Jesus's innocence in this lesson. Jesus' faithfulness to his divine calling in this narrative is Luke's strategy for showing how Jesus exercises his anointed responsibility as Christ the King who lifts or carries always the guilt of the entire human race and in so doing exhibits or brings into reality the reign of Christ.

Psalm 100

Acclaim the Lord, all human beings on earth,
Worship the Lord in gladness; enter his presence with songs of exultation.
Know that the Lord is God; he has made us and we are his own, his people, the flock which he shepherds.
Enter his gates with thanksgiving and his courts with praise.
Give thanks to him and bless his name;
For the Lord is good and his love is everlasting, his constancy endures to all generations.

SOLI DEO GLORIA!